The

CLARE C. MARSHALL

THE VIOLET FOX SERIES #2

The Silver Spear © 2015 Clare C. Marshall
Cover Design © David Farrell
Editing by Rachel Small

FAERY INK PRESS
http://www.faeryinkpress.com/
clare@faeryinkpress.com

This is a work of fiction. Names, characters, places and incidents are either the product of the author's imagination or are used fictitiously. Any similarities to real persons or happenings are purely coincidental.

Books in the Violet Fox Series:

The Violet Fox
The Silver Spear
The Emerald Cloth

One

RUN. THAT'S WHAT I thought when the guards came towards me.

I strolled by, and they barely gave me a second glance. Good, my disguise was working. It hadn't been easy tracking down peasant clothes—it was harder to find them in the castle than in the underground.

Throngs of people wove through the streets of Marlenia City. A cloak with a generous hood woven from the finest violet cloth—I could never escape the colour—almost completely covered my brown bodice dress as I dashed between the folk attending the bustling market. This was familiar. As the Violet Fox, a thieving icon inspiring hope for the Freetor people, I'd spent most of my time running from surface guards, all while trying to free and feed those forced to live underground.

That was in the past. Today I wasn't the Violet Fox. Today, I was Kiera Driscoll, future High Queen of Marlenia, just trying to hide my face while I met secretly with my future husband to quietly celebrate my name-day.

Our preappointed spot was an alleyway just off Deacon Street in the merchant district. I slipped between the buildings, relishing the feeling of being in the shadows once more. I leaned against the stone building and listened. Old habits returned: checking my hip for my dagger, shifting my weight to and fro to feel the familiar press of a hidden knife, and holding my breath for twenty seconds to adequately hear my surroundings. I stalked the length of the alley, finding the tall stone wall at the end. Good. I was alone.

Until now.

I whirled around to face the intruder, immediately adopting a defensive stance. He reacted similarly—but there was no mistaking his form, even beneath the hooked cloak.

"You came."

"I almost didn't."

Keegan pulled me close and pressed his lips to mine. I savoured his touch. How long had it been since we kissed? Too long. The politics of the castle kept us apart during the day, and when we did see each other, it was in the company of others. My hands explored beneath his hood. I enjoyed the feel of his dark curls between my fingers, and the hint of stubble lining his cheeks.

When we drew away, the white scar blazed stark against his red lips, and the guilt struck me anew within my stomach. I had given it to him when we first met. Fortunately we had taken a liking to each other since.

My gaze swept over his clothes. Although he didn't wear his crown, he still wore the Tramore colours: blue and purple. "I thought I told you to wear something less respectable. We *are* going underground."

"Sorry. This was the best—or the shabbiest—I could do. I can't stay long," Keegan said. Regret stained his green-gold eyes. He quickly took stock of our surroundings. The streets and alleyways of Marlenia City were prone to greedy thieves who would stop at nothing to overhear juicy information.

He gently pressed me against the wall and tucked my hair behind my ears. Anyone glimpsing into the alleyway would assume we were star-crossed lovers trysting away from judging eyes. It was partially true. He lowered his voice and nudged his lips against my ear. "Captain Murdock's men have just returned from the Eastern border," he whispered.

"What's the news?"

"Some odd activity from High King Leszek's men in Sallingaire. They're planning something."

My heart sank. Ever since the Gathering last month, relations between the West and the East had spiralled. The East had been more than upset when Keegan left their daughter, Lady Sylvia Frostfire, at the altar, choosing a Freetor over a Marlenian noble. Now they were refusing to trade with us, and causing trouble for the Western towns along the Eastern border.

"And the North?"

Keegan looked grim. "Still nothing."

I hated not knowing. Even though the East had the largest army in the world, I was more concerned with the North, and in particular, Lady Dominique Castillo. I had impersonated her during my mission to infiltrate the castle, but during the pandemonium of the Elder murders underground, she'd escaped and exposed my true identity. She'd sworn revenge, yet all communication with the North had been quiet since. They were planning something, just like the East, yet whether it would be war or something more covert, I couldn't say.

"Don't obsess over it now," Keegan said. "It's your name-day, and we should celebrate. Before we visit the underground, I want to give you something."

I frowned. "Keegan, I said no gifts."

"And I said I'd think about it. I couldn't *not* give you something. If you would've told me sooner—"

"It's not a big deal."

He caressed my face. "To me it is."

His kindness was touching, but name-days weren't something that Freetors often celebrated. Many didn't even know the exact day. After my parents left on a raid and never returned, my brother Rordan raised me. My name-day, he'd said, was three months and ten days after the longest day of the year. On that day, we'd go up to the surface, not on Fighter business but dressed up in our fanciest Marlenian clothes, and visit a merchant stall sympathetic to the Freetors. He'd let me pick out a sweet that couldn't be found in the Freetor underground. And we'd buy as much as we could afford with his secret stash of silver quid. Then sometimes he'd sneak me into a bar and I'd get a taste of beer, or if the surface was too dangerous, we'd travel underground to the obscure caverns, as far as we could go in a day, and try to find the underground streams. They always had the freshest water.

But I didn't mention any of that. Rordan had been a sore subject between Keegan and me ever since he was put to death in the square a month ago. To stop my brother's death I would have had to reveal myself as a Freetor. And Keegan hadn't been able to do anything because the Holy One and the Advisor had already decreed his death.

The Advisor. My father.

That was something I didn't like to think about either.

"What's wrong?" Keegan asked softly, lifting my chin.

I chased away the dark thoughts with a smile. I wouldn't let heavy feelings ruin my day.

"Nothing," I said, giving his hand a reassuring squeeze. "Let's see this gift."

His cheeks coloured as he reached into his robe and produced a hand-stitched bag from an inline pocket. "It's only one of many things I'm surprising you with today."

"One of many! Keegan...!"

"You deserve it. Take a look."

He handed me the bag. It smelled faintly like the Marlenian market a few streets over—the earthy scent of horses, a whiff of freshly baked goods. The brown leather was smooth between my fingers. A single but sturdy clasp held the bag closed. Yellow lettering stitched small in Freetor code adorned the rim of the front flap. It had several side pockets, fastened with buttons, to keep silver and other small trinkets. I hung the long strap over my shoulder, letting it dangle to my hip.

"I love it," I said.

He grinned, and let out a nervous laugh. "I'm so glad. I spent hours there yesterday, trying to figure out what you might like. When I saw it, though..." He fingered the yellow lettering. "Freetor code. I can't read it, but the lady said it wasn't anything offensive. What does it say?"

"*Freedom under the sun*," I read, placing my hand over his. "Something I used to say when Captain Murdock's men were chasing me around the streets."

"You'll have to teach me how to read Freetor code," he said. "I asked your father, but..."

He trailed off, flicking his gaze to the nearby guards. No one was supposed to know that the Advisor was my father. Not yet, anyway. Ten years ago he'd become Ivor Ferguson, a Marlenian merchant from the East, and worked his way up the social ladder in Marlenia City by cultivating several local businesses. After he saved Keegan's life in the market, he became recognized for his keen insight and was eventually offered the position as the Holy One's Advisor. He did terrible, horrible things as a Marlenian, sentencing many Freetors to death just to keep his identity safe, hoping that he would see me and Rordan again someday. Somewhere along the way, though, he really became a Marlenian, and forgot what it was like to starve and live underground.

Sometimes I wished he hadn't told me he was my father. It was better when I thought he was dead. I'd written to him in the magic journal he had given me before leaving when I was six. As a result, the father I'd envisioned and kept dear all these years was kinder and more familial than the flesh and blood version.

I tried to smile again. "Yeah, maybe someday I'll teach you."

"Has he wished you a happy name-day yet?"

I twisted my lips. "No."

"Oh. Maybe he's planning something large for you." His eyes were hopeful, even if his smile wasn't.

"Maybe."

Keegan glanced at the sky. It was growing late. "There's something I have to tell you, but it can wait until later tonight."

"You just had to tease me, didn't you."

"I have to keep the Violet Fox on her toes somehow."

As I hid my smirk, we disentangled from one another and slid into the streams of busy Marlenians. I pulled my hood further over my face. I was used to traversing these streets with a mask. Now my features were known to almost everyone, as was my secret identity.

The entry point to the Freetor underground was just two blocks up, in another alleyway. I gestured to Keegan and he followed me once again into the shadows. His hood had blown down, revealing his face. I supposed it was inevitable, though inconvenient. I had hoped for the two of us to have a worry-free, private afternoon. Keegan could scarcely go anywhere without being surrounded by people with impossible demands or cloaked threats. I would have to be extra watchful of him in the underground.

A Fighter leaned against the wall, guarding the hatch that led to the network of tunnels. He tensed as we drew near, hand ready to unsheathe his weapon. Thin, dirty, and unshaven: but in his eyes was the unmistakable, focussed look of a threatened wild animal. *I am not your enemy, I am one of you*, I wanted to say.

I drew back my hood and cleared my throat. "Open the hatch."

Indignantly, he asked, "Why?"

"Because we want to go down," I replied, balling my hands into fists. I remembered when this used to be so easy. Now everything was different.

The Fighter searched my face, and finally, a spark of recognition lit his eyes. "You're the Violet Fox." He glanced at the prince. "And… Prince Keegan."

"Yes," I replied. "Today's password is *Don't lie down to sleep*." My best friend Laoise had generously supplied the words. They changed every day to prevent unwanted guests in the underground, which was more of a problem nowadays, now that certain curious Marlenians wanted to know what the underground was really like. I had encouraged some of the Fighters to let Marlenians—in escorted, small groups—down for a few hours, in exchange for a few pieces of silver. Anything to help our people make amends, and to kick-start the Freetor economy.

Reluctantly, the Fighter unlocked the hatch. I didn't like the way he was glaring at Keegan, so I let my prince descend the ladder first.

"So," said the Fighter, his tone gruff. "How long has it been, Fox, since you went to live with the Tramores in their rich castle?"

Don't get angry. It's not worth it. "Almost two months."

"Yeah? That seems like too long, if you ask me."

"I wasn't asking." Keegan had almost disappeared down the ladder—his outline blended with the darkness.

"You promised us our land," the Fighter continued. He took a threatening step towards me. "When are we gettin' it, hmm? My ancestors used to own a few acres just south of Feenagh Forest. My mother used to tell me stories about the bounty of rabbits her great-great-grandmother would catch and cook for her brothers and sisters. 'Cause you should know better than anyone, Fox, that if we Freetors don't get what we want, we take it."

"That's the old way. Do you even know how many Freetors there are, all trying to claim the lands their ancestors lost? Lots. And right now, we're trying to figure out the fairest way to divide up the lands so that everyone is happy."

"Everyone can't be happy. That's impossible." The Fighter laughed bitterly. "Look at 'cha. In the castle barely a month and already you sound like them. Violet Fox has been choked by the Marlenian violets. The filthy Tramores have—"

"That's *enough*." I drew a dagger from my belt and held it to his throat. "I won't tolerate any more of this prejudice. We have to work together if we're going to face the true enemy."

"Kiera!" Keegan hurried up the ladder. His hand hovered at his waist where his own weapon was sheathed. "This isn't helping. You know it."

Yes, I did know it. This intolerant Fighter wouldn't listen to reason any more than most. It was hard to make people see past their own problems, especially when they were used to only thinking about themselves.

The Fighter laughed at my dagger. Funny how only a month ago, if I had been wearing my mask and a cape, pointing a dagger at another Freetor could've gotten me a severe punishment. Now what did my dagger mean? Nothing. Absolutely nothing. I was not to be feared, apparently. This made me angrier than anything else.

I sighed and retracted my weapon. "What's your name?"

The Fighter hesitated. "Why? So you can cast your Freetor magic on me?"

"Freetor magic? Since when can I command that?" Now it was my turn to laugh. "Do you want your lands or not?"

"Kiera..." Keegan's voice was full of warning now as he climbed out of the hole.

The Fighter looked suspicious. "I'm Brid Farrow."

"Farrow. All right. When I get back to the castle, I'll look up your name in the library and see what I can find." It was a long shot, as many of the records about Freetors owning land had been destroyed during the war two hundred years ago. It was possible that he had distant relatives with a similar name who owned land, however. "You know, you can go to the castle library and look up anything you want. It's available for anyone—"

"Can't read, unlike *some*."

"My father taught me to read, thanks. And it's not like you're not allowed to know how to read."

"Yeah? Sorry for not being so privileged as the Fox." He spat on the ground, next to my feet. "You know, there's a rumour that you're half-Marlenian. Sired by some rich noble. No wonder you took to the castle life so easily."

"I'm *not*—!"

"All right, that's enough. We're just here to take a look at your home, and maybe the market. No one wants to cause any trouble," Keegan said, casting a stern glance at the Fighter. "C'mon, Kiera, let this one go."

I grumbled. I hated letting go of fights. I was winning. I would've won, especially if he had dared to draw a weapon against me. I guess if word got around that the Violet Fox had pointed her dagger at a Fighter guarding an underground entrance point, well, that would not be good for Marlenian-Freetor relations.

Keegan climbed down the ladder once more, and I followed. As soon as I was submerged in the darkness, the Fighter gripped the wooden trap door and smiled wickedly down at me. "Have fun getting dirty, *Your Highnesses*."

"Have fun standing there all day by yourself," I muttered.

The trap door banged shut, sending bits of dirt and clay flying down. I spat them out of my mouth and wiped my eyes. That wouldn't have bothered me before. Maybe I was more like the surface folk—more than I realized.

At the bottom of the ladder, an ever-burning torch hung on the wall. Keegan took it and the flame spurted, as if in objection to being held by Marlenian hands. Keegan raised his eyebrows, but the fire didn't consume him. "Magic?"

"Possibly," I replied. "There's always at least one at the entrances, and they never seem to go out."

"That would be useful for the darker areas of the castle," Keegan noted.

"One step at a time. Freetor magic in use in the Marlenian castle? We'd better give everyone their lands first. This way." I pointed down the passageway, which sloped down into a maze of tunnels.

"After you, my lady."

I smiled wanly and carefully made my way down the passageway. The earthy smells were comforting, at least. My eyes adjusted to the darkness—if I still lived down here, they would have adapted immediately. I trailed a hand along the wall, and my fingers were tickled when they discovered a large patch of glowing green moss. It sprouted all over the cavern corridors, especially during the warmer seasons. I picked some and plopped it into my mouth, grimacing at the taste. Bitter as always. Yes, I really was spoiled at the castle. When there wasn't enough food to go around, this moss made up a great portion of my people's diet. Some older Freetors had horrendous green teeth.

I glanced back at Keegan, and picked some more moss from the wall. "Try some, if you want."

His face was red and shadowy from the torch. "I...I don't think so, thank you."

I spun around, walking backwards down the slope. "You're sure? It's your first time underground—you might as well experience what it's really like."

Drawing in a deep breath, he turned his uncertain gaze to the green glow covering the left wall. "Very well, if you insist."

After passing the torch to his other hand, he picked a clump of moss and bit into it. His face screwed up almost immediately as he dropped the handful to the ground. "Ugh. Kiera. That is dreadful."

"You get used to the taste after a while," I replied. I held out a hand for him to stop walking, and then bent down to pick up the moss. I put it into my cloak pocket for safekeeping. Nothing should go to waste, not even the bitter green moss. I'd eat it later, along with the apple I'd swiped from the castle kitchens.

"I'm sorry," Keegan said, touching the small of my back as we continued.

I shrugged. "Most of us don't like it either, but for some, it's all they have."

"At least it grows in great quantities."

We trudged in silence to the bottom of the slope, where I stopped to orientate myself. It only took me a few moments to map out the best way to my cavern. I guided us to the right. Fortunately the tunnels were quiet this afternoon. Maybe it was a market day, and everyone was in the Great Cavern, or up on the surface enjoying their new freedoms. I hoped it was the latter.

"Kiera," Keegan ventured after a long silence. "That man, at the entrance. Do you really intend to go to the library on his behalf and find his lost lands?"

"I guess I said I would," I replied. "We have to do this for every Freetor eventually."

"Yes, I know, that wasn't really what I meant. I was going to say...what he said about you, your ancestor being half Marlenian and that..." He cleared his throat, and it echoed in the passageway. "That really bothered you."

I wet my lips and turned a corner. "It bothered me that he was being disrespectful."

"People will always say negative things about you when you're in the public eye," Keegan said as he held up the torch higher. "You best get used to it. I'm surprised you're not already used to it, given your history."

I grimaced. "Oh, I'm used to it. I just hate it when people insult my family. And you."

"You shouldn't let it get to you so."

"I know. It just...it just does."

"Perhaps that's something we can work on."

The way he said it got under my skin. *Something we can work on?* Like I was some sort of...project? I thought he loved me the way I was. Now I was an imperfect masterpiece? Unfit to be High Queen?

I didn't voice my objection because it was my name-day, and I wanted to keep a carefree mood. I pushed these thoughts deep within me. He probably didn't mean anything by it. It was probably a joke. I hoped.

"It's just down this way," I said instead.

He followed me without further conversation through the dank tunnel. A group of Fighters passed. They eyed Keegan and me suspiciously but greeted us with curt nods of wary respect. My people didn't know what to think of me anymore. Even though I had fought and bled for them and brought them food to sate their bellies my whole life, now I was just another Marlenian, high in the mountains, making blanket decisions that did not take the Freetors into account. But I'd show them, I hoped. Soon they would see that I had not forgotten them, that I was still a Fighter deep down. Now I fought for the rights of all, not just for those who had been wronged and thrown underground.

Finding my old cavern was not difficult. I knew these passageways in and out, and soon we stood before the entrance. There were no wooden doors in the underground except for those leading to the Elders' chambers and the Great Cavern. The only thing that separated our cavern from the passageway was a tattered old cloth. I ran my hand over it, and dust flew out. Keegan coughed and I waved it away. There were no sounds from within, so I assumed that the quarters had not been reassigned, as was custom after all members of a particular family died. They probably hadn't had time to deal with petty things like that, ever since the collapse of the Elder council. Still, I wouldn't be surprised, or particularly angry, if we found lost, hungry souls behind the fabric. Everything was fair game down here.

I glanced at Keegan, but he was waiting for me. "Are you going to go in?"

"Yeah." I pushed the tattered curtain aside.

Inside was almost as I'd left it two months ago. One main cavern with two smaller adjoining caverns—bedrooms: one for Rordan, and one for me. Not all living spaces were so extravagant, but because Rordan and I were both Fighters, and I was the Violet Fox, we had been allowed luxuries. Stone counters lined the wall to my left. If Rordan had left any scrap of food here, it was gone now. I didn't doubt that our place had been raided for anything edible since our absence. One of the stone chairs had a large chip in its side—perhaps there had been a fight recently.

I dipped my head into what used to be my room. A long flat stone: that was my bed. There used to be hay too, but it was gone now. So we had been looted. Fortunately I had taken what little valuables I owned with me to the castle, namely, the magic journal from my father, and my Violet Fox cape and mask.

Back in the main cavern, Keegan examined everything with curious, quiet wonder. His boots scraped against the dirt and stone floor as he pivoted around. It was strange to have him here. A prince in the damp, smelly underground. My home.

"This is where you used to live," he said finally.

It wasn't a question. Keegan ran a hand over the smooth stone wall. The ruby ring on his middle finger made a slight scraping sound against the stone. I tensed. I'd never brought a man back to my cavern before. Three cavern rooms, dark, cold, and bare of life and character. Somewhere outside in the corridor, water dripped slowly and eternally, eroding the edge of my sanity. A worm inched across the floor. Keegan surveyed the cavern once more, trying to see everything with the ever-burning torch, and I couldn't stand it—I shouldn't have brought him here. This wasn't his place. It was Rordan's. It was...mine.

Keegan approached me. His royal boots scuffed the thin, well-trodden dirt floor. "Kiera..."

I couldn't meet his eye. "It's no palace, I know. But..."

He brushed his fingertips against my chin. I met his kind gaze. "Thank you for showing me your home."

I leaned my forehead against his. "Welcome, I suppose."

He chuckled softly and kissed my chapped lips. There were a million things he could've said—that he was overdressed, that Rordan and I had done well for having so little, that the Violet Fox was lucky to have survived all those fights on the streets so that she could end up in his arms. Instead, he caressed my cheek and stared at me as if we were not in the dank underground but in the courtyard where we'd first kissed.

"Is there anything else you'd like to show me, while we're underground?" he asked.

I moved away from him, thinking of all the places Laoise and I would wander to for fun—the half-caved-in passageways, the wooden doors that led into the Central Cavern where the Elders would meet, the underground streams filled with precious fresh water, and of course the lichen caves that shined so abnormally bright. Those were our places, though. Taking him there would be a crossing of roads too precious to bear.

"The Great Cavern has the main marketplace. I guess we could see what's there today."

"I'm sure our coins would be well spent."

Why, because every Freetor is so poor that all you want to do is shower us with coin? You think that would solve our problems? The words were on the tip of my tongue but I restrained myself. It was a poor retort. He didn't realize how offensive he sounded, and he didn't mean anything by it. He just wanted to help in any way possible. That was why he was willing to hear investment opportunities from any person—Freetor or Marlenian—much to the Advisor's dismay, for most of them were terrible. My father had been right about one thing: the miserable history between the Freetors and the Marlenians would not be solved by our marriage alone. We were a long way from healing the rift between us.

"Don't be too surprised if small hands try to pick your pockets," I warned him as I lifted the fabric curtain at the entrance. "We should've dressed in rags. It's possible they might not let us in at all."

"Even after all you've done for them?" Keegan asked, incredulous.

I sighed and said a silent goodbye to my childhood home, to the memories Rordan and I had shared there. "Especially so."

* * *

Keegan followed me cautiously through the winding tunnels that led to the Great Cavern. Torchlight became more regular as we drew closer to the marketplace; Keegan deposited his magic torch reluctantly on an empty holder on the wall. The Freetors we met greeted us with silent nods; they looked as though they had been warned of our presence. That wasn't surprising. Freetors with little to eat had to do something with their mouths, and spreading news was one way to occupy their minds and stomachs.

The Great Cavern was central to the Freetors' needs. Items procured from the surface—mainly through theft, but on the odd occasion, fairly won—were sold on tattered blankets on the dirt and stone floor. Most remarkable about the place was the tiny beam of light that shone down from the ceiling. The only place where the sun penetrated our dark world. Women and children gathered around it, praying for relief from hunger, or just relief from this life. Seeing me in this cavern used to bring them hope. The Violet Fox would alleviate some of the suffering. But as we entered the cavern, a hush fell from their praying lips as they saw me in attire devoid of holes, and glimpsed my belt brandishing a knife: my Freetor knife given to me by my brother. I was a washed Freetor in nice clothing, and that only meant you were a Fighter on an Elder mission, or you had killed someone for the clothes—in which case, they wouldn't stay clean for long.

Keegan was even more out of place, for many of the Freetors knew his face. Some of the women held their children closer, while the men gripped their knives. I didn't think that any of them would dare act against the Prince of Marlenia, not with me here. But I could be wrong.

"What?" The challenge was heavy in my voice. "If any of you have anything to say to us, now is your chance. We're just here to browse."

"Coming to see how the other half lives?" a man from somewhere in the crowd said, and others mumbled in agreement.

A reply rushed to me but Keegan was quicker. "To understand your troubles, I must immerse myself in them."

That was not the wisest thing to say. A few of the men drew their knives but I stepped in front of Keegan. "We're not here to make trouble. We've got enough of that already. You think that finding land on the surface for everyone will take a few days? Weeks? We're deep in negotiations with lords on the Western frontier to ensure that every family gets a proper lot. Kind of hard to negotiate if you have a dead prince."

A brave lie born from a kernel of truth. I had written letters, with the Advisor's and Keegan's assistance, to many of the wealthier lords in the West, the province where we resided. Many had replied graciously, eager to please the royal family but not eager to donate half an acre or two to people of their bailes who were most certainly thieves and cutpurses. Even if some of the lords were interested, I suspected their charity wouldn't be free, and that the Freetors who claimed the lands would be expected to work them while the lords reaped the majority of the benefits. Lords were fairly autonomous within their bailes—land owned by nobility—so long as they followed the Holy One's laws. There were no laws against having servants, and the regulations regarding their pay were undeveloped at best. My father considered this a fair option, but I suspected Freetors wouldn't take so kindly to indentured slavery.

Some of the Freetors returned to browsing, while the more offended at-arms men and women backed away. Muttered retorts flew through the air but were not strong enough to be heard or carried with enough conviction to make a dent in the argument. Fighters by the entrance and on patrol approached me, and one dared to lay a hand on my shoulder. I tensed, but the gesture was brotherly. "Be careful, Violet Fox. Your name no longer carries the same weight it once did. Things have changed since you left us."

I frowned, and he left with his patrol before I could question him further. Keegan raised an eyebrow and watched them leave, as if sizing them up, but even the Prince of Marlenia would be dead moments later if he were to suddenly decide to target a group of Fighters. I had sliced his lips in two when he and his guards trapped me on the streets. These Fighters would go directly for his throat.

"Don't leave my sight," I whispered as we strolled down a row of blanket merchants.

"I wouldn't dream of it."

A smile snuck through my concern. "I mean it."

"So do I."

Merchants cried to us as we passed, hawking their wares aggressively, and within minutes it was as if no confrontation had occurred. More Freetors appeared in the cavern: some delivering goods to the merchants, others clutching small coin purses to purchase clothing, hard sweets, and other luxuries sold at inflated prices. I had a coin purse tucked in my belt but was wary to spend quid, as I didn't want to show favour to a merchant only to make him a target for thieves.

"Do you see anything you want?" Keegan asked.

"I don't know yet. Do you see anything?"

It was a stupid question to ask. He had everything he needed. But he didn't make me feel like the question was stupid; he merely crossed his arms and gave the nearest merchant's blanket a fair look—she was selling handcrafted bowls made of clay, roughly pottered and some not quite dry. "I'm not sure yet."

Children flew down the row beside us. They yelled and laughed and waved at Keegan, crying their admiration for his clothes and his good looks. He smiled and waved back, but I was instantly on the alert.

Something wasn't right.

Tiny fingers slipped into my cloak pocket. As quick as a snake attacking its prey, I grabbed the offending hand and pulled the pickpocket around to face me.

A child. No more than eight-years-old, I guessed. Barefoot, gaunt, scrawny, with filth on her face. Even though Freetors were allowed on the surface now, to live and take jobs, many chose to stay underground and continue their petty crimes. This girl was not helping the Freetor stereotype.

"You don't have to steal anymore," I said to her. With my free hand, I reached into my cloak pocket and took out an apple. It was round and red and had no bruises. A prize to any Freetor. A sad prize, I realized. This girl shouldn't be worried about food. I saw a younger me in her.

I held out the apple. She hesitated.

"Go on. Take it," I said.

She grabbed it from my open palm and held it close to her face. Her nostrils flared as she took a deep sniff. Wide-eyed and speechless, the girl dug her fingernails into the skin of the apple. She whirled around and disappeared into the crowd with the rest of the children. They demanded that she share, and of course she would, as nothing could belong fully to anyone down here.

A deep quiet befell the Great Cavern. Keegan touched my arm, and I turned around, expecting to see a crowd of angry Freetor faces lusting for Keegan's blood once more.

Instead I was met by three robed Elder apprentices. They stood in a row, roughly the same height, wearing the traditional apprentice white-and-blue garb, their twiglike fingers intertwined in front of them. Since much of their faces were shadowed by hoods, I could barely detect their unblinking gazes. When the one in the centre jerked his head, the other two copied him in a forced manner, as if they were three bodies strung together and controlled by one master.

"Kiera Driscoll," said the one in the middle. He sounded a few years older than me. "Why have you ignored our summons?"

"Summons? What summons?"

"Twice we have summoned you to the Central Cavern. Why did you not come to the Undercity before?"

I glanced around the awkwardly forming crowd. Apprentices used to take a vow of silence while they trained in the ways of magic. Only Elders were allowed to command the mysterious power that had kept us safe for almost two hundred years. With the Elders gone, I had assumed that new Elders would be chosen from the flock of apprentices, but these three were...different. They didn't have the same wise presence as the Elders, a sign to me that a higher understanding of the magic also escaped them.

Some of the Freetor folk looked afraid. Magic was unknown to them, and apprentices usually kept themselves away from Freetors and Marlenians alike. I had to be strong for my people. I had to appear as if I knew what I was doing, but magic-wielders were unpredictable, especially apprentices. They could be here to taunt me because I killed their "beloved" Elder Erskina by summoning lightning from an ancient magical artefact, the Orb of Dashiell. I didn't even know how I had accomplished that. Neither did my father, and besides the apprentices, he was now the only one who knew how to command magic—though how he obtained his power, he would not say. Probably by studying ancient Freetor texts, but somehow I felt that would not be enough.

"I never got any summons from anyone," I said, both to the apprentices and to the crowd. I looked to Keegan. "Did you?"

"No," Keegan replied. He frowned at the apprentices. "If you want us to go—"

"Not you. Only Kiera Driscoll must heed the call," said the second apprentice, a young woman. They cast Keegan unfriendly glares.

Right. I supposed some Freetors might not take kindly to a Marlenian prince entering the Central Cavern, one of the most sacred places in all of the underground.

"Fine. I'll go with you to the Central Cavern." I stepped forward, waiting for the apprentices to lead the way. "Are we going, or not?"

They continued staring at me, unblinking. Then, blinking together. A smile formed on their lips.

"Heed the call," they said in unison. "Find the Spear."

"What...call?" I asked. "The Spear?" Could they be talking about the Silver Spear of legend? The one on the Elders' crest?

Hurried footfalls and laboured breathing broke through the crowd. "Excuse me, coming through! Official castle business."

The crowd parted and revealed a sweating young page, not more than ten-years-old. He doubled over, hands on his knees, panting, oblivious to the three robed apprentices beside him.

Startled, the apprentices twisted into smoke and dove into the dirt. Several Freetors who had never witnessed magic before gasped and hugged their loved ones tightly, whispering prayers. Keegan blinked several times in surprise, as if wondering if this was normal. I shrugged mildly, unable to rip my focus from the place where the apprentices once stood.

The Silver Spear. Why would they mention that, and leave without explanation?

I had to get to the Central Cavern.

"Are you all right?" Keegan asked. "And what was that about?"

"I'm fine." I frowned. "I have no clue. Maybe it's a joke...but..."

The young page from the castle cleared his throat. "Your Highnesses..."

Remembering himself, Keegan quickly addressed the boy in his most kingly tone. "What is it, page?"

The boy's cheeks were flushed. He must have run all the way down here. "The Holy One requests your presence in his bedchamber."

A pang in my stomach struck me hard. Keegan squeezed my hand. Could it be the Holy One's final hour? Keegan tried hard to hide his emotions in front of the crowd, as he'd been trained to do since birth, but even this was too much.

"Thank you, page. We'll be there right away."

"Well, actually..." The page looked uncomfortable. "He wants to see Lady Kiera."

Two

MOST FREETORS KNEW the legend of the Silver Spear. Alastar the Hero, the magic-wielder who had rebelled against the ruling Holy One and founded the Freetor movement, had travelled to the edge of the world, by the Forever Sea. There, he found a tall magic spear encased in ice. It was the most beautiful thing he'd ever seen, and he wanted it, because he could sense its power. When he tried to break the ice with his spells, the encasement shattered and marred his face. Some said he lost an eye. Others insisted that he played a game of riddles with a magical tiger guarding the Spear and lost, and had to gouge out his eye as penance, but made off with the Spear anyway. Whether he kept the Spear, or whether this happened before or during the war, I didn't know. But the story had been passed down through our people as a testament to Alastar's resilience—to remind us that when set with an impossible task, we must not falter.

A tense silence permeated Keegan's private carriage as we rode back to the castle. Whenever Keegan and I visited the bedridden Holy One—the High King Eamon Tramore—the dying ruler of the realm never acknowledged my presence. I'd stand awkwardly by the sheer bed canopy while Keegan read his father stories, or talked about the events of the day. Small nods, loud coughing, and strained whispers—that was about as much as you could expect from the Holy One. He'd given our marriage his blessing, but I remained an outsider.

My stomach jolted with the familiar sensation of ascending to a higher elevation. The castle had been built into the mountain centuries ago, forever guarding and looming over Marlenia City. The buildings below gradually became smaller, and my thoughts returned to the apprentices' strange appearance. I found it hard to believe that I'd missed such an important summons. A runner from the underground would've found me, or relayed the message to one of the castle pages. It seemed unlikely that powers such as the East or the North would interfere in such a menial affair. Perhaps the communication had simply been lost in the chaos of the underground.

Once the carriage drew to a stop, Keegan threw open the door and quickly escorted me across the bailey and into the castle. As we rushed past the historical tapestries that had once awed me, and the Tramore family crest that had once filled me with rage, Keegan's air of determination grew more urgent. He seemed just as confused as I was as to why his father would want to see me. He barely had the strength to ask for his own son—but Keegan's daily visits needed no prompting.

I reached out and squeezed his hand. There were comforting platitudes rattling around somewhere in my brain, but we Freetors weren't much for words. People died all the time underground, and even though it hurt right down beneath your gut and buried right in your bones, you just had to keep on doing what you could.

At least, that was what I kept telling myself as Rordan's fiery death played again and again before my eyes.

The Holy One rested in his royal chambers in a secluded part of the west wing. Ever since our encounter with Erskina in the Grand Square, Keegan's father had been fighting for his life. Death had seemed imminent for several weeks now, but the Holy One had always been frail and elderly, as long as I could remember.

"Go in," he said. "If he needs me...if you need me...just shout."

"I promise I will." Because I didn't want to be there alone when he died.

The door creaked open with my light touch, and to my surprise, the Holy One was alone. A sunbeam stretched across the room and draped over the bed, a streak of hope in an otherwise dark place. Lavender, roses, and other flowers covered a filthier stench that could only be death, or dying flesh. Bottles of liquid and crushed purple disciple daisies in mortars lay on a bed table, on top of book piles. Anything to keep the Holy One alive.

"You may...shut the door."

A gurgle-infused whisper overlaid the Holy One's once-powerful, booming voice. Today, it was hoarse from not speaking, but it still carried a strength that would put fear into any law-disobeying Freetor. I left the door open a crack, just in case Keegan or another attendant needed to come in.

I stepped closer to the dying man. It was strange to think of him as a man, really. For so long he was an untouchable figurehead, the leader of the surface world. Seeing his eyes glazed over, his sagging face engraved with countless wrinkles, his skin dry, and his alabaster white hair turning ashen grey—I never thought I'd feel sad for a man who had supported the death of my people. That was before I'd saved his life from Elder Erskina, though. I couldn't have feelings for Keegan and hate the man who had given him life.

I didn't want to sound rude or forward, but because death was near, I had to use my time with him wisely. I sat on a stool beside the bed. "Why did you ask me here?"

One raspy breath in, and another out. My fingers slipped under the white canopy and wrapped around the bed post. If he died before me, right now, Keegan would never forgive me. Whatever it was he had to tell me, I had to get it out of him quick so Keegan could have his father back—and so I could tend to the apprentices.

"Dashiell came to me, in a dream," the Holy One said finally.

I parted my lips to speak, but he shook his head slowly. "I know your people don't believe. I know that...that my ancestors have done violent things in his name. But seeing you...in the Grand Square..."

A violent coughing fit overtook him. I offered him a white cloth from the pile next to the collection of remedies on the night table. It came away from his face red.

He wiped his mouth, undeterred. "My dream...Dashiell, brilliant in white light. He spoke to me. He said, 'My messenger will put me back together again.' Do you know what this means?"

I shook my head.

"Your name. Kiera Driscoll." He pronounced the words slowly, carefully. "In the library, in the old texts, it says the Driscolls held land by the Forever Sea, near the western-most part of the province. The edge of the world. Or the old name: Driscoll's End."

The Forever Sea was hidden behind a row of steep, unsurpassable mountains. Rordan had always told me that the Forever Sea was a myth, that that much water couldn't possibly exist. It took a lot of convincing from my tutors and several trips to the library to make me doubt what my brother had taught me. To admit that Rordan was wrong.

He was wrong about a lot of things.

The Holy One held up a heavy hand and pointed to the tomes on the bed table. "I have been reading about before the war."

My breath caught. I found my feet and sauntered to the texts. Information about my ancestors, before the Marlenian-Freetor war. Neither Rordan nor my father had told me anything about what my family had done on the surface. All we'd known, for two hundred years, was hate.

I flipped through the pages. Most of them were faded records and maps of who held what land, who was the eldest son of whom and what daughter had married what other lesser lord. Some of the handwriting was so faded that it was impossible to decipher. But if my family history was in here, then maybe Laoise's was too, and all the other Freetors'. We would finally know what lands were really ours.

And so would the Marlenians.

"Most of these books were destroyed during the war," the Holy One said. "No one wanted any record of Freetors holding lands, in case one came to claim them."

My hand passed over the leather-bound cover. "What does this have to do with your dream?"

The Holy One coughed blood again into the stained cloth. Even his eyelids were creased with little wrinkles. I wondered how old he really was.

"Your name. *Driscoll*. It means *the messenger*. Dashiell said, 'The messenger will put me back together again.'"

"That's it?" I knew I was being rude, but I couldn't help it.

"The pieces of Dashiell," the Holy One said. "You know them. The *artefacts*." He was more insistent this time. "The Orb. The Cloth. The Slab. The *Spear*."

Yes, I did know them. The Orb of Dashiell had saved our lives, and had existed under all our noses for centuries. Wanting to keep it hidden and safe, my father had separated the Orb from the Holy One's sceptre and replaced it with a sphere of equal size and colour. The sceptre currently rested on the Holy One's vanity. I wasn't sure if anyone besides my father knew I had the real artefact in my quarters, and he didn't seem concerned that I had tucked it away beneath my bed. My chambers were as safe as any other in the castle. Perhaps he hoped that I would practice channelling its power.

I shuddered at the memory: it had felt so natural in my hands. I'd hoped to gather courage and patience to ask my father to explain how I'd activated its power, but in truth, I'd been afraid of it since its lightning killed Elder Erskina. I wasn't a murderer. I just wanted to understand the artefact and use it to help my people.

Another round of horrendous coughing ensued from the Holy One, staining his cloth a deeper red.

"I'm calling Keegan. You need to rest," I said.

I went for the door when his powerful voice overcame me. "You must find the Spear."

I stopped, and turned slowly. "The…Silver Spear?" It couldn't be a coincidence that two different factions had brought up the legend within the same day—the same hour. "I thought it was just a story."

Even Eamon Tramore could hear the uncertainty in my voice. "Not a story. It *caused* the war between us. And only it can heal our wounds. Ask Ivor."

I didn't know if I should explain to him that Advisor Ivor Ferguson was really my father, and that his real name was Conal Driscoll. The Holy One probably wouldn't remember anyway; he was too sick. He was already thinking that I was supposed to get some artefact for a man-god that I didn't even believe in.

Heed the call, the apprentices had said. The last time the magical rulers of the underground sent me on a quest, I was betrayed.

Still...

The Silver Spear was on the Elders' crest. The story about Alastar the Hero probably had some truth to it, even if it had happened centuries ago. Since the Orb of Dashiell was real, maybe the Silver Spear was as well. And if it was near the Forever Sea, where my ancestors once lived...

Maybe the Violet Fox had more adventures in her yet.

"You will do it." It was a breathy request from a dying man.

Compelled, I crossed the room again and picked up some of the tomes. The titles included: *A Record of Land Holdings: 1 HOPH to 46 HOPH, An Academic Analysis of Marlenian Legends,* and *The Futile Quest for the Silver Spear.* Well, wasn't that optimistic.

His eyes, as cloudy as they were, never left mine. "You *must*...get..."

More coughing. The door creaked open and a page peeked warily inside. "Should I call the healers?"

Cradling the tomes in my arms, I nodded. The page disappeared.

"I'll look into it," I said to the Holy One. It was all I could promise.

I didn't know if he heard me over his coughing and hacking. Two healers appeared almost at once and started barking orders at the poor page cowering near the entrance. I slipped out of the way, into the corridor.

Keegan was waiting anxiously outside. "What was it?"

I glanced down at the tomes, frowning. "He said he had a dream. That Dashiell wants me to do something important." It felt silly putting it into words. The Holy One had said it so much better. "I have some reading to do."

His gaze swept over the tomes in a passing interest as he searched for some trace of his father's influence. "I didn't give him those."

"One of the healers did perhaps, or the servants must have," I said. Or somehow, the apprentices had. Was it possible they influenced his dream, when I had somehow "failed" to heed their summons? I traced the engraved golden lettering of *The Futile Quest for the Silver Spear*, my finger digging deep into the word *quest*. "Anyway, he said that..."

But Keegan's attention was on the room. His father had stopped coughing. Quiet murmurings from the healers filtered from behind the near-shut door. Keegan's eyebrows twitched as he gently pushed the door ajar further.

"I can tell you more about it later. You should stay with him," I said.

What I didn't say: spend as much time as you can with him, because I never got to say goodbye to the person who raised me.

He turned to me, and thumbed the deckled edges of the tomes. "Thank you."

I kissed him on the cheek, and he drew me close, burying his head in my shoulder for the briefest of moments. There was no one else in the hallway, not yet.

His breath was warm. "I don't want him to die."

"I know." I grabbed fistfuls of his dark curls, willing him not to be sad. Thinking of death was a gateway to memories I wanted to bury.

"How did you do it?" he whispered. "When you thought your father was dead? When...when Rordan...?"

Too far. I drew away, holding him at arm's reach. "I just...take it one day at a time."

Golden-green eyes melted with uncensored sadness. "Me too."

From beyond the corner behind me, confident scuffing footfalls caught my attention. I tensed, although Keegan did not. I hated having my back to anyone coming towards me. Old instincts died hard. Even though I recognized the spicy scent of his perfume, and the patterning of his step, I could never let my guard down around Ivor Ferguson. I mean, Conal Driscoll. I mean, my father. The Advisor.

His gaunt face displayed a thin, twisting moustache that he'd recently trimmed and waxed. His blue coat billowed around his long legs and sported silver buttons down the front, and his bleached white tunic would make any underground Freetor woman cry out with jealousy. From beneath the coat, a silver dagger gleamed, a warning to not mess with Marlenia City's most connected, most powerful man next to the Holy One.

"Afternoon," Keegan said stiffly, glancing at the door to the Holy One's chambers once more. He looked uncomfortable. Although Keegan was the rightful ruler of Marlenia and my father had been obeying his orders ever since he came to the castle, my father had been a sort of surrogate uncle to Keegan. Learning that Advisor Ferguson was really just Conal Driscoll, a resourceful Freetor who had conned his way into the castle with a clever tongue, had upset his entire view of the man. It also hadn't helped that Keegan had announced in front of the entire city that he was going to marry me, his daughter.

"Please, Your Highness, do not let me interrupt," said the Advisor, ever diplomatic and civil, as he gestured to the door with a slight bow. "I was hoping to have a word with Kiera."

Keegan nodded again, and then cleared his throat. "Carry on."

After another bow of acknowledgement, Keegan slipped inside his father's bedchamber, while I was left to deal with a very much alive paternal presence.

Neither of us spoke. Pages came and went from the Holy One's chambers, nattering in hushed whispers about the state of his condition. I clutched the books closer to my chest. The Holy One had said to ask the Advisor about the Silver Spear. My father had a special interest in magical artefacts. But as the rough-edged pages dug into my fingertips, I hesitated. It had been weeks since we'd had a real conversation. And on this special day, my sixteenth name-day, only now in the late afternoon had he found the time to wish me well? His only daughter? My lips set in a firm, hard line.

"So," I said, surrendering to this battle of wills.

"Walk with me," he said.

Fair enough. He led me from the Holy One's chambers at a sauntering pace, his hands behind his back, head high, staring forward.

"I suppose you know why I was looking for you."

"Yes." I could run and he'd barely have any idea I was gone.

"Then what, pray, is your excuse today?"

My eyebrows shot up. "Excuse?"

He stopped. We were some distance from the Holy One's chambers now, and the faint footsteps of the pages were but a memory. "Visiting the Holy One on his deathbed, I can forgive that. But surely you weren't in there for two hours. Why did you not meet me in the tower for your history lesson?"

I was taken aback. "I don't have any classes today. I cancelled them. For my..." My gaze narrowed. "Did you...not know...?"

"Oh, I knew. Tutor Naila Pestim said that the prince told her that it was your name-day."

"It is."

He didn't look surprised. Or enthused. Mostly, just unimpressed. Frustration chewed away at my insides. I had hoped for more of a reaction than that. What could I really expect from him, though? He had left me when I was barely six-years-old.

But he'd said he'd written to me. Every day. Surely he couldn't have forgotten...

"I'm allowed to celebrate my name-day," I said, glancing down the corridor, hoping that Keegan would come and save me from my father.

He heaved a sigh. "Today isn't your name-day."

"What? Yes it is." A pang of sorrow hit me in the stomach. "Why would you even *say* that?"

"Because you weren't born today. You're still fifteen, Kiera. It is *not* your name-day, and while I was hoping you'd accompany me to a history lesson, Captain Murdock has called a meeting of the small council that I thought might interest you. *Then* I would suggest you speak with the etiquette tutor, who I believe would have a great deal to say about how to properly behave as the future High Queen. A subject you need brushing up on."

My fingernails dug into my palms, creating painful half-moon marks. "It is my name-day, because Rordan said it was."

"Rordan is dead. I am"—he lowered his voice—"I am the person who knows exactly when your name-day is. And it's not for another week, at least."

"At least." I scowled. "I bet you don't even know. How would you remember my name-day when you don't even remember which *cavern* was ours?"

He looked offended. "I would never forget the day you were born. It was one of the best days—"

"If you're so *damned* proud of it, then why won't you tell anyone that you're my father?"

My words echoed in the empty corridor, and his gaze darted with the sound, as if he was suddenly and transparently horrified that I had let the secret slip. His spindly fingers fluttered and reached for me, but I was quicker, darting from his grasp. Freeing one hand, I went for my dagger, but he didn't try to touch me again.

"The only thing keeping you safe, besides Keegan's love for you, and perhaps some of the Freetor sympathizers, is that some Marlenians see me as Keegan's guardian. As the true person who holds the crown," he said slowly, as if trying to calm a wild animal. "I'm supposed to be an upstanding Marlenian. If I didn't have the support of the Freetor-hating Marlenians, they would overwhelm the castle and slit your throat. Not to mention the East would kill for that sort of intelligence."

"They wouldn't make it past the guards."

"Spoken like a Marlenian noble. I remember a young fiery girl who used to think she could survive anything."

I gritted my teeth. "A Marlenian noble would lie there and let her throat get cut. I would get to them first."

"That sounds more like the daughter of a man I once knew."

My skin crawled. It was still odd to think of the man in front of me as a father. A man who had been absent for most of my life, who had put thousands of Freetors to death because he didn't want to sacrifice his cozy position on the surface. I thought of my mother, and what she'd think if she were alive to see him now. But she and Rordan were dead, and we were the only Driscolls left. Even if my father didn't like to think about it that way.

He adjusted the gleaming silver buttons on his long coat. "We have kept the captain waiting long enough, don't you think?"

I bristled once again. This conversation wasn't over. It was never over. I glanced once again over my shoulder.

"But...Keegan..."

"He is well aware of his schedule." Realizing the harshness of his tone, he rephrased. "He will be along when he's ready."

I relented—for now. I didn't want to follow this man anywhere, especially after he'd insisted that my name-day was a lie.

His coat billowed behind him as he spun, but he turned his head to the side. He was waiting for me.

The tomes were a heavy reminder of a dying man's request. Fine. I'd ask him about the Silver Spear later tonight, once my emotional wounds had time to heal.

* * *

After a brief stop at my chambers to drop off the tomes, I followed my father to the council's meeting room.

The council was comprised of a group of Marlenians handpicked by the Holy One to serve as advisors in their realms of specialty. Six people were on Eamon Tramore's council: my father, Keegan, Captain Allan Murdock, Marlenia City's steward Barra Volcain, the castle's head scholar Rois Cassidy, and most recently myself. Membership would fluctuate based on the needs of the realm, but that was the core group. Normally Keegan's role on the council would be one of observation, but as he was the regent, his role had become crucial. Since Keegan and I became engaged, the council had met at least twice a week to discuss Marlenia's current concerns. Sometimes Captain Murdock or the Advisor called more meetings when the need arose, and no matter what Keegan was doing—spending time with me, or tending to important documents in his study—he would have to drop everything and cater to these men.

A wall made of thick curtain separated the council room from the throne room. Two guards were posted on the other side, and one stood at attention by the side door, the only other entrance to the room. The guard saluted the Advisor solemnly as we entered, though he gave me little more than a passing glance. They didn't completely trust me, I knew, but they wouldn't dare oppose me, not with the Advisor and Keegan giving me their full support.

An unassuming wooden table with seven chairs sat in the middle of the room. Captain Murdock was already seated. The stress of a real war looming on the province had taken a toll on the captain. His usual full, sated cheeks were drawn and gaunt. Even his dress uniform, worn in the castle on days when he was not actively on duty in the city, seemed baggy around his portly figure.

Steward Barra Volcain dipped his head in greeting to me and smiled warmly at the Advisor. I didn't know him well—he didn't attend all council meetings—but he and my father apparently had a great friendship. That was not a surprise, given my father's history as an affluent Marlenian businessman. They sat next to each other—Volcain on my right at the head of the table, and my father to his right across from me.

"Crawled out of your book pit to join us?" Volcain asked my father good-naturedly.

My father looked amused. It was not a secret that he was a voracious reader. "An easier crawl today. I seem to have misplaced some of my favourite volumes."

"They're probably at the bottom of one of the hundreds of piles you got in that tower. You should return some of them to the library."

"True, but where is the fun in that?"

They shared a chuckle, and then Captain Murdock cleared his throat. "Rois Cassidy will not be joining us," he said without preamble. "And His Highness...?"

On cue, the door flew open and Keegan rushed inside. He hastily shut the entrance and composed himself. My heart fluttered. His dark hair, normally groomed, appeared dishevelled, possibly from his running halfway across the castle to be here.

"My apologies for my tardiness," Keegan said, nodding to the men around the table. His gaze arrested mine for a long moment as he sat across from me, next to the Advisor. The council acknowledged him appropriately, and then Captain Murdock leaned back in his chair, resting his large hand across his diminishing gut.

"A report arrived this morning from our forces stationed in Sallingaire."

I pursed my lips. Sallingaire was a town on our northern border with the East. Since Keegan spurned Lady Sylvia Frostfire, announced our marriage, and outlawed Freetor slavery, Sallingaire had been the site of great tension between the East and the West. Not only did the town import most of the East's goods—silk, glass, and sweet fruits such as bluesberries—but it was also an important military holding. The lands surrounding Sallingaire had the easiest roads in and out of the East, but also in and out of the North. Situated in an elevated valley, surrounded by rocky, mountainous terrain that gave way to treacherous desert in the east, Sallingaire was the only town for leagues. If we were to lose that town to the Eastern forces, an offensive would be out of the question—they'd see us coming and strike us down with no trouble.

"Three more fights between the platoons. Everyone was restless. Until five days ago. When around seventy-five percent of the Eastern forces stationed at Sallingaire up and left."

"Headed west?" my father asked.

"Our watch says they left in small groups of five. Some went west. Some went north. Others, south."

The Advisor leaned back in his chair and sighed. "To confuse us."

Captain Murdock nodded. "Towns and villages along the route to Marlenia City have also reported suspicious activity. Increased presence of Eastern forces. Strange shipments arriving in the middle of the night at the barracks. Soldiers disappearing soon after. All within the past few weeks. A ploy to weaken our forces, and get a jump on us."

"Has any of that been happening here in the city?" I asked.

My father waved his hand. "It was. Until I found out and put a swift end to it. Only two men suffered. They had disappeared from their post in the merchant district and were found dead in a nearby alley. Throats slit clean." He made the motion dispassionately across his neck.

Only two men. To him, that was a victory. I wondered how he had found out about it, and *taken care of it* in the first place. I shivered. He had always said that knowing the goings-on in the city and the castle was his job.

"We're actively recruiting new members to the city guard, and the Western Army," Captain Murdock said. "But the idea of war with the East frightens people. With their numbers, they could overwhelm the city."

"Even with increased defences?" Keegan asked.

"See, here's the thing. The castle is safe. It's built into the mountain—a very defensible position. If an attack happened, and even if we had no hope at keeping the castle, we could escape through the tunnels, which lead into the cathedral, and into remote parts of the city. But the city itself..." He slouched in his chair. "It wasn't built to defend against an invasion. Only the castle. The wall would keep out some, and it may withstand quite a bit, but a long, drawn-out effort would eventually exhaust us."

"Not if we used the Freetor tunnels to refresh our supplies," I said. "There are tunnels that lead in and out of the city, known only to certain Fighters. They could be collapsed when needed. We could last longer than you think."

"It is not a long-term solution," Volcain replied, leaning forward. "The tunnels might be of use for evacuating citizens, or for retrieving supplies. But the fact of the matter is, the East has more numbers, and they will scale our walls and break down our infrastructure, and then storm the mountain. The city is our weak point. We don't have enough manpower to defend it."

"What about recruiting Freetors?"

Captain Murdock coughed, and Volcain looked uncomfortable. It was a sore point. Every meeting, I had to be the one pushing the

Freetor angle. No Freetors had come forward wishing for a place on the small council because they believed that was my job. *Why are Freetors still being denied service in our establishments?* and *The land two leagues outside of Feenagh Forest is being turned into royal hunting grounds. Why can't we turn it into residences for Freetors?* There was always an excuse for our lack of progress. *If any customer, Marlenian or Freetor, dresses inappropriately, the vendor has a right to deny him or her service so long as he or she stands on the vendor's property*, and *The city can't afford to build residences for refugees. They are welcome to buy the land if they wish, but it is currently more valuable as a food resource.*

My people had long used Feenagh Forest as hunting grounds, but dangerous beasts roamed the area. Even Baile Gareth, land in the southern part of the forest, did not see many visitors. Freetors had tried to settle in the centre of the wood in the past, but they were never heard from again.

My father had been right. Just because the Freetors were legally allowed to live on the surface didn't mean that they had the means.

"Some Freetors have joined our ranks," Captain Murdock said slowly. "And we denied none of them. We need everyone we can get. But the rest of them have spat on our efforts. Way they see it, surface affairs aren't their concern. Doesn't matter if the East takes over—they're still not all going to have lands. That's all they care about."

You try living underground and tell me that's not a big thing to care about, I wanted to say. Instead: "But if High King Leszek takes Marlenia City and proclaims himself the new Holy One, he will repeal the antislavery law. I don't even think they follow it now."

The High Kings of the South, the North, and the East had autonomy over their realms, but the Holy One in the West was the ruler of all Marlenia, and the other High Kings answered to him. If the Holy One passed a law in the West, he expected the other realms to quickly fall in line; otherwise, they would face the wrath of the man-god—or more secularly, lose the favour of the Tramore family. Yet abolishing slavery in the other provinces would have its costs to the various economies: the North relied on slave labour in their mines, and the East was known to sell hard-working slaves to the highest bidder. Not following a law was punishable enough, but if High King Leszek were truly planning to usurp the Western throne, drastic action had to be taken immediately.

I could see Captain Murdock's point, though. Most Freetors wouldn't consider surface politics any of their concern, especially if the royal family was not meeting their needs.

"I've heard the Freetors have been listening to a couple of apprentices since the Elders are gone," Captain Murdock said.

"Have you reached out to them?" Keegan asked.

"Tried, via my new recruits. They refused. Apparently they're more selective about their audience than their predecessors were."

I wondered if the apprentices were waiting for me to reply to their summons first. A summons that I had no idea about until today. "I could arrange a meeting with them to discuss terms. I should have no trouble doing that," I said.

Captain Murdock looked wary. For him, and most surface dwellers, anything magic was to be feared. He wasn't wrong. "And what might they want? Because land is out of the question right now. Extra rations for Freetor recruits, maybe I could swing that, though it might make the surface lads a bit miffed, and I don't want any more infighting, not now."

Food might be enough for some. But it wouldn't sway the apprentices. They already got the biggest share of food rations as it was. Freetor magic was not well understood. If the apprentices stood with the Marlenian armies, the East would turn tail and run, and think twice before making a move against us again. The East with their large population and the North with their secretive fighting ways would be no match for us. We would be invincible.

No, I needed something big to convince the apprentices to work with us. Something legendary.

"What about the Silver Spear?"

The Advisor's lip quirked slightly, brows furrowed intently as he leaned forward. "What about it?"

I drew a deep breath. "What if…I found it, and brought it here. As a gesture of goodwill for the Freetor people. As it is, not all of them are sure that the Violet Fox has their best interests at heart." The encounter earlier today had solidified that. "But if I retrieved for them a weapon, a symbol, that Alastar the Hero brandished, it would convince them to follow me. Follow *us*."

A confused silence descended upon the room. Then, Captain Murdock's belly shook, and he could not hold in his amusement in any longer. A bellowing laugh escaped him. Volcain let out his own guffaw, slapping his hand on the table repeatedly as he rocked back and forth in his revelry. Keegan frowned, giving me a questioning look. My father was strangely quiet. His stare burned into me so intensely I was afraid he'd use his ill-gotten Freetor magic to reduce me to ash.

Finally Captain Murdock regained control of himself, wiping tears from his eyes. "Ah, Lady Fox. Good one. Haven't had a laugh like that in days."

"But I—"

My father pushed back his chair and commanded the attention of the room with a quick, sharp look. "Yes. Very good. If there is no other business?"

"No. That's all for now," the captain confirmed, getting the last of his laughter from his system as my face heated with embarrassment.

"Adjourned, then," Keegan said.

I stared at the floor. Stupid, stupid, stupid. How dare they laugh at me? My suggestion, although completely outlandish, had been genuine. Whether the Holy One's dream had been divine, or the apprentices had somehow wormed their way into his ear, I couldn't banish the idea. The small council wouldn't help me give my people lands, and they wouldn't take me seriously. To them, was I still a dirty Freetor, elevated to a royal position by chance? I just wanted to help, however I could.

A gentle hand on my shoulder just barely lifted me from despair.

"Are you all right?" Keegan asked quietly.

I nodded, but I didn't meet his gaze.

"I was going to sit with my father for a while," he said. "Then I'd like to spend the evening with you, if you're free."

I thought I was free. But living in this castle...destined to be a High Queen...

"It's all right," I said, putting on my bravest face. I covered his hand with mine, acutely aware of the Advisor standing on the other side of the room. "You should be with your father."

"You're sure? I...I was hoping to discuss something—"

"It's fine. We can talk later tomorrow, if it's not urgent."

Conflict clouded his face, but then he relented. "No, I suppose it's not. Thank you, Kiera. I...I appreciate this."

No matter my mood, I always liked it when Keegan said my name. It reminded me that regardless of my origins, he still loved me for me. He kissed me chastely on the forehead, and left the room.

I stood and glowered at my father, who guarded the door. "Anything else, *Advisor*?"

"Yes, actually."

My gaze narrowed. "You have a witticism about my Silver Spear suggestion?"

He sneered. "A witticism, no. Advice, yes. I am the *Advisor*, after all."

Among other things. "Then say it."

"Gladly: not everything can be solved with a quest for a legendary artefact."

"Nothing will be solved by sitting here and pushing papers. If we could strike fear into the East and the North so that they don't *dare* touch us, we might have a fighting chance!" I circled the table. Words tumbled out of my mouth faster than I could form them. My ambition owned me. "Getting the Spear will help us win!"

"A weapon does not win wars," my father said in a patient voice, as if he were explaining the concept to a simple child. "Strategy and the faith of men gains us victories. If you go gallivanting off across the world just because the Holy One insists that a holy artefact exists out there—let's just say that the people are no longer forgiving when it comes to crusades." He must have guessed the topic of my conversation with the Holy One from the books I had been carrying. Or, one of his agents had eavesdropped. His sharp gaze flicked over me. "You haven't convinced Keegan that this is a good idea, have you?"

"What if I have?" Part of me understood his point. Leaving Marlenia City when we were on the brink of war to sate the notion that something powerful out there could help us win was insane. But I couldn't let him be right. I wouldn't let this nation fall apart just because no one dared to try something radical. Pride swelled inside me and hungered for justification.

"No you haven't, have you. Well, he has enough sense to deal with the situation in a rational way." He sauntered around the table, trailing his fingers on the wood as he went. "Do you know the story behind Alastar's involvement with the Spear?"

"Of course I do. It's one of Dashiell's legendary artefacts. The Elders have it on their crest."

"Yes, they do. Do you know *why* the Elders might revere such an instrument, one so beloved of a surface god?"

"Because Alastar the Hero found it, in a cave, and...used it." My details on the story were sketchy at best, and my father picked up on my failing confidence like a predator sniffing out weakness in its prey.

"Alastar the *Hero* offered it to the ruling Holy One, the High King Peadar Hightower, to appease him—an attempt to persuade the monarch to lower the high taxes and treat the greater populace with mercy. Alastar was already feared and hated by the monarchy because of the rumours of his magical abilities. Perhaps they came from the Spear itself.

"High King Peadar did not believe that Alastar could have found the real Silver Spear of legend. Alastar, eager to prove that the Spear was Dashiell's artefact, threw it across the throne room to demonstrate its great power. His aim was unfortunate. The Spear pierced the skull of the High King's favoured son. That was how the Marlenian-Freetor war began."

I gripped the table to prevent myself from falling over. No wonder the Elders idolized the Spear. Given that fact, I was surprised the council hadn't demanded I leave the room. Perhaps they didn't know the full story. "I didn't realize you were so knowledgeable about the Spear."

"Ancient artefacts are my area of interest." He pushed his shoulders back. "But the legend loses the location of the Spear after Alastar's followers were driven underground. Some scholars say Alastar destroyed it, some say Marlenians destroyed it...and yet another tale says that Alastar returned it to its original resting place, deep in the mountains beside the Forever Sea." He held up a finger. "If you were Alastar, suddenly the father of a rebellion and the bringer of magic, would you go traipsing off to the other side of the world just to hide a powerful weapon?"

"I...no. I would use it to fight my enemies." My eyes widened. "But that means you're saying you think the Spear is here. In Marlenia City. Or underground."

"What I'm saying is that if it were here—or anywhere—then it would have been found, if not destroyed by now." He sighed. "No weapon that powerful could remain under our noses for two hundred years. The Orb of Dashiell was a carefully guarded secret. Elder magic is also whispered secretly but known to everyone as a dangerous force in the wrong hands. But the Spear? There have been no sightings, no reports of it since it was first used. Believe me, Kiera, fools have gone searching before. Out West, here in the city, but also to all corners of the world, carried by the slimmest possible hope that it might be hiding, forgotten somewhere. Volumes upon volumes have been written, speculating about it, and none of them has concrete proof that it exists. No one has found it." He offered me a sad smile. "It is not for lack of believing in you that I say this. But believing that something is true and then discovering that it isn't—it is hard. I don't want you to leave and return feeling like you've failed."

"I wouldn't." He was trying to shelter me from dispelled hope. *Just let it go. There must be something else I can do to get the apprentices to join us instead of chasing after a dream.* But try as I might, I couldn't force it from my mind. The seed the Holy One and the apprentices had planted had sprouted in my brain. I wasn't sure if the ruler's dream was legitimately a sign from his god, but if something as powerful as the Orb of Dashiell existed out there, that could be controlled with greater ease, I had to at least try to locate it.

"I'm going to find the Spear," I told him confidently. "And I won't let you stop me."

"I suppose you won't, but even the Violet Fox cannot escape the castle once the Advisor has her on lockdown."

My lips twitched. "Is that a challenge?"

"I wouldn't *like* to see my only child running off into the mountains on a fool's errand. At the very least, she should have other fools to accompany her."

"I'm not an only child. But it's easy for you to forget that, isn't it."

I regretted the words as soon as they left me. It had been an easy blow, but I'd hurt myself in the process. Rordan was still a tender subject—perhaps because deep down, we both shared equal responsibility for his demise. Neither of us had been willing to give up our respective ruses to save him from a slow, public death at the stake.

The hurt was plain in his eyes. "Kiera..."

"Sorry," I said.

The silence grew between us for a time. I ground my teeth, chewing on the memories of my brother and the man I thought he had been. I sighed. Arguing with my father would get me nowhere. He was as stubborn as I was, if not more. I stormed for the door, and at the last moment, turned towards him. "By the way. I met some apprentices while I was in the Undercity today. They said that they had been summoning me. Do you know anything about that?"

"Yes. I ignored it."

"You *ignored* a summons from the Elder apprentices. The people who are now speaking for the Freetor people. Whose help we need now more than ever."

"*You* are speaking for the Freetor people now, as much as they like to ignore that." He dusted off his pristine tunic. "Remember how corrupt the Elders became, Kiera. One does not summon a lady of the castle to the darkest parts of the underground—even if she was a Freetor rat only a month ago."

I scowled. "The Freetors are my *people*. If they've got something to say to me, I'm going to listen." I wheeled around to leave, and then spun around again. "And don't you ever hide something like this from me again. When I am the High Queen of Marlenia, I'll strip you of your title and tell the world who you really are."

He chuckled, but his laugh didn't meet his eyes. "We will see."

Three

Donning my Violet Fox cloak, I stole away from the castle, down the mountain, and disappeared into the streets of Marlenia City.

It was like slipping into another, more familiar skin. The more distance I put between me and the castle, the more I felt like myself. The Violet Fox had been part of me for so long that it was hard to believe that I would rule over this land one day as High Queen.

It hadn't been easy, but I'd obtained the evening password and entrance point to the underground from Bidelia's network of Freetor spies. Bidelia was a Freetor spy who had been working at the castle for years as Mother Margaret, a head servant. Even though Freetors were allowed to be open about their heritage, many opted to remain in their Marlenian roles in fear that prejudice would threaten their jobs or the lives of their families. I wondered if any of them felt as trapped as my father had. I gritted my teeth. Certainly none of them had done as much damage.

After thirty minutes of searching for the right alley, and avoiding the suspicion of the evening Marlenian guard patrol, I eventually found the correct trapdoor and performed the special knock of the evening. The wooden entrance flung up, sending bits of dirt and dust into my face. I coughed and sputtered as a Fighter—not the same one we'd met earlier today—appeared at the top of the ladder and demanded, "Who are you? What do you want?"

I recovered quickly, and relayed the password. "I was summoned by the apprentices. Let me in."

It was something I'd never thought I'd be doing, asking to be let into the underground—for the second time that day no less. My violet cloak billowed in the wind as the Fighter paused, considering. Everyone knew my face now. I did not wear my mask tonight, as the darkness did the job just fine. No doubt the word had spread about the trouble Keegan and I had caused earlier.

He slipped down the ladder and gestured for me to follow.

I disappeared into the darkness with him. The grainy wood of the ladder sunk splinters into my hands as I descended. The air grew steadily colder as the familiar, earthy stench wafted through my nose and infected my clothes. It took my eyes a few minutes to once more adjust to the eternal twilight of my former home.

"They're expecting you in the Central Cavern," the Fighter said, and led me on without further explanation.

I followed quietly, matching his footsteps in the dark. The occasional ever-burning torch mounted on the cave walls cast eerie, twisting shadows, engaging my imagination in frightening ways. Despite this, the twists and turns of the underground tunnels grew familiar. By the time we arrived at the wooden doors of the Central Cavern, the Fighter and I walked side by side.

When the Elders had summoned me before, the Central Cavern had been locked by a small silver key. No more. The Fighter knocked—*rap, rap, rap-rap*—and with a sudden click, the door was unlocked.

He gestured. "Inside."

"Oh." I had expected him to come in with me. Rordan had accompanied me last time, because I was not of age. I was my own guardian now.

I treaded into the Central Cavern. Turning to thank my escort, I found the door slamming shut in my face. So much for hospitality.

The cavern was void of life. My flats scraped against the gritty floor as I moved, and the sound bounced off the smooth walls. When I called the underground my home, seven Elders ruled from the Central Cavern. It had seemed so magnificent the last time I was here, with Rordan, receiving my mission to infiltrate the castle and retrieve a stolen treatise that ultimately did not exist. Now the stone chairs collected dust before me, and the glow of the smooth walls was subdued, like the remnants of sunlight as night overtook the sky.

This wasn't the way things were supposed to be. Why wouldn't the apprentices be here to greet me?

"Hello?" I called. "I'm Kiera Driscoll. I was—"

Three apprentices drifted in from the side entrance. Their white-and-blue robes draped to the floor and obscured their feet as they moved, creating an eerie floating effect. Based on their heights and their movements, I suspected they were the same apprentices I had met earlier. Their synced entrance was reminiscent of a dance, and I realized with a touch of sadness that we had so few apprentices to carry our magical secrets to the next generation.

The light was low here, but as they drew closer, they pushed back their hoods. I recognized their faces, though it took me longer to recall their names. The tallest apprentice was Lorcán: a few years older than Rordan, and possibly the more senior apprentice of the three. His sister, Sinéad: they shared the same dark, stringy hair and high cheekbones, but otherwise it was hard to tell whether they were related by blood. It wasn't uncommon for newly orphaned Freetor children to band together and claim each other as siblings. It was easier to receive rations and Fighter benefits if you had a living, breathing family. And finally, Apprentice Orrin: the shortest, and possibly the youngest of the three. He walked with hunched shoulders, head drooped low like a frightened dog, uncertain about its future or place. He mirrored Sinéad's movements and wore his hair long like hers, though his was more of a dark brown than cinder black.

The three of them stood side by side, barely touching each other. I hadn't noticed earlier, but their matching robes were tattered and faded. Were there no attendants to sew for them? Although Lorcán's eyes were green, Sinéad's, dark blue, and Orrin's, light grey, a bright cyan outlined their irises and gleamed similar to Freetor artefacts teeming with magic. It simultaneously unsettled me and reminded me that although they might not have all of the powers of an Elder, they were still very much in charge here in the underground.

"Welcome to the Central Cavern," Apprentice Lorcán said, his long fingers gesturing to the large, empty space. Sinéad and Orrin copied the gesture a split second after Lorcán completed it.

Awkwardly, I dipped my head. Typically the Freetors bowed to the Elders. But the three of them had not completed their apprentice training, and all of the Elders were dead. Apprentices trained for years in the secret art of magic before they were initiated fully and recognized as Elders. With the Elders gone, the Freetors were making do with what they had, as they always had.

"I'm sorry I didn't come earlier," I said, choosing my words carefully. "Your messages were intercepted."

Apprentice Sinéad shared the briefest of glances with her brother. "We assumed that might be the case. But we are—"

Orrin finished her sentence without skipping a beat. "—thankful you came."

I frowned. The apprentices I knew were skittish, silent, and obedient. These three weren't a shining example of normality. "Before you tell me why you've summoned me, there's something I need to ask of you."

Lorcán nodded. "We know."

I raised an eyebrow. Could they read my thoughts, gauge my desires, and know that deep down, I burned for an adventure? Although Elder Erskina had trained for decades, I didn't think that even she had had that power. "I wish to secure an alliance between the Freetors and the surface people of Western Marlenia. In exchange for help against an invading army, what would you want in return?"

"There is only one thing we want," Orrin hissed, throwing a glance at Sinéad.

"What?" I asked.

"Our freedom," the three of them said in tandem, in perfect harmony.

I frowned. "You have your freedom."

"No, there is only one way to be free," Lorcán said.

"Our freedom lies with the instrument that bound our ancestors to these caves," Sinéad added.

I felt queasy. "You think that the Silver Spear will grant you your freedom?"

One nod from the three of them: curt and coordinated.

"Retrieve the Silver Spear," Lorcán said.

"Bring it back to Marlenia City," Sinéad added.

"And free us from oppression," Orrin said.

"Otherwise, no help will be given," Lorcán finished.

The hair on the back of my neck rose. Were they playing into my curiosity? Did they know I had come to the underground to propose this very plan? Or had they guided me here, to be their pawn? Even so, hope swelled in my chest. My father had been wrong. "So it exists. It wasn't destroyed."

"Of course," Sinéad said dismissively. She shook her head, and the other two mirrored her just seconds later.

"We feel its power," Orrin added, smirking.

My stomach curled. "The last time an Elder told me to retrieve an artefact, I found out I was being used. Why should I trust you when Elder Erskina tried to kill me?"

"She tried to kill us all," Lorcán began.

"Took us to a room—"

"—sealed us in—"

"Stole the warmth—"

"—told us it was a test—"

"All right, all right, just stop!" I waved my hands and the three of them recoiled, as if I were about to cast a spell. I took a deep breath. "Why are you acting this way? Finishing each other's sentences...it's...odd."

"We are not free," Lorcán replied. He looked to Sinéad and Orrin to finish his thought, but they simply nodded—one nod, both of them dipping and raising their chins without consulting the other. Then he stared at me, as if his answer sufficiently satisfied the question. When I didn't reply, Lorcán continued. "We have a...strong bond. Some sensitive apprentices develop it during training to communicate during the silent years. Common among apprentices who were close growing up."

"Very close," Orrin chimed in. He opened his mouth and showed his clenched teeth. He was trying to grin, yet there was nothing amusing or sincere about the gesture.

"The apprentices depend on one another to survive. Eldership is not guaranteed. It is the only thing besides freedom we strive for. To finally be in control," Lorcán said. "We were told not to speak. When to eat. What magic is safe, and what magic is unstable. Now, the Elders are gone. And we have no one. No one to give us the freedom we were promised."

Being chosen as an apprentice was a high honour among Freetor youths. The training was long and arduous, but I had had no idea it was so...consuming. "But you *are* free now. To lead, to go onto the surface, to live. You can learn whatever magic you want now, right?"

"It is difficult," Sinéad admitted. The pain was palpable in her voice. "We are the most senior apprentices left. We try to lead. But the secrets died with the Elders. Magic is primarily an oral tradition. We will only be free once we have mastered the magic we have trained so hard to control." Speaking in long sentences without the others interjecting seemed to unnerve the three of them. They exchanged urgent looks for support and reassurance.

I bowed my head. "I'm sorry. I wish...I wish things could've been different."

Lorcán nodded. "The Violet Fox will wield the Spear, once retrieved, against her enemies, as she wielded Dashiell's Orb."

He already seemed sure that I would undertake the task. They could read me too well. "If I have the Spear, do you think that would be enough for the Freetors and the apprentices to fight with me against the North and the East?"

"We will follow anyone who wields the Spear—"

"—hiding deep in its place, at Driscoll's End, by the Forever Sea—"

"—deep in the icy cavern."

Just as the Holy One had said. I heaved a deep sigh. Even if the Spear was on my ancestors' lands, mounting an expedition to the end of the province would be resource heavy and time consuming.

"Why don't the three of you go get it"—I tossed a suspicious glance at Orrin—"since you can *feel* its power."

"We must stay here to keep the Freetors safe," Lorcán replied.

"If we leave, no one will watch the children," Sinéad added.

"Fighters, not to be trusted," Orrin said.

Lorcán and Sinéad turned suddenly to him, as if he had spoken a forbidden thought. "We cannot trust anyone but our own."

"The Fighters are your own. All Freetors are united and equal," I said.

"The Freetors are divided just as much as the surface people," Sinéad said. "We cannot live in harmony with the Marlenians if we cannot live in harmony ourselves. Some scramble to take land in Feenagh Forest. Others think that just because a Freetor lady—the Violet Fox, no less—sits next to the throne, they have the right to take land from farmers and nobles of all social statures. This is not unity. One Freetor ruling the realm does not make all other Freetors free. If Alastar the Hero were alive today, he would be ashamed of us all."

"*Ashamed!*" Orrin shrieked, eyes suddenly wide with terror and delight.

Lorcán and Sinéad nodded again, as if this outburst were not completely mad. "We are not acting as one force with one purpose. We are thousands of tiny forces with our own selfish needs. The Spear will unite the Freetors once again under one power, and then you will have thousands willing to fight for their right to have land once again, against the enemies that oppress everyone."

That did strike a chord with me. I chewed on their words.

"Unite us once more, Violet Fox," Sinéad said, with an imploring smile.

"Under your command!" Orrin added.

"The Spear, for the Freetors' support against the Fox's enemies," Lorcán promised.

"You will embody the Hero once more," they said together.

I didn't know how I felt about *commanding* an army of Freetors. Participating in the fight, being a symbolic leader to inspire our people—that I could do. But me, doling out orders? In the underground, everyone usually worked together, as a team. No Freetor had greater importance than another, except the Elders—and they were gone now.

The apprentices would be our best asset. No matter how many soldiers the Frostfire family threw at us, they would be no match against magic lightning. It would mean a quick victory—and that in itself was valuable.

Having the Freetors' full support—the support of *my people*—that was what we really needed to unite everyone, Marlenian and Freetor.

My father was not going to be happy with me. It was going to take a lot of convincing and explaining to Keegan the cost of the Freetors' support. My father would probably think I put the idea in the apprentices' heads. Maybe I had.

I tried to push this from my mind, and heard my father's voice urging me to ask them if there was anything else they'd want instead. What else was worth their loyalty? The question lingered, kept at bay by my overwhelming guilt and pride. Retrieving the Spear wasn't just something that I needed to do to unite my people—all of my people. It was something I wanted to do. I wanted to see the lands of my ancestors. That selfish desire, coupled with the need to save my people, had driven me here tonight.

Otherwise, with the way the things were going along the frontier, we would be slaughtered.

My hands clenched into fists; my sharp fingernails dug deep into my palms. "We have a deal."

***

The moon was beginning its descent when I finally crawled out of the underground. I didn't know if I trusted the apprentices, but I did trust in our common goal to unite the Freetor people. Their odd tendency to be united in action and in thought gave them a naive energy. The Elders had controlled them for so long. Only now were they learning to think for themselves. They had promised to send a pack of rations to the castle when I was ready to leave—their contribution to the journey.

My footsteps scraped against the dirt as I ran down a quiet residential street. I cursed the noise. The shoemaker hadn't finished altering my castle shoes yet so I was stuck with inferior, loud flats. I slowed my stride. At my change of pace came the sound of running footsteps behind me. Just as quickly as I noted it, the sound blended with my canter.

Someone was following me.

In the darkness, I smirked. Just like old times. I knew these streets like the back of my hand. Better than the back of my hand. If they thought they could catch the Violet Fox, they were sorely mistaken.

I dipped into the nearest alley. The alleys in the residential district were more cramped than I remembered—probably because of the weight I'd gained since living at the castle. This sobered my ego as I struggled to slip unseen, sideways, through the space between the buildings.

A shadow darkened the alley. A large figure robed in black was upon me. He—or she—grabbed my arm and threw me to the ground. There was barely enough room to struggle. I was pinned. I kicked and grunted but at first, I did not scream. Screaming meant giving away your position to other predators.

The attacker pressed all of his bodyweight on me, and it was next to impossible to throw him off. My father's account of the guards found dead in the alley pushed to the front of my mind. An Eastern assassin?

I kicked the attacker in the stomach and he was momentarily stunned. I struggled to get up but my feet caught on my cloak, which pulled at the string on my neck, choking me.

A soft scraping sound caught my ear. Robes rustled. Silver glinted in the moonlight. A knife.

I drew the dagger from my ankle sheath as the attacker lunged once more. The silver knife flashed white in the moonlight as it soared towards my chest. I scuttled backwards, the right half of my body scraping against the wall. The attacker's knife sparked against the stone and hit dirt. Leaping to my feet, my dagger at the ready, I prepared to pounce.

Another figure appeared behind my attacker, as if the darkness had conjured him. My heart raced as I rethought my attack. More silver glinted, but it was too small—too square—to be a weapon, and it was inside his mouth. A silver tooth: his left canine. The second figure grabbed my attacker by the neck and threw him to the ground. I couldn't get a good look at either of them, but I knew an opportunity when I saw one. I bolted over the low stone wall that separated the alley from the next street.

I chanced a glance over my shoulder. There were no sounds of struggle. Just incoherent shadows dancing on the wall. Part of me itched to run back. To demand answers. Another part of me, the part of me that I had grown to trust over the years of surviving on the Marlenian streets, persuaded me otherwise.

Someone had tried to assassinate me, but I had gotten lucky. Maybe Keegan or my father was keeping tabs on my nightly adventures, and had hired Fighters to protect me from afar. That was the best-case scenario. Whoever the assassin was—North, East, Extremist, or otherwise—he or she had known I was going to sneak out, and had the ability to hide from me, the Violet Fox. I didn't know what was worse: not knowing which enemy had tried to kill me, or knowing that I had a mysterious rescuer who was hiding in the shadows, watching my every move.

Four

BIDELIA HELD UP a blue gown. "This one. It complements the Tramore colours, but it is not as garish as some of the other noble gowns the dressmaker sent over. It will appeal to the Freetor public."

It was the middle of the morning, and I was expected at court. After the previous night's adventures, I had slept fitfully on the floor, fearful of another attack. I was not about to be assassinated in my bed after narrowly escaping my death in an even narrower alleyway. Fortunately Bidelia had roused me later than usual. Finding me propped up against a chest of shoes and belts, a pillow under one arm and a dagger in the other, she had only cocked an eyebrow at my strange behaviour, and proceeded to draw the curtains and unhatch the locked window. I'd get a piece of her mind later, no doubt, after my appearance in the throne room.

The Holy One held sessions three times a week for the general public to bring their legal disputes before the Crown. Even when the Holy One had his health, the Advisor had run these sessions, as they mainly dealt with trivial crimes like theft and property disputes—and before my engagement to Keegan, any Freetor-related activities. Sometimes the Holy One would settle larger crimes like adultery and murder, but special trials were often arranged and were held in the cathedral, not the castle.

Now Keegan ran these sessions, under the Advisor's watchful eye. And even though I'd rather attend my studies than sit in a large, stuffy room filled with Marlenians complaining about petty crimes, it was my duty to show the Marlenian people—those who lived on the surface and those who were born underground—that Keegan and I had a strong relationship in the face of adversity.

I examined the dress that Bidelia held up. "I like the colour, I guess."

Bidelia nodded curtly. "It matches your eyes."

She helped me into it. It was tight around the waist, and the petticoat didn't help. I felt sweat beading on my forehead already. Bidelia sat me down in front of the looking glass and called her daughter, my best friend, Laoise, in to help with my hair. Laoise carried a white pocket fan, one you could buy for four silver quid in the marketplace. I grinned as she fanned herself dramatically, the back of her hand resting on her forehead as she made a silly face.

"That's enough, Laoise," her mother scolded, though she was smiling.

"You'll need this," Laoise said as she closed the fan and handed it to me. "Sorry you can't put it in a belt or anything. I don't think it would be ladylike to tie it around your thigh."

"Certainly not!" Bidelia said. "Carry it with you. The other ladies will have similar fans." Bidelia frowned. "I thought I told you to get one from Lady Merrilyn. She has mountains of fans in her closet."

Laoise shrugged, tucking a short lock of dark blonde hair behind her ear. "I thought we were trying to make Kiera seem more likeable to the merchant class and the Freetors. We can't have a shiny fan and a simple, unadorned dress."

I rolled my eyes. "It's just a fan. I like it, it will serve."

"Thank you, my lady," Laoise said with a silly voice, and bowed deeply. I giggled, and then gasped for air, because my dress did not allow fun, or breathing.

Bidelia gave us both disapproving stares. "If your father saw you acting like this…"

That sobered me. "Well he's not here right now. And this is my room, therefore my domain, and I say we can do whatever we want."

"I shall be the premier lady-in-waiting of Queen Kiera's chambers," Laoise declared, sitting carefully on the edge of my bed with a false smug look on her face.

It was good to see her in such high spirits. It distracted me from the previous night's events, among other things. I wondered how deep her giddiness ran. Perhaps like me, she was hiding the pain of my brother's death. If he had lived, they would've married. That is, if Rordan hadn't gotten involved with the Extremists. Laoise would've been my sister for real. But none of that was to be. I hoped that when I had real power, I could find her and Bidelia some good land outside the city walls, and they could have their own life instead of serving others in the castle. Bidelia kept their Freetor roots a secret, but I hoped there would be a day soon when they could roam free, as I did. Maybe I could even find Laoise a lord to marry, and then she could be nobility too...

Bidelia pulled my hair with such force that those ridiculous thoughts ceased. Already I was thinking like a Marlenian politician. Scheming, plotting. I was more like my father than I thought. I could never arrange a marriage between my sister and a man she might not love, just to advance her standing. She would never forgive me for even suggesting it. Rordan's memory would never forgive me.

Once Bidelia had reined in my hair—half of it arranged neatly in a bun on top of my head, laced with blue ribbons, and the rest neatly curled around my shoulders—she tucked the silver circlet that was my crown into place. It scraped my scalp, but I bore the pain. It was a reminder of the responsibilities weighing on me. Of all the pain I had caused to get here. I stood when Bidelia was finished, and she appraised my appearance.

"You look lovely," she said, nodding at her handiwork.

"And Prince Keegan will think so too, I think," Laoise said shyly.

I pursed my lips and blushed, wondering when and how I would broach the subject of the Silver Spear with him. "Hopefully."

Bidelia muttered something inaudible. I knew she had mixed feelings about the marriage. It was hard to shake off two hundred years of prejudice. Laoise had confided in me that it was hard for her mother not to think of this as a political match, instead of a love match. Being in the castle even for a short time, I understood her concern. If I was going to survive and be a good queen to not only the surface-born, but also the Freetor-born people in Marlenia, I had to be mindful of all viewpoints in the land.

Laoise walked me to the door. She pointed to a pair of shoes resting on top of a chest. "Flat shoes. Like you wanted. I had to pay the shoemaker an extra thirty silver to smooth out the bottoms, but he told me that they shouldn't make much of a sound when you walk. I charged it to the royal account."

"Thanks, Laoise," I said. I wished we were alone, so that I could tell her about the attack. But I knew I should probably tell Keegan first, and find out if my rescuer was working for him. If not—if I had truly gotten lucky with the encounter—Keegan would probably be angry with me. My father would be furious. My sneaking-around days were numbered. That didn't mean I was going to let these shoes go to waste. It wasn't like anyone was going to be looking at my feet.

I slipped into the flats and Bidelia hurried me out the door. I thought Laoise would accompany me, but she scurried off to the kitchen to run other errands. I sighed. I rarely got to see her anymore. And once I was married, I'd have even less time for socializing.

And less time for adventures. Secretly I fantasized of taking Laoise along on my journey to the Forever Sea. It would be just like old times. We used to explore the underground tunnels alone. Sometimes we'd get lost, but that was just half of the fun. Perhaps Keegan would agree to come along. Yes! I would gather a small trustworthy party, and we'd go on horseback or by carriage to the sea to find the Silver Spear. Bandits, Northerners, and Easterners be damned if they tried to attack us. The Violet Fox and her allies would crush them all.

I was grinning like a fool as I approached the throne room. Passing nobles curtsied to me, and I almost curtsied back, forgetting my position. Focus, I told myself. I still had to convince everyone that retrieving the Spear was a feasible way to secure our alliance with the Freetor apprentices. And uncover my would-be assassin. Both substantial tasks.

Traditionally Keegan, the Advisor, and I entered the throne room through the council chamber. The tittering and not-so-quiet whispers of the ladies-in-waiting, the anxious lords, and the other folk attending today's session seeped through the thick curtains separating the rooms and filled the council chamber with a nervous energy. Keegan paced the room with his hands behind his back, looking regal in his traditional blue dress jacket and dark fitted trousers. A silver circlet crown similar to mine encircled his head. He bore it better than I did, for I could feel its weight pressing on me with every small movement. His thick, wavy black hair shone brilliantly, even in the dim torchlight. When I entered the chamber, his pensive expression gave way to a smile. For a moment, all of his worries seemed to melt away.

I was about to go to him, and hug him, kiss him, do something physical to acknowledge his presence, when my father gestured to my attire and rose from his spot at the table. "Yes, I suppose that will do."

My gaze snapped to his. "What do you mean?"

"It means you are more suitably dressed for court than I had anticipated. They're out there waiting for you." He straightened his vest, a lime green colour with buttons larger than my eyes. "Your Highness, we have a rather long list of cases and complaints today. If you would rather I handle it—"

Keegan held up a regal hand. "I'm fine. Let's just get this over with."

Before I could interject and tell them I'd met with the apprentices, Keegan swirled around and pushed back the heavy curtain, and entered the throne room. A hush fell over the crowd, and, frustrated that I hadn't gotten a word in, I hurried after him.

Keegan stood on the platform before his people. Ladies curtsied deeply, with red flushes looming over their cheeks. Men bowed. There had to be at least a hundred people, all huddled near the front. Admiration shone on their faces, and their devotion made Keegan light up like a lone candle fighting the dark. The people loved him. Or, at least the people who had attended court today did.

Face it. He's not going to want to go on some mission to find an artefact.

I pushed the thought away as I walked further onto the platform.

Keegan glanced over at me and, to my surprise, offered his hand. Some of the ladies in the front swooned.

"Kiera," Keegan said, gripping my hand. "My lady."

Though it was likely no one could hear us, Keegan wouldn't let his princely guard down in front of his loyal subjects. Fine. I would have to accept that. He kissed and squeezed my hand. I saw he wished we could be alone.

"I need to talk to you later," I whispered.

He squeezed my hand again. "So do I."

Right. He had said he wanted to tell me something.

We sat in the twin thrones. My father, the ever-present solemn Advisor, stood to the right of the prince with his hands behind his back. I shifted uncomfortably. These meetings were tedious at best and boring at worst. My father's gaze flicked to mine and I straightened my posture without hesitation. I could see the criticism written all over his face. *Pay attention, Kiera. Your future and the future of the Freetor people depend on it.*

Taking a deep breath, I thought of my people. I nodded at Keegan. He began the session.

More like torture. The first few cases were thefts, and all of them merchants blaming one Freetor or another. Keegan listened carefully to each one without betraying his emotions. Most of them hadn't even bothered to find out the name of the alleged thief—they'd simply come to court with baseless accusations. For each one, Keegan told them they needed a name and more proof that it was one thief or another, and asked Captain Murdock to assign a man to the case.

I kept my mouth shut, just to make the whole process faster. The sooner this was over, the sooner I could properly lay out a comprehensive plan to retrieve the Spear. I propped my head up with my hand before the Advisor cleared his throat, and I was immediately stiff once more. My thumbnail dug into my hand, my one coping mechanism that kept me in the present. The dull press of the nail imprinted on my palm—I felt incredibly unprepared for all of this.

A young page boy stepped forward to announce the next case. He looked incredibly nervous. "Sss...s...Sir Monju Farin."

Keegan looked intrigued. *Farin* was a Southern name. I wasn't aware of any official diplomats visiting the castle, though my father might have said something and I might have *accidentally* "forgotten" it to avoid hearing his voice at one time or another. We had sent a few envoys to the South to improve our relationship with High King Kamal Zaman and the royals there—we would need their support for the impending war. We'd had some tentative dialogue about their military force, but nothing committal.

This young Southern man was not a noble. He was well dressed, and had an innocent, almost joyous, air about him. Darker skin, and even darker eyes—people hailing from provinces other than the South had lighter complexions. His hair whispered around his ears, straight and thin, as was the Southern style. His light blue shirt was made of an airy, expensive fabric, but his pants were well worn, suggesting that perhaps it was his only pair. A guitar hung on his back from a strap that crossed his breast. If he was a bard, he was the cleanest one I'd ever seen. Perhaps he was a Roamer, presenting evidence of an injustice in our city? Or he was simply offering his services to the Crown? I leaned forward. Whoever this man was, I couldn't place him, and that made me anxious.

"Lady Kiera Driscoll," he said, bowing deeply. "This bard has come to solve all the problems."

Yeah. Right. All of the problems. I resisted snorting. "Really. What problems do you hope to solve, Sir Monju Farin?"

"Please. The lady will call the bard Monju. Not a soldier, or a knight, not by Western standards." There was a mischievous glint in his eye that the Freetor in me liked. He avoided referring to himself in the first person, which was common of the peasant folk from the South. Selflessness was a highly praised attribute in Southern society, and one of the hallmarks of their mother tongue. Only the Southern nobles referred to themselves using "I" and "we" and "you"—and even that was a recent development as trade with the West and the South had grown more prosperous.

"Monju is hearing that the queen to-be wishes to journey to the Forever Sea, to the home of her ancestors."

A deep fear unsettled my stomach. Who else knew about my desire to find the Spear? Surely the council members had said nothing. Perhaps a servant or a healer had overheard my conversation with the Holy One? Or the Holy One, in his dying state, had told someone else of his dream?

Or word of my meeting with the apprentices last night had reached unworthy ears.

Amazed whispers broke out among the attendance. *The Freetor Queen wants to lay claim to her home in the West. How novel.* And: *Of course she wants to abandon the throne. Freetors were not bred to rule.*

I leaned forward in the throne. "You've seen the Forever Sea?"

"Yes, Lady Kiera. Monju has gazed upon its gentle waves and stared into the great expanse, and felt small in its presence. If the lady wishes to also feel this, Monju knows a safe way to go. Can take her there, to find what she seeks."

A bold offer from a bard. He knew something. Perhaps he was just fishing for more information on a half-baked rumour about the Spear. Or it was a less-than-covert invitation to get me alone. I played it safe and gave him a pleasant smile. "I've never seen the Forever Sea."

"Whenever the lady wishes, Monju can take her there." He flashed a smile. His left canine tooth was silver.

My stomach clenched and I fought to suppress my fear. My rescuer last night had had a silver tooth. No, it couldn't be…

To have a silver tooth like that, either he was very wealthy and chose to make his living playing on the streets, or he was into some shady business in the South. The South had a reputation for their underground drug trade. One drug in particular, Race, rotted your teeth and slowed your organs until they stopped working altogether.

"Thank you for your offer, Mr. Farin, but I don't think it's necessary," Keegan said. There was a hint of coolness in his tone. He wasn't *jealous*, was he? He wouldn't be acting this way if he had hired Monju to follow me and protect me from attack.

Maybe he was working for my father. But to have a silver tooth? It made you too easily identifiable. He couldn't be a hired shadow hand, not by trade.

I frowned, struggling to keep calm. I had to keep Monju in the court for as long as it took to get answers. "Is there anything else you'd like to share with us?"

"Yes," Monju said. He swung the guitar around and flicked his fingers across the stings. A harmonious chord echoed in the court. "The people, they are pleased with the lady's engagement to Prince Keegan. In the lady's honour, Monju composed a song to celebrate her love for her prince. *The Violet Fox on Mountain High*. She has heard this, yes?"

"Actually, yes," I said. It had become a popular song, played by some of the local musicians and even hummed in the marketplace. "You wrote that?"

"Yes, Lady Kiera. Have heard many versions of this song, but Monju's is far superior. If the lady does not mind the humble bard saying."

I smiled at Keegan. "I would like to hear it."

Keegan relaxed and shared my smile. "Please, play it."

Monju's fingers caressed the strings as he played the opening bar. Ladies of the court fanned themselves as he acknowledged them with a slight smile. Even as he charmed the crowd, his music never faltered. His voice rang pure and sweet. Otherworldly. As if the love Keegan and I shared had been ordained by something higher and godly.

There once was a maiden fair,
With rosy cheeks and raven hair.
As the Violet Fox she took to the sky;
She charmed the prince on Mountain High.
To free her people, she had to be strong,
Hold her head high, and do no wrong.

She called lightning to evil's lie,
And won the prince's heart on Mountain High.
Once separated by earth, united
Once enemies, now wrongs are righted
For one brave heart,
Who chose to depart.
He climbed the ladder and felt the sun
She'll have everything when she's done
But her people are safe
and the morning draws nigh
In her castle up on Mountain High.
Oh, there once was a maiden fair;
From the streets, head held high, she did stare.
For she knew one day she'd venture there.

When Monju finished playing, the court applauded politely. Keegan was smiling, holding back a grin, even. My cheeks were on fire. I'd heard the song before, but never in its entirety, and never from its creator.

Perhaps my rescuer was simply a skilled admirer, with no one's hand in his pocket but his own.

Monju knelt on one knee. "Humbly thanks the prince regent and his fair lady for their attentions."

"You certainly have talent," Keegan said, nodding.

"And we do not have a court musician," I added, lifting an eyebrow at Keegan.

Keegan leaned towards my father. The two exchanged quiet words while I tried not to look awkward in front of the ladies and lords before me. Of course Keegan would rely on my father's judgment, at least in front of the court. They still thought the Advisor was an upstanding Marlenian. Monju's eyes sparkled as he regarded me. I focussed on erasing fear and uncertainty from my face. This was my domain now. I had to act as though I owned it, even if Keegan did not consult me directly about decisions. And I had to pretend, for the moment, that I did not recognize Monju from last night.

Keegan's fingers curled around the throne armrest. "We do have a position available."

"And we would love to have you," I said. So that I could find out what he knew about the Forever Sea, and who had attacked me last night, and why he had rescued me.

Monju found his feet and strummed a pleasing chord. "The prince and the lady have made Monju's day a happy one. Generous offer is accepted."

He grinned at me, and his silver tooth flashed again. I returned his smile and nod, and then found Keegan's hand to give it a squeeze in thanks.

"Advisor Ferguson will have someone show you to your quarters," Keegan said to Monju. "He will discuss with you the details of your stipend."

As a page announced the next complaint, Monju bowed again and skipped backwards to rejoin the crowd. I blinked, and he had all but disappeared into the throng of courtiers, merchants, and nobles. A skilled shadow indeed.

* * *

Once court business had concluded, many of the nobles, peasants, and visiting dignitaries dispersed from the throne room. My attempt to escape unnoticed was futile. Three men and two ladies approached the base of the platform, their eyes full of hope, wishing to win my favour. Their pandering grated on my nerves, but I patiently listened to their empty words, keeping an eye on my father. He summoned a servant to his side, and pointed to the other side of the room, where Monju Farin was entertaining a group of tittering noblewomen. Likely the servant would show Monju to the east wing, where nonnoble visitors were lodged.

My etiquette classes were paying off, for I managed to placate the insistent nobles with no more than a half-dozen words. By then, my father and Monju had disappeared, but Keegan was still present. A crowd of courtiers—all women—surrounded him. He didn't look like he was urgently trying to escape their company.

I approached cautiously. It didn't bother me to see him surrounded by women. Everyone wanted a piece of him—he was the regent, the Holy One to-be. To be in favour with such a powerful ruler boosted their fragile egos. But a twinge of jealousy tugged my heart when one of the courtiers boldly plucked a stray hair from his blue jacket.

All right, ladies, I thought, steeling myself. The prince had more important things to do than suffer your attentions. Like preparing for war.

"Hey—I mean, Your Highness, a word," I said, quickly recovering my good graces before I made a fool out of myself in front of the resident ladies-in-waiting.

Keegan barely contained an amused smile, but he did not wave away his posse. "Yes, my lady?"

I stifled a sigh. Time alone was as rare as sunlight in the Undercity. "I was hoping to discuss a *development* in our relations with the—"

"Your Highness!" An out-of-breath page appeared at Keegan's arm from the corridor a few stone-throws beyond us, to the right of the thrones. "Please, forgive me, Your Highness, but a messenger from the East has arrived. Urgent."

Keegan turned his full attention to the page, his eyes suddenly alight with concern. "I'll see him in my study, thank you."

"News from Sallingaire?" I asked.

But the page ignored me, and rushed off to deliver Keegan's wishes. *Don't stop on my account.* Again, I suppressed my frustration. This was to be expected. I must practice patience and choose my battles carefully. "My prince, I—"

"My lady," Keegan said, taking my hands in his. His affectionate tone was laced with the page's urgency. "I must attend to this messenger. I'm sorry."

I set my lips in a firm defensive line, if only to hold back a scream. "Of course. Tonight, at dinner?"

He squeezed my hands tighter. "I'm meeting with Captain Murdock to go over provisions and rations for the new troops we're stationing at Sallingaire."

Oh. I didn't need to attend that meeting, did I? "Morning tea?" Keegan was fond of taking tea before noon, after his morning appointments, but before visiting his father.

"Don't you have a lesson?"

Right. "Lunch?"

"I…" His gaze flicked to the door. "I may have a meeting."

My face reddened. The courtiers were pretending not to listen as they engaged in small talk, but I knew they could hear every word.

"I will make time for you, Kiera. I promise," Keegan whispered. "But right now, I need to get to my study."

But I'd still see him sometime this afternoon, wouldn't I? The question barely had life before Keegan dipped his head cordially, killing the words on my lips. The courtiers curtsied as Keegan rushed by as dignified as a one-track-minded man could, and disappeared into the hallway.

I turned away from the ladies to avoid their sympathies and their company. I had bigger things to worry about. I had less than an hour before my geography lesson, and now that Keegan was busy, I intended to use that time to find out more about Monju Farin, my mysterious rescuer.

Thankful that Laoise had had my shoes augmented for stealth, I stole down the same hallway. I was met and well wished by several healers, tutors, and courtiers, but when I hurried up the servant staircase and down a narrow corridor that led to the east wing, the number of people around diminished to zero. Good. My dress was not meant for this kind of sneaking around. Not that I was really sneaking, was I? The castle was supposed to be my home now. And if anyone dared question what I was doing in the east wing, I'd—

The hair on my arm rose. I slowed my stride. Someone was watching me. I held my breath. I wasn't doing anything wrong. To my left was a wall. Before me, the hallway turned and led to an archway, then another corridor that led to the visitor guest rooms. Behind me…

"You have lost your edge. And in such a short period of time."

I whipped around to face my father. "How did you...?"

He smiled and sauntered towards me. He snapped his fingers, and a yellow flame danced in his palm. "I've been practicing. My shoes are more silent than a whisper, but the magic aids me to move unseen at great speeds."

"Put that out," I hissed. Even the smell of smoke took me back to Rordan's execution. How could he not be sensitive to that? To his own *son's* death?

Concerned, he cupped his palm and the flame extinguished, along with his arrogance. "You're right. I shouldn't be reckless with this power. My apologies, *my lady*."

Now he was mocking me. My fingernails—longer now that Bidelia had urged me to grow and paint them—dug fierce half moons into my palms. Still, my curiosity got the better of me. "How are you able to use the Elders' magic without the training? The apprentices, they—"

"I would prefer to discuss this in my tower, at a later time," my father said, waving his once-on-fire hand. "If you're looking for our new court musician, I've put him in the northwestern part of the castle. Much quieter there, near the courtyard, so he may amuse the courtiers to his content."

I hid my frustration. "Yes, you would do that, wouldn't you."

"I was only thinking of your safety. He was much too interested in you. You handled his attentions as delicately as you could, though now half the city suspects you're ready to gallivant to the edge of the world. How convenient for him to appear, at this most critical time."

"I didn't invite him, if that's what you're trying to ask me."

"I was wondering, though I highly doubted it. More important is if others think it. Word in the city is that you wish to abandon the castle on some grand adventure because you can't keep your *Freetor inclinations* in check."

Freetor inclinations. A fancy way of saying that I was some kind of animal!

I sighed. He had a point. Even though I personally didn't care for public opinion, I did care about how my actions reflected on my people. Which was why it was more important than ever that I secure the alliance with the Freetors, so that they and the Western Marlenians could fight side by side against the East.

"I snuck out of the castle last night," I began, trying to remain calm.

"You..." Now he looked surprised. "You did?"

"Yes. You didn't know?"

"No," he admitted, sounding mildly impressed. Concern stole away his fatherly pride. "You could have been hurt, Kiera."

And I almost was. But I didn't want to give him the satisfaction of knowing that. Not when I'd managed to accomplish something without his realizing it. "I spoke to the apprentices. They want the Spear."

He shook his head disapprovingly. "You convinced them that that was what they wanted."

"No. They brought it up first."

"They are *using* you, Kiera, as the Elders used you before!"

"Our interests are aligned this time. The Spear is a powerful weapon, and the East is a powerful enemy. They won't help otherwise. They know they hold all the cards."

"Do you think it was a coincidence that the Holy One had that dream, piquing your curiosity about the Spear, the same day that they asked you to retrieve the Spear?"

"Does it matter?"

"Of course it matters! They probably have an agenda."

"We made a *deal*. They promised to help!"

"People don't always do what they say just because you ask or tell them to. It is easy to think of people as sheep when you think yourself a shepherd."

"I'm *not*—"

Frustrated, he advanced on me. The scent of magic—smoke and fresh earth—wafted over me, and a hard kernel of icy fear crystalized in my stomach. I clenched my hands into fists, ready to defend myself if necessary.

"Is there anything I can say," he said slowly, "that would persuade you to reconsider?"

"I thought you were a master of persuasion," I said, just as carefully. "So you tell me."

As he drew himself up to his full height, the smell of smoke and despair dissipated. He sighed in defeat.

"What?" I asked.

"Nothing." He stepped away from me suddenly. The faraway look in his eyes took me back to when he had divulged his identity to me. He was living in a memory, seeing something in me that reminded him of his past. "Did the apprentices say anything else about the Spear?"

Slowly, I shook my head. Tell him about the attack, part of me urged. He deserved to know.

"I should get to the library," I said instead, averting my gaze. "I don't want to be late for my lesson."

"Of course."

I brushed past him, and had made it halfway to the servant staircase when he called my name. It brought me instantly to a stop.

"You'll tell me if the apprentices say anything else about the Spear, won't you?"

It was a request. Not a command. Frowning, I nodded slowly.

He looked relieved. "Thank you, Kiera."

The attack. Tell him.

My lips parted, ready to release the tale, but he turned and headed deeper into the east wing, away from me.

***

Thunk, thunk, thunk. The door wobbled under the weight of the knock, shaking me from my study of the Holy One's tomes in my comfortable bed.

"I've had enough tea, thank you," I said, covering my head with a pillow. The evening servants had a tendency to bring me fragrant herbal teas an hour before bed. At first I wondered if it was because they thought I somehow smelled like the underground, though I bathed as regularly as any other lady at the castle. Later I gleaned that it was Bidelia's doing, for the teas aided in restful sleep.

Silence from the other end. Good.

But then, again: *thunk, thunk, thunk.*

"Who is it?" Bidelia wouldn't be troubling me this late, and Laoise would already be in bed. My father wouldn't want to speak to me now, would he? Part of me wished he'd try.

Light footsteps scurried away from the door. All right, now I was curious.

"Father?" I whispered. Calling him that made me queasy. "Advisor?" Not stellar, but it would do for now.

No response. Now sure it was Keegan, I crawled from my bed and threw open the door. No one. I peered around the corridor. The castle was eerily quiet. If I strained hard enough I could hear some revelry outside, and the stifled giggling of servants as they prepared the guest beds in the adjacent quarters for the various visiting diplomats and messengers.

I crossed the threshold and was met with cloth binding instead of stone underfoot. I gasped and leapt backwards, instinctively feeling for my knife, and then felt extremely silly and remorseful for stepping on an abandoned tome. Not one of mine, I thought, as I bent to retrieve it. Was this a gift from Keegan, to make up for his lack of time for me? More likely it was my father's doing—another game, or lesson. My suspicious gaze roamed the corridor for the person who had left it here, and once no one came forward, I opened the volume to the first page.

Handwritten in the neatest penmanship I'd ever seen was:
Notes from the Pilgrimage
by C. Driscoll
Alternative title: How to Find the Silver Spear

I snapped the volume shut and ensconced myself even faster in my room.

C. Driscoll. Conal Driscoll. My father's real name. He wouldn't have written it out if it weren't important, if he thought he would be compromised in some way.

How to Find the Silver Spear. Was it a joke? After our talk, I was sure he was still reluctant to encourage me.

What if the volume was fake? There was one way to ensure it wasn't.

I rushed for the bureau drawer I had been too cowardly to broach for the past few weeks. I had kept my promise to my father to write in my journal daily. As it happened, he had a twin volume, and had done the same. Recently he had given his volume to me, possibly to make up for all of his years spent living a lie here in the castle, or to prove his goodwill towards me. I hadn't brought myself to read it, afraid of what I might find. More afraid, perhaps, that I would become less angry with him for keeping me in the dark all these years. The anger was still somewhat of a comfort, and I wasn't completely ready to forgive him.

I could brave the pages if I didn't read them. I removed my father's journal from the drawer and opened it to a random page. I spread the new volume out as well and compared the shapes of the letters.

They matched. Not only that, I realized, but both were written in Freetor script. Only a handful of books written in the Freetor code existed, and many of them had been destroyed by Marlenians over the years to prevent us from penning any of our traditions and stories. There was little doubt that this was my father's work.

But why show this to me now? And why leave it at my door, especially after our conversation today?

I hid away my father's journal and took the expedition notes over to the bed. I buried my legs in the covers and read.

Day One:

I am recording my findings during my journey to Driscoll's End. The court believes I am visiting family in Marlmuth, a story I have used before to leave the confines of the castle on extended periods. After cutting away from the main road, I rented a horse, and I have now travelled two leagues into Feenagh Forest. With any luck, I will find the Spear and return it to its proper place among the Freetor people.

Maybe then, maybe then...?

Other notes: wild berries discovered in a patch not—

I thumbed the page and shut the book. He took a leave to "visit family" and didn't bother to visit us, underground?

More importantly, my father took a secret leave to find the Silver Spear.

"Why didn't you tell me?" I asked the empty room, and immediately the answer was apparent: he'd wanted to save me from the pain of failure. Because he had presumably felt that pain? I reopened the volume and skipped ahead a few entries, now more curious than ever to see just how successful my father's journey had been.

Day Six:

Attacked today by beasts. I will heal but had to abandon the horse. The creatures of the forest will eat hearty. Horse meat is tough anyway. Only berries and dried venison from the kitchens left. Could turn back, but to return to the castle injured would raise suspicions. I have three more weeks before my absence will raise concern and a search party—or worse, an envoy—to my "family" may be sent out.

Day Seven:

This bloody spear had better exist, for I am sacrificing my last meals. Why didn't I take the main road? If I was recognized by a peasant, I could surely alter my story? Tell them I left my "family" early to study the region, show them my sketches? Where do the lies end, and where does the truth begin? Ferguson, Driscoll, Ferguson. I have taken to repeating my old name in the mornings upon waking—a ritual I have not undertaken since my first days as Ivor Ferguson the merchant, before I became the Advisor. Being here in the wild has returned me to my Freetor self. Just as well if my trip ends early...I cannot return to the castle with my Freetor habits and name on my mind. This region of Feenagh Forest is particularly thick and uninhabited, dominated by vicious beasts, and who knows what else.

Pages of crude maps followed the entry. A yellowed parchment map was also tucked inside—a more official cartographer's rendition. Looked like my father was fleshing out the official version with his own renderings. The next few entries detailed the terrain, and there were more rambling, self-convincing entries about the Spear's existence. I skipped over them to look for anything concrete. Closer to the end of the volume, I stumbled across a scrawled entry:

Day Twelve:

Good thing I didn't turn around yesterday! THE CAVE OF LEGEND—*I FOUND IT. Icy, cold, and uninviting. Just like the story! I'm venturing inside. I'm a Freetor again, mapping my way through the sunless terrain.*

I will track my movements on the next page.

I flipped the page, eyes wide.

Two pages were missing from the journal.

Gripping the blankets with one hand and running my fingers along the jagged, ripped pages with the other, I fought a frustrated scream. Why give me the journal, and then tear out the navigation, the directions *to* the Silver Spear?

Assuming it even was the correct cave. But why tear out the directions otherwise?

This was typical of him. He didn't want me to go on the journey when we were preparing for war, but he wanted to assure me that it was out there, and that he had come so close…

His writing picked up on the pages following the missing entry:

…icy floor. Scraped my knees, can't feel my fingers, starving, but am alive. The Spear—real. Saw it with my own eyes, could not get at it. Is safe, at least, and that is all I needed to know. Someday, will return to the labyrinth. For now, rest.

The Spear was real.

My father *saw* it.

He *lied* to me.

I almost threw the book across the room. No wonder he had been so pensive this afternoon. He had seen himself in me.

I reread the entries, even the ones about his identity struggle that pained me, but there was no other clue about the Spear's whereabouts. The information only confirmed what the apprentices had told me: that it rested at Driscoll's End. It had taken him twelve days to get there from the castle. But he had also been attacked, and spent at least three days recovering and moving slower than usual. I could probably do it in nine days, perhaps eleven if I had others with me, adopted a strict sleeping schedule, and travelled with strong horses.

Surely Keegan could live without me for a few weeks? The East's suspicious behaviour could escalate into a full-blown attack at any moment. Wouldn't the apprentices help defend the city if they knew I was in the middle of retrieving the artefact? And if we were quiet about it, no one would have to know I was gone. There remained the matter of getting at the Spear—perhaps it was stuck in ice—but he wouldn't have left the journal if he weren't willing to help me.

Beneath my bed, in the bag that Keegan had given me as a nameday present, I kept my most precious belongings. I shoved the expedition notes inside. It was late. I thought about seeing if Keegan was still awake, and sharing the news with him, but the blankets were invitingly warm and I didn't want to leave my bed. Tomorrow, I told myself as I blew out the scented candles and settled into slumber. Tomorrow, I'd confront my father and get to the bottom of his mysterious journey to uncover the secrets of the Silver Spear.

Five

AFTER TAKING AN early breakfast, I climbed the stairs to the Advisor's tower, only to find the door locked. I knocked, listened, and determined he was either not taking visitors or was somewhere else in the castle. So I rushed back down towards Keegan's study, startling some servants carrying a large load of clean sheets as I ripped down the servants' staircase.

This early in the morning, if he didn't have a private lesson, Keegan would be in his study conducting private meetings. Well, he was about to have a private meeting with me—I resolved not to be brushed away like yesterday. Sometimes my father attended these meetings as well, and if he was there, that would be a bonus.

Unfortunately, Keegan's study proved empty. Undeterred, I circled back around and up the servants' staircase—a much faster route, all around—and found the balcony overlooking the north side of the castle. Sure enough, he was there. It was not uncommon on nicer days for him to take his morning tea here, or see visiting nobles, as the vista showed off the twisting maze, the miniature garden, and the northwest expanse that led to the stables, the forests, and far beyond that, out of sight, the Forever Sea.

Keegan was on the far side of the balcony, speaking in calming tones to three men dressed in Southern colours. They surrounded Keegan, which put me on edge. He should not let himself be cornered so—his only way out if things turned violent would be to jump off the balcony to an untimely end several floors below.

Only a month ago, here on this balcony, I asked Keegan to save Rordan. He failed.

The thought retreated to a dark corner of my mind as the three scowling Southern nobles turned from my prince and strode right for me and the exit. I hurriedly stepped aside. Their colourful bright blue-and-pink capes fluttered around their ankles as they threw distrustful glances at me, muttering their grievances under their breath. Keegan leaned against the railing, doing his own muttering as he overlooked the courtyard maze below. His brilliantly blue shirt whipped in a sudden gust of wind, and his dark hair tossed at the wind's mercy, but he did not shiver. I rubbed my arm, hoping to rid it of goose prickles.

"There you are," I said, hoping to lighten the mood.

Surprised, he turned, and greeted me with a smile that didn't reach his eyes. "I didn't expect to see you this morning. I have meetings—"

"I know. I was hoping I wouldn't have to schedule one just to see my husband-to-be, but here I am."

He sighed. "Kiera, I'm sorry, that's not what I meant." He flicked his gaze to the entrance. "The South refuses to send us more provisions or troops. They don't see the East as a threat. They think High King Leszek is just blowing smoke."

"Is there anything I can do?" I asked. "I hate meetings, but I'll sit in on them if it makes you feel better. I can be very persuasive, you know."

This time his smile was genuine. "Only if you want to. Most of them are fairly dry. Financial reports, trade agreements...and not all of the sit-downs are pleasant. They want more, I tell them I don't have more, or vice versa."

"My father or someone should be helping you. You don't have to face this alone."

He nodded, but he waved my concern away. Faint worry lines embedded his brow, and bracketed his tired yellow-green eyes. My fingernails dug into my palms. The stress was tearing him apart. My solutions as the Violet Fox involved daggers, sneaking around, theft, and liberation. That wouldn't help here.

"Have you visited your father today?" I asked, hoping to change the subject from politics.

He shook his head, the barest of movements. "I haven't had a free moment."

"Until now. And I'm taking up that time. I understand." I turned and headed for the door, partly to avoid his seeing me so ashamed. "I'm sorry for ambushing you. We can talk later."

"Kiera," he said quietly.

The tenderness in his tone stopped my stride. How long had it been since I heard him speak to me that way? "Yes?"

"I didn't mean to avoid you yesterday. Please forgive me."

I turned to face him once more. "Only if you forgive me for being frustrated."

"I'd be worried if you weren't," he admitted, launching himself from the railing. "So is this a social visit? Should I call for tea? I have fifteen minutes until I must meet Captain Murdock in the council room, and he's likely to order lunch, though it isn't yet midday."

I drew as deep a breath as my dress allowed. "No tea. I can be brief. There is something I need to tell you." I smiled grimly, and told him about my conversation with the apprentices, and the attack in the alleyway. I watched for telltale signs that my father had told him the first half of the story already, but instead, he became concerned.

"Did you get hurt? You would have gone to a healer if you had been, right? Did you get a good look at who it was?"

I shook my head. "Not the attacker, no. He...I think it was a he, at least. He was strong. Fast. Well trained. I...I was lucky to escape." I hesitated. My suspicions about Monju wrapped around my tongue, jumbled, desiring to be released.

Keegan pressed his forehead against mine. "Every time you tell me stories like this...I wish I'd been there to help you."

"I know," I said. "But...but this time, I would've been dead if someone hadn't saved me."

I told him about the silver-toothed man who had rescued me in the alley, and my feelings surrounding Monju's appearance in court.

"You think Monju Farin, the musician, saved you?" Keegan looked uncertain.

I glanced around the empty balcony for potential eavesdroppers. "I'm almost certain it was."

"That was why you wanted him to stay," Keegan said, his eyes narrowing with suspicion.

"You didn't object."

"How could I, with that song?"

"You're the regent, aren't you? You don't have to accept someone into your home just because they've sung something nice about you." Basic Freetor logic, I almost added.

He ignored the jab. "I suspected he might be a Southern spy. Now that I know he has other...skills...he's more of a potential threat," Keegan said. "We're not yet sure of where the South's loyalty lies."

"All the more reason to let him stay," I argued, venturing a step closer. "If he *is* a spy, we can keep an eye on him and see where he's passing information, and try to feed him false information."

Keegan raised his eyebrows. "We?"

"Well, me. Or my father."

"I'm having the Advisor look into him. If he has any connections with the North or the East, or even the Extremists, I'm confident he'll be able to suss that out."

Yes, of course he would, I thought sourly.

Keegan noted my expression and cupped my cheek. "There are those who could come and whisper lies in your ears just for the chance to..." He set his lips in a firm line, unable to utter the words. "I don't want them to take advantage of you."

"I don't think Monju is here to do that."

"Just because he saved your life doesn't mean he's innocent," Keegan warned. "Everyone has an agenda."

"I trust him."

He gave me a funny look. "Why?"

I was about to reply when I realized I didn't have a legitimate reason for what I felt in my gut. Because he's like me, was what I had almost said. "He wouldn't have saved my life if he meant to kill me later. It would have been easier to end my life in the alley."

"And if he means to get you to lead him to the Spear, for his own glory?"

"No one except the council and the apprentices know about the Spear."

"Unless he followed you underground, overheard your conversation with the apprentices. The attacker could have just as easily done this as well."

I considered this. "I don't think so. I think the apprentices would've known if someone was listening in. There's so much magic in the underground, and there are Freetors guarding the entrances and the Central Cavern. I don't think anyone could've snuck in."

"But your father managed to get underground, when he wanted to, without the Elders' knowing."

"He has magic. That's different."

Keegan leaned against the railing once more. "I don't know, Kiera. This Monju...if he saved your life, I am forever in his debt, but I don't know if I can trust a man who sneaks around in shadows and turns up at court begging for a job."

I crossed my arms. "I sneak around in shadows and showed up at court. And you're going to marry me."

He smiled at this. "Yes, but you are a good deal prettier than Monju, or any mysterious shadow for that matter."

"That's not a high bar to reach."

"All right, all right." He became serious once again, and drew closer to me. "You don't think it's a tad convenient that he shows up just as you're ready to pack up and leave? That he offers his *services* as a guide to parts unknown?

"That's what my father said." Even though their concern was warranted, I couldn't keep the disdain from my voice. "I don't suppose a certain prince would care to join me on such an expedition, to parts unknown, to retrieve an ancient weapon of power?"

I phrased the question lightheartedly, but the heaviness of the ordeal had weighed upon my words. The edge of Keegan's lips drew downward, and sadness clouded his gaze.

"I can't go with you, Kiera."

I knew he'd say that. He was a prince, soon to be a king. The sense of responsibility for our people that we shared drove us in different directions. Me, to find the Spear and use it to form an alliance between the Freetors and the Western Marlenians. Him, to stay put and rule in his mountain castle. I swallowed my pride and my anger. It was a big ball of dirt in my throat.

"My father is dying," he said softly, more to his shoes than to me. "And if I'm not here when he draws his last breath...I don't think I'd be able to forgive myself."

"I understand," I replied, trying to keep my voice void of emotion. Here came the hard part. My stomach clenched with all of the emotions I was holding at bay. "But what if I told you that I *wanted* to go?"

He furrowed his brows. "Do you know where it is?"

"My father knows where it is. He's been to the cave. It's somewhere close to the Forever Sea, in the west."

Keegan's eyes lit with interest. "He's been there? When?"

I told him about my discovery of his notes outside my chamber. "He put them there. I didn't think he wanted to encourage me, but...it's proof that the Spear is real. If he, and myself, and a team—"

"I can't spare the both of you. Not now. Travelling to the Forever Sea would take a fortnight at least, each way. Assuming you don't run into trouble. Our rule is not as firm that far west as it is here in the capital. Bandits on the roads, creatures in the forest..."

"The beatag are just made-up stories told to Freetor children to prevent them from leaving the underground and sneaking out to the forest."

He set his lips firmly, refusing to take up *that* argument, and turned away to overlook the garden once more. His fingers obsessively brushed grit from the railing.

I was being stubborn. But I also knew I was *right*. If I didn't retrieve the Spear for the apprentices, then the Freetors would never truly follow our leadership. They would continue to ignore the true threat on the surface. The last thing we needed was someone *else* to oppose us.

"What if you never come back?" He glanced over his shoulder, his eyes heavy with sadness and fear. "I...just can't stand the thought of losing you, Kiera. I know that going off on an adventure somewhere doesn't seem like a big ordeal for you, but for me, to leave the city at such a critical juncture would be the worst decision I could make. Tell me you understand, that if you were in my shoes..."

If I were in his shoes, I would still want to go. How could I make *him* understand my thirst for adventure?

He glanced at the sky, and then at the entrance to the balcony. "Captain Murdock is probably waiting for me in the council room." He drew in a deep breath, lifting his chest high. "I wish I didn't have to leave right now. I can't stand to have you mad at me."

"I'm not mad," I said, taking his hands in mine to stop his compulsive balcony brushing. "I know you're thinking of your father, and what's best for our people."

"We'll talk more about the Silver Spear later," he promised. His thumb traced the outline of my jaw, sending shivers down my front. A hint of a smile touched his scarred lips. "Try not to get into any more trouble between now and dinner."

I grinned. "How else am I supposed to keep things interesting around here?"

"Well..."

He leaned close and grazed his lips against mine just as the heavy balcony door burst open.

"Oh...many apologies..."

Keegan stiffened and immediately recoiled from me, holding my body an arm's length from him. Monju Farin stood awkwardly in the doorway. Apologetic he might be, but he made no move to leave us be either.

"Is there something you want?" Keegan asked. His grip on me

tightened. The future king of Marlenia spoke now. Keegan could not simultaneously be my affectionate fiancé and the prince of the realm.

Monju averted his gaze from Keegan and looked instead to me. "Monju apologizes, many times, to His Highnesses. Lost, in this vast labyrinth."

I stroked Keegan's arm, not just lovingly, but to get him to loosen his iron grip. "Maybe I can help you," I offered.

Keegan frowned, then thought better of arguing about the better things I had to do. "Of course." Finally, he released my arms, and cleared his throat. "I'm late for my meeting."

"Go, then," I said playfully, pushing him away, but he caught me again and squeezed my hands in a sincere goodbye gesture. A kiss that was not a kiss, just because Monju stood in the doorway. I pursed my lips. I'd have to work on that. Freetors were more liberal with their affections—a ruler of a realm shouldn't have to be afraid of showing his true feelings for his queen.

Monju respectfully stepped aside for Keegan, dipping his head as the prince strode past him and into the corridor. The slight tilt of Monju's head, the way he leaned against the heavy wood of the door, propping it open: he was following Keegan's footsteps as they travelled deeper into the castle.

I wandered across the balcony towards the mysterious Southern bard. Servants must have provided him with some proper castle attire, as the tattered street clothes he'd worn yesterday had been replaced by a bright green tunic that complemented his dark skin, and fresh dark pants. A whistle peeked out of his pocket, and with one hand, he held tight onto his guitar.

His stare was unchallenging, but held a curiosity that would be considered inappropriate for a man of his social standing. A slight blush coloured my cheeks. He had charmed the court yesterday with his songs, and distracted us from the looming cloud of war, but that was because he twisted words for money and the entertainment of others. Although he may have saved me in the alley, Keegan was right: I had every right to be cautious.

We were alone, however. It was the perfect opportunity to bring up the attack.

I gestured to the hallway, and we returned to the interior of the castle.

"Were you looking for some place in particular?" I asked Monju, breaking our cordial silence.

"Oh. Hmm," Monju replied thoughtfully. "The courtyard. To play while the sun shines—feels like home."

"I hear it's sunnier in the South." We began walking down the corridor at a leisurely pace. Already I grew tired of the small talk. I needed to bring up the attack.

"Yes, the lady is correct. Someday, she should visit."

"There are a number of places I'd like to visit, though the tensions between the provinces will make that difficult." I felt dirty dancing around the issue. I wondered if this was how my father felt all the time: like a snake, circling its prey, waiting for weakness and then striking.

Monju didn't miss a beat. "Travelling the great land, Monju's speciality. The offer to be the lady's guide still stands, should she require."

I pursed my lips and dug my fingernails into my palms. "Monju...how did you know that I wanted to go west to...explore the lands of my ancestors?"

"Oh. The lady's Freetor heritage is widely known. Whispers in the shadows bring news of Driscoll lands by the Forever Sea. Fortunate to know her ancestors' lands, yes?"

Yes, but not so fortunate that everyone else knew. That would not sit well with other Freetors. To them, I had used my influence to benefit myself, while they continued to toil away underground without a legal claim to anything on the surface.

Whispers in the shadows. Did we have a spy in the castle? In the council? Perhaps someone had been listening to my conversation with the Holy One.

"This way, to the courtyard?" Monju asked, interrupting my thoughts. He pointed down a rampway that spiralled down to the first floor.

"Yes," I said absently.

Monju bowed courteously, sporting a handsome smile. There was that silver tooth again. "A pleasure to walk with the great Lady Kiera on Mountain High. The lady will come to listen to music later, hope?"

Despite the glinting tooth, his smile was infectious, and the reference to the song made me somewhat giddy, distracting me momentarily. "Yes, I will. Thank you."

"The thanks is Monju's, Lady Kiera."

With another quick bow, Monju spun around silently and hurried down the ramp towards the courtyard. Another pair of soundless footsteps I had to worry about. But again, Monju seemed harmless enough. We had been alone, and he could have used the opportunity to harm me—and since I was dressed in layers and layers of fabric, he would have had agility on his side. Yet, nothing.

I continued down the corridor. My morning lesson in the library was due to begin shortly, yet history was the furthest thing from my mind. My thoughts returned to Monju's assertion that *whispers* had told him of my plans to journey west. Hearsay from a bard wasn't enough to interrupt Keegan's meeting. Servants, after all, were known to eavesdrop and whisper.

Keegan's study was nearby. I could leave him a note saying that I wanted to see him later, before dinner, as he often returned to his private space several times a day.

I hurried as fast as the dress allowed to the door, and once again found it unlocked. Inside, the room was quiet except for the occasional creak from above and below. Unease churned in my stomach. Although the generous room with a large, open window opposite me, wall-to-wall bookshelves, and a century-old desk to my right had the styling of an older man, this was Keegan's space. I shouldn't be in here—a glance to determine his presence was all I should've allowed. I would speak to Keegan at dinner.

As I swirled around to leave, my long sleeves brushed against a feeble stack of papers, sending them flying from the desk and onto the floor. No! With everything going on lately, no wonder Keegan's desk was a mess. Since the Holy One was incapacitated, Keegan was lending his signature to every bill or allowance that passed through the castle walls. Grunting in frustration, I bent to retrieve the documents, hoping that they didn't need to be in any special order.

All of the retrieved documents bore the Tramore family crest at the top—official royal documents—except one. The parchment was thick and the handwriting was not the neat penmanship of a scribe. It was hurried; more personal. I'd only seen Keegan's handwriting a few times, but from the large loops and the tight packing of the letters, I guessed it was his.

My dearest,

I cannot stop thinking of you, even though you are close by. Even though we are from different worlds, we see Marlenia as one united nation, under our rule. But you know this. On our wedding day, we will begin a new journey together—

I drew a sharp breath and pressed the letter to my breast. What was this? Another name-day present? A wedding present? It was early to start working on that—we'd agreed to delay our ceremony a year to focus on the war. A draft for a wedding speech? I bit my lip. I was never good at keeping things a surprise once I knew them. I should just put it back on the desk...

I lowered my eyes and kept reading.

Do not fear, dearest Sylvia. With a slow, steady hand, our alliance shall be sealed in the sacred bonds of marriage. We will not be interrupted again.

The parchment tumbled from my hand.

Dearest...Sylvia? *We will not be interrupted again.*

Although my hands instinctively repelled from the parchment, I snatched the letter from the floor and reread it.

"How?" I whispered.

Speaking seemed to make the threat more real. I crumpled the letter and threw it across the room. It almost flew out the window. Keegan had written that? No. He couldn't have. He wouldn't consent to a marriage with the East. Would he?

I was Keegan's intended. He *cared* for me.

But he was always busy. He barely made time for me anymore.

He had said that he had something to tell me.

He almost married Sylvia. He was so close to saying yes at the altar.

What if...when I stood up and revealed my identity during that ceremony, sacrificing my mission and effectively preventing him from marrying Sylvia, I'd gotten in the way of what he truly wanted?

No. No, that was impossible.

And yet, it was his handwriting. And the words he drafted on that parchment, intimate.

Footsteps ventured near the room. Knowing I shouldn't have entered, I followed my first instinct and hid beneath the desk, training my breathing to be low and slow. My dress splayed out beneath the desk, singing my position. Muttering, I gathered the hem and hugged it close to my chest just as the door swung open.

As clean, pointed, decorated boots—Keegan!—strode into the room, I realized my first impulse had been foolish. I was the prince's bride-to-be, not a thief! He wouldn't chide me for being in here. He had told me I was free to roam the castle. I could have been in here to leave my own love letter, as far as he knew. It was his fault for leaving his *business* on the table. Considering the scandalous letter, I was completely justified in confronting Keegan.

The door shut after another pair of boots—rounded, simple, and silent as they met the floor. "Thank you for seeing me." My father's voice was unmistakable.

"The hours are hurrying by so fast. I don't even see Kiera much these days."

I tugged on the collar of my dress and squeezed my eyes shut.

"I'll be brief," my father said bluntly. "There has been a lot of talk in the small council about how to handle the tension between the East and the North, but we are getting nowhere."

"And you have a suggestion? One that cannot wait until the next council meeting?"

"Yes, Your Highness. Remember the conversation we had when Kiera was in the dungeon?"

"Yes," Keegan said hesitantly.

"We need to reconsider that option."

"I cannot submit to the East's demand. Not that one!" Keegan's voice was suddenly deep, commanding, and in control. "It would break Kiera's heart."

"It is better to break the heart of one young woman than send good Marlenian men off to die on the Eastern border. They *will* slaughter us. That is a fact."

"She's your daughter. You would ask me to give her up?"

I stifled a gasp and bit hard into my fingers to prevent a noise. No. No, this couldn't be happening, not after all I had sacrificed.

"Don't try to play that card with me, Your Highness. She may be my daughter, but we—*you*—must do what is in the interest of the realm. The arrangements can be made within days. The East will remove their garrison at the border, and take the Violet Fox with them to do what they wilt. We can keep our men from the slaughterhouse. And perhaps the North will remove their spies. Or at least, once I am sure of their identities, *I* can take steps to remove them."

Take the Violet Fox with them, to do as they wilt. Each second that Keegan didn't reply multiplied the doubt that had seeded in my mind. To prevent a war with the East, my father would give me up—as a hostage, or a prisoner? Or worse: Keegan would annul our engagement.

According to the letter on his desk, that was exactly what he wanted.

"Think about it," my father said firmly.

"I...will. Thank you for your time." Keegan's reply was formal, but full of hesitation. That was good, right? No, it did not excuse the letter. "Murdock should be back from his post by now. Excuse me."

"Of course, Your Highness."

Keegan crossed the room and left, slamming the door behind him. The Advisor remained, stalking the room. Silently, I urged him to leave—this wasn't even his space! I heard him snapping his fingers each time he took a slow, lumbering step. The familiar glow of Freetor magic lit the room momentarily and then flamed out.

Abusing Freetor magic, in the middle of Keegan's study! What sort of spell—?

He rounded the desk and paused near the entrance. "I know you're there."

I gritted my teeth and said nothing. All right, so he used Freetor magic to discover he wasn't alone, but he wouldn't be able to tell for sure that it was—

"Kiera."

And then I lost control.

Screaming insults, I leapt from beneath the desk and tackled him. My father hit the wall with such force that all the air escaped his lungs. My grip tightened on his collar. He was stronger than I was, and could easily manoeuvre out of the hold, but he didn't struggle.

"Why?" was the only sensible word that fled my lips.

His eyebrows furrowed, but only slightly. "It's what's best for the realm."

Unblinking, I stared up at the man I had first feared, then despised, and now feared again. My anger transcended into an unstable calm, one that shook my hands and clenched my chest so tightly that I could barely breathe. Slowly I released my grip on his shirt and stepped back. My lips parted but there was nothing appropriate to say.

Every instinct told me to unsheathe my knife. My fingers inched for the thrill of the fight.

Seemingly unafraid, my father regarded me coolly. "I would handle the arrangements. Just one or two appearances to show the East that we are willing to cooperate, and then you could continue on with your life."

"My...life." It was hard to force the words out. My anger choked me. "This. *Is*. My. Life."

He drew closer to me. "Kiera..."

Shaking my head, and ignoring my Freetor instincts, I covered my face and darted for the door. Before I could leave, he caught me by the wrist.

"Let me go," I said in a low, dangerous tone.

Pushing his lips together in a determined line that suddenly reminded me of Rordan, he released his grip. "I can make it up to you."

How could he say that? Cornering Keegan, convincing him that handing me over to the East was the only option for a peaceful realm?

I coated my words with every venomous thought in my being: "I hope you rot."

I ran from the room, and I didn't look back. Even though the scared six-year-old within me who still loved him desperately wanted him to shout my name, he did not call after me.

Six

THE SMOKE THICKENED, taking me back to Rordan's execution.

Danger.

My dagger flew into my hand and my bare feet touched the floor in half a heartbeat. The bedroom was as dark and as cold as the underground. I had fallen asleep hours ago, before the curled sliver moon reached its peak. The roaring fire I'd cultivated while refusing all visitors and meals had suspiciously died. The window: closed. My door: also closed, and locked. For hours, my father had tried to persuade me to leave, but I couldn't face him. Even when Keegan came around in the evening, I treated him with silence. If Keegan didn't want me as his wife—even if he did have feelings for me—he should've had the courage to say so before, instead of putting it off like it wasn't important.

All of this was irrelevant in the moment, for I was not alone.

Dark, thick clouds slowly rolled in from beneath the crack in my door. A fire at the only proper exit to my chambers, to dissuade me from escaping—or to fill my lungs with smoke while I slept. I kept my breathing shallow and quiet as I studied my surroundings for the intruder.

Movement in the corner, from behind the vanity. Night shrouded the attacker; I could just barely distinguish his form. He—perhaps she—leapt nimbly from side to side, soundless on the floor, attempting to anticipate my next move.

"What do you want?" I demanded, stifling the need to cough.

He lunged, and I rolled out of the way. A blade nicked me in the shoulder, tearing the fabric. The attacker tried again. I leapt out of reach of the offending blade—not much larger than a dagger, but more curved than the Freetor shivs and not as refined as a Marlenian blade—and gripped the bedpost for purchase. The smoke obscured my sense of smell, and the past month living on the surface had dulled my ability to see well in darkness. Just as I dove on the bed, the attacker swung again, tearing my nightgown. I gasped, and instead of blindly swinging my dagger, I grabbed the nearest potential projectile: a pillow. I threw it in the attacker's direction, and the knife tore through the plush fabric. I yanked another pillow from the bed and hugged it to my chest as faux armour while I scrambled across the mattress to the other side.

I needed to get to the bag underneath my bed.

I tried reasoning with the shadow once more. "Whoever you are, you're going to be swarmed with royal guards in about two seconds. That is, if I don't stab you first. Tell me who sent you and I may be merciful."

Nothing. A soft *plat* to my left as the attacker leapt onto the bed, and I circled around again. Light. I needed a candle, a fire—something. Darkness was no longer on my side. It was the tool of an unknown enemy. I kept still, with my dagger at the ready. Where did Bidelia put the candles? Right—in the vanity drawer. But how would I light them? Useless, useless...

More smoke filtered in from beneath the door and thickened the air. Coughing was inevitable, and gave away my position immediately. The attacker lunged and caught his blade in the pillow. I seized the opportunity. I stabbed him, sinking the blade to the hilt into his body. I was certain that I had mortally wounded him—and yet he made no sound. A small gasp for air, as one might take before speaking—and then he jabbed his knife once more into my pillow armour. The blade poked through the fabric and nicked my skin through my nightgown.

I stumbled back towards the door, coughing, and abandoned the shredded pillow. The attacker slumped to the floor. He wasn't dead yet. Shallow breaths dominated the silence. I jumped over him and quickly retrieved my sack from beneath the bed. There were four important things in there, besides two days of clothes. One: my magic journal. Two: the Orb of Dashiell. Three: my Violet Fox mask and cape. And four: the expedition notes my father had allegedly written. My dagger trembled in my hand as I slung the bag over my shoulder. Escape routes drew bright lines in my mind.

I gave the still-breathing assassin one more chance as I ran for the door. "Who sent you?"

Another shallow breath, and I leaned in to listen. He drew his blade across my calf. I grunted and stomped on his hand; his dagger clattered to the floor. I kicked wildly until I heard the satisfying sound of metal scraping on wood as the weapon flew across the floorboards, finding a new home under the bed.

I pulled the door open, intending to run as fast as I could down the corridor. Billows of dense smoke hit me and I doubled over, coughing like mad.

Focus!

After pulling my nightgown sleeve over my hand to use as a breath filter, I closed the door to my chamber. There was no resistance from the assassin on the inside.

I could not stand. A memory of Rordan floated back to me. Once, we were on the surface together stealing bread and fruit in the early evening and a bakery suddenly caught fire. Accident or Extremist activity, I didn't know—but we were dangerously close to the building and guards began to evacuate people from the street. We needed to get by, as our safe point was only two buildings down, and the Fighters would only hold it open for a few more minutes. Thick smoke, just like the smoke I waded through now, drifted across the way, creating a thick barrier. Rordan had forced me to my knees and shouted over the chaos: "Crawl!" We'd lost almost half of what we'd stolen that day but we made it to the safe point with only minor bruising to our knees and lungs full of smoke. I was coughing for a day afterward.

I crawled on my hands and knees now over the riveted stone floor, keeping my head down and trying not to breathe. The smoke filled me—even down this low, it was blinding. My eyes watered and I no longer knew whether I was crawling away from my room, or even in a straight line. Where was this smoke coming from? Was everything on fire? Sweat dripped from my forehead and coated my nightgown. I was not used to this heat. I would lose consciousness.

"Kiera. Kiera!"

My name, called from the lips of someone who I thought had loved me. I struggled to form a reply. "Keee...gan..."

"Kiera! Kiera...are you...?" He descended into a coughing fit and fell somewhere near me, disturbing clouds of smoke.

"Here," I rasped. One hand over another, and I touched his leg, then his side. Did he know that I knew about his love letter to Sylvia? Later, I'd think about it later. "Get...up..."

He grunted but complied, feeling my arm, and then my face. "Fire...everything..."

Silent warnings flared in my mind. The scuffing of shoes on stone—the assassin was not dead. I bent over, gripped Keegan's arm tightly, and ran. He protested but I silenced him—had he not run into any shadowy figures on his way to my chambers? Was this the same assassin who had attacked me in the alleyway?

Where was Monju, and would he save us?

Sylvia would never do something like this for Keegan.

Light fought the smoke off to the left—a servants' hallway, which would take us around the Great Hall, bypassing most of the major routes, and out the postern. From there, we could potentially hide in the large hedge maze, or make it to the stables. Or, we could go the other way, around the castle, through the bailey, and climb down the mountain...

Movement in front of us. More attackers? I tugged on Keegan, urging him to stop, but he resisted and limped on. My stubborn prince. The assassin behind us was gaining, but his wounds slowed him. Smoke devastated my senses with every passing second.

"Down!" I managed to shout, inevitably pulling more smoke into my lungs as I urged Keegan to the floor.

A large, lumbering force leapt from the deep darkness, wielding silver steel and wearing heavy armour. But it wasn't interested in us. It came down hard on the assassin behind us, whose life ended with a muffled, strangled whisper.

I was crawling slowly away from the fight when someone grabbed my ankle. I struggled and kicked, feeling once more for my dagger.

"Violet Fox, get up!"

Captain Murdock's commanding tone sent surprised chills through me. I kicked one final time, and he relinquished his grip. He was gentler with Keegan as he helped his monarch to his feet.

"Your Highness, the castle is under siege," Captain Murdock sputtered. "Both of you, with me."

"Under siege?"

"Please…" He descended into a brief coughing fit. "This way, before we choke…"

No time for arguments. Captain Murdock took the lead and led us through the servants' hallway, and down a set of stairs I'd forgotten about, connecting us to a low-ceiling cellar. The air was earthy and clear of smoke. I coughed and sputtered the thick ash from my lungs, though I didn't dare stop moving. After three tries, the captain kicked open a thick wooden door, which led to an old storage room. He quickly gestured us inside, and barricaded the door with heavy, cobwebbed barrels filled with sploshing liquid.

Keegan bent over, coughing violently. "I haven't been down here in ages."

"No one comes here much," the captain explained curtly. He moved around the room with one hand on the wall. There was another exit on the other side, blocked by barrels and crates. Natural light was but a memory. The captain cursed under his breath, and I heard him turn around to address me. "I don't suppose you can see in here?"

"Outlines. Shadows," I said. Now would be a really good time for my father's hand-fire. Though I'd had enough fire and smoke for one night. The earthy smell of the cellar reminded me of the underground, and the longing for my former home surged to new heights.

Now mostly recovered, Keegan rose to his full height. His hair brushed against the stone-and-earth ceiling, causing tiny rocks and dirt to rain upon him. He reached for me, blindly groping the dark. I hesitated, not wanting to be found.

"Kiera?" he asked. "Are you all right?"

I took a slow step backwards to avoid his wandering hand. The wound of his betrayal festered inside me, annoyingly present in our more threatening circumstances. "I'm fine. A few scrapes from the assassin in my quarters, but I'm all right."

"Assassin." Keegan's concern was palpable. He turned towards the general direction of the captain, who was still mapping the room. "Where is my father?"

"The Advisor and the healers are evacuating the Holy One through the secret passage that goes into the cathedral. They should be safe there."

I frowned, recalling my limited knowledge of the passages within the mountain. "Why do I get the feeling we're not joining them?"

"Your Grace, if you would explain." Captain Murdock's voice was strained as he shifted around more heavy barrels.

Keegan stepped towards me. "Having all the royals in one place, it's too dangerous, Kiera. The passage through the cathedral is only one of many beneath the earth. It's not as deep or as sound as your Freetor tunnels, but it serves. We will go this way, through the back, to the stables. In the thick of Feenagh Forest, there is land owned by a lesser lord loyal to my family. Lord Ansel Gareth. We will be safe in Baile Gareth, for a time."

"And what of everyone else in the castle?" My father might be escorting the Holy One to safety, but what about Bidelia and Laoise? And Monju? I did not like this. The castle was under siege; it could be the beginning of an all-out attack on the city. My people—the Freetors and the Marlenians—were in danger. The Violet Fox would never run away and hide herself when an innocent's life was threatened.

"Each person in the castle follows an emergency plan, just as we do. Have faith in me," Keegan pleaded.

This time his hand found my face. It was warm on my cheek. I closed my eyes. He cared about me.

But he didn't care enough. He loved another, and I was a convenient pawn to trade for an uncertain peace.

"Captain, what is going on?" Keegan asked. "How did things get so terrible so quickly? Who's attacking us?"

Murdock grunted and then sighed. "An hour ago, Eastern forces flooded the city. Advisor Ferguson was right to suspect something fishy with the imports. They've been smuggling in men, positioning them in key places for at least the past month. Even some of my own men wore Eastern colours beneath their Tramore crests." He scoffed and spat on the floor. "There was no warning. Some of my men reported hearing a noblewoman scream in the west wing. I chose two of my men to come with me to investigate. We cut through the Great Hall.

"One second, it was a normal night watch. The next, chaos. Ten men strode towards us, with their weapons drawn. Men I thought I knew, had trained, had supped with. Then they tore the Tramore crest off their sleeves, revealing their true Eastern reds and blues, and attacked. I ordered men some to protect the Holy One, to begin emergency procedures for evacuation if necessary. Managed to slay some of the bastards but they just kept coming. I barely escaped, and ran for your quarters, but you weren't there, so I figured you'd gone to the Fox's chambers to…check on her."

"Yes," Keegan admitted sheepishly. "I was already awake, and when I smelled smoke, I was worried about Kiera."

My face reddened at his concern, and I crossed my arms. In the chaos of our escape, I hadn't noticed that he was wearing his day clothes: a white tunic, tight pants, and boots. I was woefully underdressed in comparison. I touched my sack; at least I had that.

"Fires sprang up out of nowhere," Murdock continued. He pushed another heavy barrel out of the way. "Thought it might be the work of the Freetor apprentices, somehow in league with the East, unleashing their magic in anger at us."

I swallowed uncomfortably over the growing lump in my throat. "It wouldn't be the apprentices. They don't want to hurt the Tramore family, as far as I know. They just want to unite the Freetors under one banner."

"And killing the royal family wouldn't do that?" He sneered. "Doesn't matter, I knew it wasn't Freetor work. Far too organized, even for your lot. They had all the time to do that before, if they'd wanted. This was the work of the East. At least...most of it was. Until them shadow killers came for me." His voice grew chilly. "I'd only seen movement like that once before, when I visited High King Matís's castle. The Northern killing arts. Silent, deadly, and effective. Our suspicions of their working together proved true."

"And now they're working together to take over the castle," Keegan said under his breath.

Captain Murdock shoved a crate across the floor. "Always wondered if Matís was building a small army up there. Even one trained assassin could bring down dozens of men without breaking a sweat. Trained from near birth to kill a man in the least number of moves. Only escaped the ones I did because I know the castle better than they do." He grunted, and the door gave way with a loud bang. "Not sure about their physical strength, but we should get moving before they get through the barricade."

I felt Keegan's stare. The assassins in the alleyway must have been from the North. Yet Monju had managed to cut them down. If Monju could face off against deadly, trained killers, he must be just as deadly. I wondered if he had escaped with the rest of the castle nobles, or if he had taken up the Eastern or Northern colours. I prayed it was the former.

"This way, Your Grace," Murdock said, more insistently this time. "Down—"

The raddling of the barricade behind us startled me into action. My grip on the dagger tightened as I whirled around. Even the heavy barrels filled with liquid and who-knew-what trembled before the shouts of the men outside the door.

"Come on out, Murdock, you coward!"

"Give us the prince and we'll give you a warrior's death!"

The barricade wouldn't last long against the East's constant hammering, and we wouldn't last long if the Northern shadow killers got through.

"The tunnel leads out?" I asked.

"It's a maze," Keegan said, retreating behind Murdock and into the dark, dank passageway. "But one exit is by the stables."

Murdock grabbed me by the shoulders and roughly escorted me into the tunnel. "How many damned times do I have to tell you to run, Fox? You used to do it so well."

"You're not going to last long enough against them," I said. "There could be dozens out there. And I can run, but we can't run forever. We need to seal this passageway."

The captain's features softened. He knew I was right. "How?"

I swung my pack around and withdrew the Orb of Dashiell.

"Why do you have the Orb in your pack?" Keegan asked, incredulous. "Did you detach it from the sceptre?"

"The Advisor did," I said. So he hadn't told Keegan. "If I figure out how to use it, I can collapse the entrance to the tunnel. Prevent them from coming through and capturing us."

"Figure fast," Murdock said. "Go on then, and I'll hold them off for as long as I can." Keegan looked ready to object, but Murdock continued. "We don't know if this will work. Better to have both plans than only one. Listen to your lady, Your Highness. If I survive, I will join your father beneath or in the cathedral. Get to Baile Gareth, and remind Lord Ansel of your safe-haven treaty."

My palms warmed with the artefact's mystical power just as the men broke our barricades. First one man squeezed through, slipping on some of the liquid spilled from the barrels. Another shoved him aside, and then another. Their weapons clanged as they fought to establish themselves in the darkness.

"I'm over here, idiots," Murdock muttered.

Keegan and I escaped deeper into the tunnel, and I concentrated on the artefact. It hummed and slowly filled the area with its warm blue light, calling attention to us immediately.

"There!" one of the attackers shouted.

The only time I'd used the Orb, my will had been to save Keegan. Perhaps my conviction to save us was all that was needed. Yet I had called lightning *from the sky*. Would it even work underground?

I had to try.

"I won't let them take us!" I said, and pointed the Orb at the vulnerable entrance to the tunnel.

Murdock, protected by heavy maille but armed only with his silver steel blade, braced to meet the dozen or so invaders storming into the storage room.

"We should run," Keegan said, pulling the fabric of my nightgown. "Captain, you can—"

"Go!" Murdock shouted. "Long reign the Tramore line. Long live—"

Though Murdock and I never saw eye to eye, and he'd spent the last few years chasing me around the streets of Marlenia City, wishing me dead, I would not let his sacrifice be in vain. I squeezed my eyes shut as the ground rumbled. Rocks and clay fell from the ceiling. The Orb lit up a familiar bright blue and the interior clouded in a brewing lightning storm. The magic cast an eerie blue light on the attackers' faces, illuminating their fear and dread of the unknown.

One raised his sword against Murdock, and swung.

Lightning snapped from the Orb and connected with the door frame, and the rocks above, collapsing dirt and rocks between us. Two men tried to get through the rubble, but the more they dug, the more rocks collapsed until they were buried. Keegan dragged me backwards, glancing at the tunnel ceiling, fearing we would meet a similar fate.

Soon we could see nothing of the storage room. Swords clashed, men cried, and Captain Murdock's bellowing howl echoed off the walls. Whether it was his last cry in this world, or a call for strength in the midst of battle, I didn't know. But where the Eastern men were younger, nimble, and agile, Murdock was weathered, lumbering, and unbalanced with his stocky frame.

"Thank you for your sacrifice," Keegan said quietly as the last of the rocks sealed us in the dark, earthy tunnel.

I set my lips firmly as the Orb's unnatural light dimmed, leaving us once again in darkness. "We should go."

Seven

IN THE UNDERGROUND passage of stone and clay, it was hard to tell how long and how far we had run. I led the way, one hand latched to Keegan's arm and the other bracing my bouncing pack. The sooner we found the surface, the sooner I could resume my quest to find the Silver Spear. With the East controlling the castle, there was nothing left for me here. Especially if Keegan didn't really want me.

My throat tightened at the thought.

Once the clanging of swords was a distant sound, Keegan wrenched his arm from my grip. "We...we should...stop..."

I was out of breath too but I wasn't about to show it. I whirled around and Keegan hunched over, hands on his knees, while he recovered. He coughed, trying to be quiet but failing. These walls took every sound and multiplied it by three.

"We shouldn't stay in one place for too long," I whispered.

"I know," he said shortly. He sucked in a deep breath and cleared his throat. "How were you able to use the Orb of Dashiell like that?"

"I felt its power," I replied slowly, reaching around and feeling the bulge in my pack. It radiated heat and warmed my back. "I'd always thought that apprentices and Elders were the only ones who could use magic. But maybe there's potential in all Freetors."

Maybe I didn't need the Spear after all. If I could use the Orb against the East...

It would be me against hundreds of thousands of soldiers. I might be able to take out some of them, but it wouldn't be the same as having a team of skilled apprentices at my side. I needed my people's support. Better to die fighting than as an imprisoned hostage of the East.

"I don't recognize this passage," Keegan said after a minute of terse silence. "We may have taken a wrong turn."

"We can't go back. It's too dangerous."

"I am aware of what is and isn't dangerous."

"Really."

My sarcasm wasn't lost on Keegan. His boots scraped on the dirt as he stepped away from me. "There was a turn back this way, maybe thirty paces. I felt a draft. I think that was the passage that will take us to the surface."

"And if we keep going this way, where does this lead?"

Keegan inhaled sharply and coughed some more. All these sounds, all this discussion, it made me nervous. If it were just me and Rordan, we wouldn't need this deliberation. Sure, I'd put up a fight, but ultimately he'd drag me in the right direction and I'd mumble an apology later. My brother was an ass, but he never failed to protect me.

"I'm not quite sure, but if I recall my studies correctly, a number of these passages were sealed a hundred years ago by my grandfather, after an ambitious Freetor raid. The tunnels stretch deep into the mountain, and exit behind the castle, in the fields. Perhaps some of these passages once connected with the Undercity. It was said that the skeletons of Marlenian and Freetor alike could still be found down here, and that would explain the smell." Another sniff, another cough. "Though that was a story my father would tell, to discourage me from exploring down here as a boy."

"Well your exploring really could've come in handy now."

His hand brushed my shoulder. "Kiera, are you...angry at me for something I *failed* to do as a boy?"

I sighed and ran my hand along the rocky tunnel wall. "No."

He relented. "We'll backtrack then, to where I felt the draft. Once we get to Baile Gareth, I'll remind Lord Ansel of his old treaty. He'll rally his troops, and perhaps send word to the South. It will be our new base to build our resistance. I will not let the Frostfire family take my home from me. Our home."

"I can't go there with you."

"Why?" Then: "Because you want to go after the Spear."

"You don't need me with you," I replied, more quietly. "Getting the Spear is the best thing I can do for the realm." Unlike my father's plan to ship me off to the East. "I won't be in your way. I'll have the Orb with me, and then when you're able to...*settle*...things with the East..."

"Kiera, what are you on about?" Keegan exclaimed. "Of course I need—"

"Don't pretend," I snapped. I couldn't keep the hurt from my voice. "I know about the letter you're writing to Sylvia."

Even in the darkness, I saw his features twist with confusion. "Kiera, what—?"

A rock tumbled from a cavernous passage off to our left.

My heart skipped at the sound. Keegan tensed beside me as he drew his sword from the scabbard at his hip. "Show yourself, or prepare to be slaughtered."

Rock scraped against metal, and flame was born in the adjacent tunnel. Magic. No—pocket flint and a blade, held in skilled hands, gave birth to the fire atop a handful of long twigs.

"Monju," I uttered beneath my breath. "How did you get down here?"

"Found it while escaping the smoke. Seek deeper ground, that is the way when fire strikes," he said, bowing deeply first to Keegan, and then to me. "Is this all that survives? No escorts?"

"My captain...he stayed to fight," Keegan said. He lowered his sword but kept it at the ready.

Monju closed his eyes briefly and muttered a prayer. "Monju is sorry for the prince's loss. A good man sacrifices everything for his prince and his land."

"Yes," Keegan said slowly, sliding his gaze to me. I read everything there: *What is this man doing here? Can we trust him?*

I stepped deeper into the darkness, my footsteps scratching the stone and dirt. "We need to get to the surface. Have you come across an exit?"

Monju shook his head. "If the exit to the surface is behind Monju, then safe passage is not guaranteed. These earths, foreign, but not the sounds of hurrying solider feet. These invaders, they are coming, from all tunnels they are searching from behind. Narrowly evaded some of them. The prince does not know the way out?"

Warily, Keegan glanced behind us, and then returned his suspicious gaze to Monju. "I...might know a way."

This was not good. If there were other ways into the tunnels, then the East and the shadow killers could be on us in any second.

"Quickly, then," Monju urged, and bowed again to emphasize his submissiveness to the monarch. His makeshift torch was burning low—where had he gotten those twigs? He took a few steps to where Keegan's gaze had indicated, and then turned towards us. "Something the matter, Highnesses?"

"Stay ahead of us," Keegan said, gesturing him to keep moving. "Light the way."

"Right. Yes, Highness."

Monju was barely better dressed than I was. His good pants were covered in dirt and clay, and his bright blue shirt was ripped at the collar. Around his waist, a thick belt with a side pouch likely housed his flint and hopefully other useful supplies. His flat shoes gave off the barest of echoes as he scouted ahead for us. The small guitar, slung over his shoulder, hung loosely on his back. I squinted, looking for his blade. As Monju dropped the once-lit twigs and produced shorter ones from his pouch to light, I spotted his weapon. Hanging on his right hip was the curved sword, almost as dark as his pants.

Keegan's mistrust seemed misplaced, but no matter how unarmoured the foreign bard seemed, I couldn't forget the way he'd moved in the alley. He'd beat a shadow killer wearing only a little more than he was now.

And now we were moving through a darkened old tunnel with him. And he was holding the only light source.

"A draft," Keegan said finally, about a hundred paces later before a narrow passageway off to our right. "This way."

The cold air was barely strong enough to lift my tangled hair. "You're sure...?"

Monju turned right down the new passageway, holding the light above his head. Every few seconds, he turned his head for Keegan's next order, but Keegan waved him on. Just as I was beginning to doubt our choice of direction, Keegan lifted his hand.

"It's coming from up here," Keegan said, squinting. "Cut the light."

Monju obeyed without question. Once again the darkness enveloped us. The three of us stared at the ceiling. There was a slight *whoosh* of movement as Monju pointed. "There."

It took me several moments to see it. A slight square outline of a trap door, lit by the faint yellow of torchlight. It would have been obscured by Monju's much more powerful flame, and would take a keen eye to spot.

"Your darkness vision is impressive," I said. "A month above ground and I feel I've gotten rusty. Used to take me only a few seconds to transition."

"Lived and travelled underground at times, Lady. Freetors do not pay for Monju's songs, but they make appreciative audiences. How would the prince like to proceed?"

It took some awkward manoeuvring, but Keegan knelt to give Monju a knee up to the trap door. With a loud *whoomph*, Monju pushed the dirt door ajar. A shower of tiny rocks, dust, and manure rained on Keegan. Despite the situation, I stifled a snort.

Keegan spat on the ground and grimaced as yellow light spilled upon his handsome face. He shifted, allowing Monju better purchase. "How are we up there?"

"Clear," he said.

I listened for potential intruders in the nearby tunnels, but heard only the echoes of our efforts. The more distance we put between us and this cursed castle, the better. Monju pushed the door open all the way with another *thump*, and Keegan hoisted him through the generous opening.

For a brief, torturous moment, I thought that Monju might shut the door and leave us trapped down in the tunnels.

His helping hand dispelled my doubts.

I was next. Keegan's strong grip kept my core steady as I climbed on top of him. I closed my eyes, savouring his touch, realizing with a deep pang that it could be the last time I felt his hands on me. I had gotten so used to him touching my shoulder, my wrist, my face in reassurance. Yet with the war preparations, we'd had barely a moment to ourselves to express any kind of deeper affection.

Now we'd never have that chance.

Monju grabbed my arm, and I gripped the wooden edge of the opening to wedge myself up. My bag briefly caught—the opening was barely large enough for my slight form and my full sack—but I shifted the contents and eventually it gave way. The early morning air was cool but still, Monju's grip was warm and calloused. His fingertips were especially rough; tough skin was required to perform daily.

His touch reminded me of Rordan's. Skilled, and always there.

"Thanks," I said to him, with the barest of smiles, finding my feet quickly on the hay-covered wooden floor.

"Welcome, Lady Kiera," he replied, with a slight dip of his head.

One second. Two seconds. Only then did he release me.

Three torches lit the walls, casting odd shadows about the stables. Horses rustled restlessly in their stalls, perhaps wondering about the sudden, unexpected intruders from beneath the earth. The smell of smoke wasn't as strong as it had been in the tunnels and in the castle itself, but it permeated the air, reminding us of what was burning. To our left, the large stable doors were wide open, displaying the slight decline of the hill, and the stretch of fields and forests beyond.

Freedom.

And foes. I mustn't let down my guard yet, not until we were clear of the castle grounds. There were far too many shadows in the stable. Suitable for the Violet Fox, but she was not the huntress today. I gripped the strap across my body. I carried everything of value with me, and I was too vulnerable a target.

So was Keegan.

"Some help from the lady?" Monju implored as he knelt before the hole.

I crouched beside Monju as he lay flat on his stomach. Very few words passed between us. Evidently I was not the only experienced one helping people climb in and out of holes in the earth. I placed most of my weight over his legs, holding him steady as his upper body disappeared into the hole to help Keegan up. Keegan himself was not heavy—if anything he'd lost weight in the past month under his new stress. Monju quietly strained under Keegan's weight until the prince gripped the edge of the opening, and was able to pull himself up the rest of the way.

As Monju closed and covered the trap door, I took count of the horses. In a stable that held at least thirty, seven horses remained in their stalls. The other stalls were open, and in the darkness, I thought I could see more outside.

"If we're quick, we can get the horses ready and be out of Tramore territory before dawn," I said.

The idea of leaving our people behind struck an unpleasant chord in my stomach. The brief sting of regret flashed upon Keegan's face as well. But to stay was to be under the East's control, and we could neither rally forces nor retrieve magical artefacts without leaving the comforts of home behind.

"It's barely two days' ride to Baile Gareth on horseback. Three or four through the forest and less-travelled routes," Keegan said, mostly to me.

"Yeah," I said, crossing my arms, glancing at the horses again. "You'll be safe there."

Keegan frowned. He was working hard to contain his frustration in front of Monju. "The Forever Sea is at least a fortnight's ride. We have no food, no water, and no sleeping supplies."

"If Monju may interject," he said respectfully. "If the lady wishes to head to the Forever Sea, to seek refuge in the lands of her ancestors, can happily lead the way. Very good at foraging, surviving with little but the fruits of the land."

"No, I think you'd better stay with me," Keegan said just as I replied, "I'd be happy for the company."

I pursed my lips. I knew he didn't trust the bard and that he was thinking it would be better to keep him in his sights than send him back to the castle, where he might report our whereabouts to eager Eastern ears.

In his most respectful low tone, Keegan said, "If I may have a moment alone with *the lady?*"

Monju bowed his head. "Will begin preparing horses."

Keegan dragged me to the opposite side of the stables to his favourite horse, a shiny black stallion affectionately named Lord Beauty, and began preparing the beast for riding. He lowered his voice. "Tell me what's wrong, Kiera. You know I can't stand to have you mad at me."

"I told you. I'm not going with you. Finding the Spear is important."

"Yes, and then you said I apparently don't need you."

"You don't. I don't," I said quietly, trying hard to keep the hurt from my voice.

He grabbed my hand. "Clearly."

"Let go. I'm going."

"Just like that?"

"Yes, just like this. You don't need to worry about me anymore."

He sighed, and glanced over at Monju. He had his back to us and was going through a saddle rack at the other end of the stables. Keegan's grip loosened, but he would not release me. "I know how important the Spear is to you, and your people. You're right in that the apprentices likely won't help us without it. But you're mad at me for something that I don't know anything about. Whatever *letter* you're referring to, me and Sylvia—"

"Were you and my father going to sell me to the East?"

Keegan was taken aback. Then, afraid. Another fitful glance at

Monju. "Kiera, it's not what you think. And it was the Advisor's idea. Not his best."

I wrenched my arm from his grip. "You're right about that one."

Before he could retort, I crossed the stables and retrieved a saddle. Keegan impatiently paced as I prepared the horse. Apparently he was too flustered to make Lord Beauty ready himself.

"I'm sorry, Kiera. I was meaning to tell you. I should have made it more of a priority."

Yes, he should have. Once the saddle and the reins were prepped, I leapt up onto the horse and sat side-saddle, facing the prince. I had a change of clothes in my pack, but that could wait until we were out of immediate danger.

"Would you...look at me, at least?"

I wanted to. But I feared if I did, he would see the hurt in my eyes, and I'd melt and apologize, when I wasn't sure if I could.

"Kiera, just *listen* to me for one *moment*!"

The horse whinnied and jostled me, sending flurrying anxiety from my core to my extremities. I was still new to riding, and any sudden movement from the horse startled me. The horse was clearly already displeased, possibly for being chosen for riding in the middle of the night.

Keegan petted the horse's side to calm him. "Yes, there was a plan to *trade* the Violet Fox to buy us some time to prepare for war. But not *you*, Kiera. A doppelgänger, who would escape the East's clutches two or three days after the exchange. Or, she would stay and feed the East incorrect information. Your father hadn't worked out the details, and I didn't want him to. The whole idea was full of holes and risks. Not to mention, the biggest risk of them all: that the imposter would be discovered, killed, and the East would attack anyway."

One or two appearances, and then you'd be free to live your own life, he'd said.

He hadn't wanted to put me in danger. Just my name.

My pride festered, making it hard to admit that I'd misunderstood the plan—making it hard to forgive Keegan, and forgive myself for treating him this way. He took my silence as permission to continue.

"Tell me about this letter you saw, from Sylvia?"

I allowed him a furtive glance. "Not from. To."

Monju led his chosen horse, a handsome mare with black and brown colouring named Song Spirit, towards us. "If His Highness does not have a favourite horse, this one is ready. Possibly better for Lady Kiera than the black stallion, considering size."

Keegan blinked as if waking from a dream. "You may have that one. If you would ready this one here"—he pointed to an adjacent brown-and-white horse named Winnie—"the quicker we can depart."

"Yes, Highness."

I didn't protest as Keegan led me and Lord Beauty outside the stables, into the night, though I hated being exposed. He stared up at the castle, an oddly shaped shadow melded with the contours of the mountain, partly aglow from the raging flame. We were not close enough to hear sounds, but I strained, and I thought I heard the shouts of determined guards, but whether they wore Frostfire or Tramore colours could not be known.

It was his home, and we were watching it burn.

I was so reminded of the image of Rordan suffering in the Grand Square that I looked away, torn.

"I..." What could I say? "I just...I know that I'm not the easiest fiancée to have...I'm of low birth, and my only value is in my name. Sylvia is a better match, politically."

"Kiera, what are you on about?" he asked again. He reached up and took my hands in his, and I stiffened. "Do you think this attack has something to do with my feelings for you? Or my relationship with Sylvia?"

My eyes flared. "Then you admit it."

"Admit what?"

"Your relationship with Sylvia. You intended to marry her."

"I almost did." He frowned, and amusement crept over his face in the yellow light. "This is old water, Kiera. I chose you."

"You were going to marry her, even when you had feelings for me."

"I almost married her, despite my feelings, to appease our respective fathers and forge a strong alliance between the East and the West. But none of that matters now." He gestured up to the castle. "They have made their position clear."

I looked away. I realized with a sudden, anxious pang that both of our fathers were still in grave danger—possibly dead. "If you had married her, none of this would have happened."

"We can't think like that." He squeezed my hands tighter. "We are respected figures for our people. We can't dwell on what-ifs. We can only move forward."

I glanced to the west, to the looming, shadowy forests.

"So this letter," he ventured once again, "it was to Sylvia, from me?"

I nodded.

"In my handwriting?"

"And in your study."

"Professing my love?"

Again, I nodded.

"Look at me, Kiera."

Slowly, I shifted my gaze to his. In his yellow-green irises I saw the sincere look of a man who could only speak truth.

"I don't know how that letter got there. But I swear on..." He thought for a moment. "I swear on my father's life that I didn't write it. You're the only one, Kiera. The one that I—"

Monju's urgent voice, suddenly behind me: "Lady Kiera, look out!"

From the shadows of the distant forests, four men, dressed head-to-toe in tight black wrappings and wielding long, thin, curved swords materialized on the sloping plains. There was nowhere to hide; the men seemed to have spontaneously appeared. One of them leapt in front of Lord Beauty, spooking him, and causing him to rear. Keegan jumped backwards and drew his weapon. I was thrown from the saddle and landed hard on the grass.

I grabbed my knife from my sack and found my feet, once again terribly aware that I was in my torn, dirty nightgown. One of the men lunged at me, whipping his knife. It whizzed past my ear as

I ducked. He didn't hesitate and struck again: this time, the blade dove into my left shoulder. A blinding, burning pain rippled through my body. My attacker stole the knife and raised it to strike again but I rolled out of the way just as he brought the blade down hard onto the grass.

I crawled away, my fingernails digging into the dirt. I couldn't feel my left arm. Blood seeped from the wound. Keegan was up ahead. He wielded a one-handed sword, but his attacker wielded two small knives, and Keegan had no shield. The prince swung. The attacker ducked and jabbed Keegan, but my prince hit the man in the arm with the blunt side of the knife. He wasn't trying to hurt them, I realized. Perhaps he hoped to negotiate. That kind of approach would get him killed.

My head pounded. Someone grabbed my legs and pulled. I shouted nonsense and implanted my fingers into the ground, tearing up the grass as I was dragged along.

Keegan's head snapped in my direction. "Kiera!"

My eyes widened as Keegan let his guard down. "WATCH OUT!"

The attacker lunged. Keegan swung his sword with both hands. His blade caught the man in the neck. I squeezed my eyes shut and looked away as steel sliced skin all the way to bone.

The shadow killer dragging me suddenly released his grip as Monju tore into action with his long, curved blade. Within moments, his opponent was in pieces on the grass.

I wasn't down yet. I refused to be out of the fight just because my shoulder gushed blood with every small movement. But instead of climbing to my feet like a Fighter, I cowered on the cold ground in the fetal position. My head swam. Shouts, thuds, steel clanging on steel—another man down.

Up. Get up.

Finally, I pushed myself to a sitting position. I squinted. Two figures remained standing. Two lumps on the ground. Several horses, minding their own business.

The figures came closer, and I fumbled for my knife before realizing the men were Keegan and Monju. I frowned and tried to save face, pressing on the wound both to stop the bleeding and hoping Keegan wouldn't notice how badly I'd been hurt.

The ruse was foolhardy. "Kiera! You're wounded," Keegan said urgently, cupping my face. "We have to get you somewhere safe."

I bit my lip. I couldn't let him see me in pain. I couldn't let Monju see me in pain. "I'll be all right."

The conflict was written all over his face. It was possible that some of the castle staff and nobles were holed up in the cathedral, or in the tunnels beneath it. It was also possible that some of the healers escaped. If we went back into the tunnels, there was a slim chance that we could find them.

"Can find healing herbs in the forest. But cannot go back," Monju said quietly as he slid his blade back in its scabbard on his hip. "Those assassins, too powerful. Trained shadow killers of the North. Not masters, lucky for the prince. Masters train from birth. These were good, though their moves...they are not fluid. But powerful enough to overwhelm the uninitiated." He picked up the nearest killer's blade, and sniffed the sharp edge. "Lucky the blades are not poisoned. Potent venoms and antidotes are the North's secret weapons; they are the best in the world."

"You...saved me in the alley, didn't you?" I said, looking up to Monju.

Monju's silver canine glinted as he smirked and tossed the shadow killer's blade on the ground. "Yes, Lady Kiera."

"Were you following her?" Keegan asked bluntly. "You seem rather *initiated* yourself in these arts."

"Monju is familiar with the teachings. A blended style, from many teachers, practiced over many years on many soils." His expression soured as Keegan's insinuation sank in. "Monju would not do anything to bring danger to the prince or the lady. Is only here to serve."

"He saved us," I said. "If he hadn't been here..."

Keegan curled his lips, but said nothing. I hadn't meant to undermine him.

"Shadow killers never travel alone," Monju said as his gaze travelled from the burning castle to our position. "They attack in spades. Eastern men invaded, gained trust, and betrayed the prince, yes? Saw the men, wearing East colours. Barely escaped the chambers. Castle, overrun. East, they are a spurned lover. North, want revenge for the lady impersonating the Northern daughter. If East and North share common cause, and the South have no part, then Monju Farin of the South has no ill wish upon the Prince of the West, rightful Holy One of Marlenia."

Keegan's hand wrapped around the hilt of his sword as he stood to face the bard. "What are you saying?"

Even in the dim light, I saw Monju's furtive glance at me. He turned to Keegan, stern-faced and determined, and knelt on one knee. "Monju Farin swears fealty to the rightful prince of Marlenia. Will help him to regain his throne. Will help his lady, brave Kiera Driscoll, the Violet Fox, on her quest to hold the Forever Sea in her shining blue eyes."

"Monju Farin, I am...touched...by your devotion," Keegan said slowly. His gaze darted around, searching for more shadow killers, and settled on me. I nodded encouragingly. "But why me?"

Again, Monju smiled. "The prince and his lady are players in an epic. Monju writes, sings such tales. The song, sung to His Highnesses and so loved by all? Much fame upon Monju, much silver. More silver, if another such song were spun. But not just about the silver," Monju said quickly. "Believes in the prince. Believes in the lady. Would not wish to see them come to harm. Monju will protect His Highnesses. See them to their final destinations." He looked between Keegan and me. "Wherever that might be."

"There is something buried on my family lands that might be able to help us take back the throne, and defeat the East," I said, not wanting to explain everything while I was still bleeding in unsafe lands. "But we should keep moving, before more shadows come to life."

"Agreed," Monju said. "What say the prince?"

Keegan heaved a sigh. "Normally royal protectors are knighted, and have lands of their own."

"That is unnecessary. Silver and steel are enough, if the prince agrees."

"All right," Keegan said finally, urging Monju to stand. "I accept your fealty, Monju Farin. Where we're going, we'll decide once we're out of Tramore lands."

As Keegan and Monju helped me to my feet and onto a horse, I stole one last glance at the burning mountain castle. Smoke billowed out of the Advisor's towers and several other windows. Where was my father? Did he have enough magical knowledge to keep our people safe?

The sun peeked from behind the mountain, adding to the red and yellow illuminating glow. I turned my cheek to the castle, and looked to the west.

Eight

SWEAT POURED DOWN our backs as we rode hard through Tramore territory. More than once, an Eastern search party caught our scent, and we took advantage of the thick Feenagh Forest trees to conceal ourselves. We only stopped to hide, and for Monju to forage for berries and disciple daisies, the latter of which he tore apart and placed directly on my shoulder wound. I also consumed the bitter purple flowers to ease the throbbing pain. Although Monju was no healer, he said the attacker's knife hadn't pierced the vital bundle of nerves that controlled my arm movement.

"Likely deliberate," he added as he used my nightgown as a temporary bandage on the wound. I had since changed into my familiar Violet Fox clothes. "Shadow killer would know where and where not to stab. May have wanted to take the lady alive."

"Lady Dominique did say she wanted to cut out my tongue and feed me to her dogs," I muttered.

Keegan looked worried, but transformed the emotion into steely determination. I supposed I hadn't told him about that either.

By midafternoon, we passed out of royal lands and into the thick of the Western province. Patrols seemed thinner—perhaps the East and the North were more concerned with holding the castle they'd just burned, and controlling the hopefully rebelling citizens.

Finding water was our priority. Keegan's knowledge of his family's surrounding lands aided us in finding a stream where we could refresh ourselves, and clean my wound. I recalled our romp many weeks ago to a similar but larger stream, when I had unknowingly thwarted my brother's attempt to assassinate Keegan and almost drowned in the process. I quickly squirrelled Rordan from my mind, as I didn't know how to reconcile my love for the brother who'd raised me with the image of the traitor who would kill innocents just so he and his kin could live on the surface.

This part of the wood was thick, and Monju was adamant that we abandon our horses soon. More than once they had almost given us away. "Will run back to the stables, find hay there," he assured me.

"Without horses, we'll have no hope of traversing the stretch of land that leads into Baile Gareth with haste," Keegan replied bitterly, stroking Lord Beauty affectionately. He'd taken to riding him, as he could handle his size better than I could. "Assuming my topographical knowledge of the region is correct, the forests will continue to thicken if we stay south of the main road. And as for the journey west, to avoid the roads and the villages, you'll need to stay in the treed areas until you reach Iar Bunsula, marking the start of the Shoulder Mountains."

Monju's eyes flickered with respect. "The prince knows his lands."

He nodded curtly. Of course he did: they were his to govern. Only I seemed to note Keegan's use of *you*—meaning he was undecided about accompanying me to find the Spear. I realized that of the three of us, I was the least knowledgeable of the region. Yes, I had looked at a fair number of maps since my tutoring began, but a month's worth of studying was no match for years of schooling. And no doubt Keegan's knowledge—assuming he hadn't travelled extensively through the area—was no match for Monju's keen woodsmen skills. I didn't know how well-travelled our bard was, but from what I had been able to glean from him so far, I figured he knew how to survive in and adapt to any situation he found himself in.

Nine days to a fortnight, then. Most of it through the woods, until the forest thinned and we approached the rocky baile that housed the holy town of Iar Bunsula. Then, through the windy Throat—the pass between the mountains that led to the edge of the world: Driscoll's End. According to Monju, there was nothing but sea beyond that.

But only three, maybe four days until Baile Gareth. Would Keegan trust Monju enough to allow him to accompany me to the Forever Sea while he went and rallied forces at Baile Gareth?

Moreover: would Baile Gareth even be safe, now that the East had control of Marlenia City?

These thoughts plagued me as we rode, and kept me from thinking about the pain in my shoulder. In the late afternoon of the following day of our escape from the castle, after many hours of silence save the sounds of our horses, we stopped briefly to rest. Our sleep had been fitful in our quest to escape Tramore lands. Now that we had passed Wending River, which marked the divide between royal hunting grounds and the beginning of Baile Chadwick (the land was worked by a lord of a newly made noble family—Keegan was unsure if their loyalty was sound), we could find a suitable place to camp. So long as we stayed in the thick of Feenagh Forest for shelter.

"Has the lady ever seen the sea?" Monju asked in a calming low voice as he stroked our horses. The three of us had barely spoken since leaving royal grounds, and had just stopped to allow the horses a brief rest.

I shook my head and leaned back against a thick tree trunk, massaging my upper arm tenderly. "No. It's hard to imagine so much water in one place."

"Beautiful sight," Monju replied, inclining his head and ducking beneath a large fir-tree branch as he approached Keegan and me. "Peta took young Monju to Xelliim Harbour for the Festival of Lights." *Peta* was a Southern term for *father*. "Islands are spread in the harbour. Have fishermen, others who live there. Further out still, boats, and the fishers who live on them. But not quite Driscoll's End. There, no boats, no fishers. Just...sea and sky, and where they kiss." He brought his hands together gently, his reins trapped between his grip, and he smiled at me.

"Sounds lovely," I said, glancing at Keegan.

The prince merely nodded. His mind seemed elsewhere.

"The lady mentioned," Monju said slowly, "that she suspected something was buried in Driscoll family lands?"

Keegan's fierce gaze narrowed on Monju. A warning.

"Yes," I said, just as carefully. From my sack, I withdrew my father's expedition notes and splayed them on my lap. Monju didn't dare venture too close, out of respect, but he leaned in with curiosity to peer at the strange Freetor symbols. "An ancient weapon. An artefact."

"Emphasis on ancient," Keegan added. "If it's there at all. We have no way of knowing if the information we have is current, or correct. It may just be a story."

I gritted my teeth. Was this his way of trying to convince me to go to Baile Gareth, or did he truly believe the journey to the edge of the world to be futile?

"Stories bring silver," Monju replied, stroking his chin. "But an ancient weapon, if well-cared for, worth more in a warrior's hand."

I didn't want to argue with Keegan in front of Monju, and it seemed that Monju and the apprentices had the same view of the Spear. "It *is* there," I said finally, casting a glance at Keegan. "These are notes from someone who has travelled this path before, and found the...artefact."

"Oh?" Monju appeared genuinely curious. "A reliable source?"

"Yes. Very." I opened it to the section where my father described the forest. Reading through it quickly, I thought we were around the same place. It had taken us less time to travel through the Tramore lands, since we'd made fewer stops.

"What script is that?" Monju asked.

"Freetor code. You can't read it?"

"No. Not really. A rune or two is familiar, but the combinations were never taught to Monju. Can get by just fine with Marlenian letters and Roamer shorthand." He smiled, and his silver tooth gleamed. "The lady would teach Monju someday, perhaps?"

"Oh. Sure, I guess." But not with this text. If Monju was telling the truth, then the expedition notes were safe from his potential prying eyes, as was my personal journal. "Maybe later."

Keegan leaned in to inspect the book. "What does it say?"

"Several leagues ahead of where we are now, the...man in the notes...was attacked by what he describes as *creatures*. Wolves, maybe?"

"It doesn't seem like their sort of territory," Keegan said slowly, unsure of himself.

"The prince is correct," Monju said. "Though there are some packs in the South. Sometimes the Roamers capture them as pets, bring them up, only to have them escape into the wild. Perhaps those are the creatures?" He looked thoughtful as he mused. "Though...there are stories of beatag nesting in this region of Marlenia..."

"Those are just stories," I said, amused that Monju also knew of the mystical, dangerous beasts.

"Predators aside," Keegan said, "we should keep moving to find a proper place to sleep so that we aren't discovered by Eastern scouts or Northern assassins."

That we could agree upon. Half a league later, we arrived at a patch of somewhat flat terrain that was less root infested than its surroundings. It was already late in the evening, and I was exhausted. The sun was saying its last goodbyes. Keegan had been nodding off in his saddle for the past half-league, and although I knew Monju was trying to hide it, he was yawning into his left sleeve every few minutes. To spare their prides, I suggested we rest for a few hours.

We had only what blankets Monju had nicked from the stables to lie upon. The grass was relatively comfortable, by Freetor standards. While Keegan tethered the horses to the nearby trees, Monju and I quietly built a small fire in tandem. Barely a word was exchanged between the two of us. We knew what to do to survive, he more so than I, as I was not a Forest Freetor. The evening had brought a sharp chill, and although I hated to admit it, I had gotten used to the castle's near-constant warmth.

The firepit we built was small but adequate: it could be easily scattered in an emergency—a circle of stones surrounding a small pile of dry twigs and leaves. Monju set to work creating sparks with his flint and blade. If my father were here, he could light a fiery blaze in his palm. My stomach felt queasy just thinking about him.

My prince slumped against a nearby tree, staring mindlessly into the forest. Briefly I thought about working on convincing him to come to Driscoll's End. In a day, maybe two, we'd be faced with that decision. But he could barely keep his eyes open, and my own head was spinning. He needed rest. We all did.

After about ten minutes of awkward silence, Monju finally managed to make fire with his flint. I cheered, then slapped my hand over my mouth, afraid the noise had carried. Keegan jolted into action, startled. His gaze darted around the clearing as his hand went for the hilt of his sword.

"Sorry," I whispered. "It's fine. Go to sleep. We've got a lot of riding to do."

"I know." There was a bitterness to his tone that I didn't appreciate. He hadn't wanted to come on this journey. Who knew what High King Leszek was doing to the castle, to our people now.

I needed his support. But he also needed mine.

"Shouldn't one of us keep watch?" Keegan asked, rubbing his eyes.

Monju bowed his head. "The lady and her prince need their rest. Monju will watch the forest."

That didn't placate Keegan. "You're our guide. You should be the one who has the most rest. I'll take the first watch, and Kiera can take the second."

"Prince Keegan, with respect, Monju's sleeping is secondary to the prince's safety."

"Yes, *our* safety"—he gestured between me and him—"is vital. Which is why I'd like to take the first watch."

"Monju does not think—"

I grabbed a nearby fallen branch and whipped it through the air, striking one of the boulders off to the right between the trees. "Stop it. *I'll* take the first watch. At the first sign of trouble, I'll wake the both of you."

Keegan's eyebrows drew up, but he was too tired to argue further. Monju deferred to my judgment immediately, and so it was decided. Keegan was asleep within minutes. He didn't seem to mind his grassy bed and starry blanket as he rolled onto his side. Gentle snores escaped him. I sighed with relief. Monju lay next to the fire a few feet from Keegan. He slept on his back. Or at least, he closed his eyes, and his breathing slowed.

I leaned back against the rough bark of the nearby tree and let out a slow, long sigh. It'd been a while since I'd been expected to stay awake for a long watch. Most of my Violet Fox escapades had been during the day. And not all of them had involved staking out places—though usually I wouldn't be watching a place alone, I'd be with Rordan or Laoise.

A gentle wind swept through the trees, bringing with it the scents of the unfamiliar forest. The flames of our fragile fire wavered. It was a cloudy evening, and the fire was likely too small to give off enough smoke to be discovered. Beside the warmth, it would be easy to be lulled into sleep.

Writing—that would keep me alert. Just thinking about putting the quill to the magical pages of my journal awakened the urge within me. The desire arrested me, perhaps because I was finally alone with my thoughts, and outside the confines of the castle and the bustling streets of Marlenia City. I surrendered gladly.

I rose and slung my pack over my shoulder. Keegan and Monju breathed slow and peacefully in the depths of sleep. I didn't want them to wake and discover me penning my secrets. I wouldn't go far. They'd be all right for fifteen minutes or so. I hoped.

My eyes, now fully adjusted to the overwhelming darkness, still had trouble navigating the forest's thick growth. I took it one footstep at a time, ever conscious of the crunching of the leaves underfoot, and the snapping of the fragile branches jutting out from the large overgrown trees.

I counted forty paces before I turned around and realized I could no longer see the camp. Far enough. The untamed forest pressed against me and stretched for leagues; I wasn't going to find a cozy clearing to curl up in. Although many of the trees sported fragile branches closer to the ground, the branches further up appeared larger and sturdier.

Perfect.

Climbing a tree was like scaling a wall, but a lot more convenient. At least after I cleared the first few stone-throws. Branches stuck out like helping hands as I gripped their sappy, rough limbs and pulled myself up. The moonlight glinted through the collection of leaves. After a few minutes of climbing, my arm ached fiercely. With Monju's knowledge and skillful application of herbs, the wound was healing quicker than I'd anticipated, but I didn't want to aggravate it and undo the progress.

The pain became too great for me to go any farther. I settled for a long, thick branch five stone-throws from the ground. I wrapped my legs around it and leaned against the rough bark. Balancing myself on a tree wasn't the easiest thing in the world, but I'd trapeezed on much narrower surfaces at greater distances from the ground. It was nice to be away from the men, and up here in the tree, I began to feel a lot like my old self. The one with fewer responsibilities and worries. The Violet Fox only had to worry about protecting the Freetor people and giving the Marlenians a run for their silver.

Swinging my pack around and placing it between my legs, I undid the binding to check on the valuable contents inside. I breathed a sigh of relief. The Orb of Dashiell appeared undamaged. I drew it out of the bag, admiring the beauty and the power of the ancient artefact. The Orb was slightly larger than my fist and burned fiercely in the night. Cradling it to my chest, I couldn't look away. I had made this work, more than once now. Did that mean I had an aptitude for magic?

The Freetors were descendants of Alastar the Hero and his followers. Alastar was said to have great innate power, and he had awoken this power within those who shared his aptitude. What was required to wield such power, I didn't know. But Alastar's blood was surely in my veins, and it had helped to save the people of Marlenia when Erskina threatened us all.

The Elders carefully selected potential apprentices around their eleventh or twelfth name-days. I hadn't been one of them, and I'd assumed that like most of the Freetor population, I just wasn't gifted enough to wield the unique Freetor ability. Yet because of my father, I was beginning to believe that anyone could learn. Perhaps Erskina and the Elders had chosen their apprentices not based on magical aptitude but on individual will—easier to control meek, mature apprentices than unruly, outspoken youngsters.

I returned the Orb to the bag. I'd figure out its secrets later. It rested in a nest that I'd created out of my Violet Fox cape. Better for me to have it in Feenagh Forest than for it to be in the hands of the North or the East.

My hand touched the leather-bound journal. It tore me up inside to avoid writing. I had been in the habit of recording each day's events as if I were really talking to my father, as that was what he had made me promise I would do just before he left.

And now, the idea that he might really be gone this time weighed on me.

I pulled it out of the sack. The quill marked the page where I'd last written. My handwriting and the worn pages glowed faintly of Freetor magic. Though I had written thousands of pages of content since my father's disappearance, the journal itself wasn't more than three hundred pages. One of the few sacred Freetor-magic items to be treasured—what my father had done to acquire this, I didn't know. I splayed the tome across my lap.

Usually it was easy to figure out what to write. But now, even though so much had happened, I found it hard to put my experiences into words. On a fresh, blank page I allowed my hand to guide the magical quill to create what I could not express.

I wish that things were easier.

I rolled my eyes at my naivety. My father would scoff at such a statement. Complaining never got anything done.

Maybe I was more like him than I thought.

I was about to give up on the whole affair and return to camp when a bright yellow light on the page caught my eye.

Kiera.

There it was, my name, written in tight cursive. Not my sprawling handwriting. This was the script of someone highly organized. Someone who kept secrets close to his chest.

And someone who was a Freetor.

I knew this handwriting.

But how...?

The runes shone gold before fading into a dull black. I grabbed the quill and let the tip hover over the page. Ink dripped beside my name. It hissed as the paper absorbed the black ink.

Is someone there? I wrote.

It was silly, thinking that someone was inside my magic journal. But it held all of the words I'd written since my father left. I couldn't dismiss its other potential abilities.

A sudden longing squeezed my stomach. *Let Rordan's soul be in this tome,* I prayed, *so I can tell him I'm sorry.*

More words appeared on the page, as if someone were slowly burning them into existence.

Today is your name-day.

I clenched my teeth. So my initial instinct had been correct. My father.

I thought about closing the book, climbing back down to the campsite, and going to sleep. If I didn't go back soon, Keegan might wake, see me gone, and come looking for me. Or worse, Monju might come out. He might actually be able to find me.

As if the words could read my urgency, more appeared.

I know you're reading this. I augmented our journals so we could talk this way, just in case. Don't leave. Tell me where you are.

Augmented our journals—just in case I ran off without consulting him further about the Spear. A gentle breeze fluttered the pages. I wondered if he could read all the other entries in the journal. I had written them for him, but my insides twisted at the thought of his eyes upon them now. Through the thick stream of branches and boughs, I thought I saw the embers of our fire burning out, though it could have been my imagination.

Is it really my name-day?

The reply was swift.

Yes. I can only assume you're safely away from the castle if you're writing to me this way.

My thoughts went to the castle, and the smoke that had billowed from the Advisor's tower.

We're safe. Where are you?

The question seemed so personal. He'd been gone from my life for so long that I hadn't had to ask it. When he'd entered my world again, sitting there on my bed in the castle, declaring his true identity with our identical journals splayed on the sheets...I hadn't had to ask again. Yet he weaved in and out of my days, lecturing me on the castle ways, always there, but never really present. He wasn't my father. He was trying to be a ruler. A teacher. An Advisor.

Someone I didn't need.

I escaped through a tunnel in the cathedral, he wrote. *I'm underground with the Elder apprentices. They are shielding Undercity entrances with magic. Please tell me that Keegan is with you.*

The desperation in his words. For *Keegan.* He just wanted his precious prince to be safe so that he could stay in the city. My now-short, bitten nails dug deep into the black leather that housed the magical pages of the journal.

Kiera? Both of our futures depend on Keegan's life. Is he alive?

I thought about lying. Not like he could do anything to find out if I was telling the truth. My handwriting was shaky. Hesitant.

Of course he's alive. We are safe away from the castle.

Then, from him:

You're not taking him to the Spear, are you?

I gritted my teeth.

Maybe.

Something crunched the dead leaves on the ground. I slammed the book shut, trapping the quill in the folds of paper, and froze. Waiting. One second. Two seconds. Then, another crunch. I squinted through the boughs. A dark figure stalked the forest floor. I couldn't see his face, or make out the details of his clothing, but he moved as though he didn't understand the forest. Breaking branches underfoot, making a racket as he lumbered through the dark greenery. Searching.

Keegan?

I sucked in air slowly through my nose, thinking about turning it into words. He stopped at the base of the tree. I hugged the journal close to my chest. The Orb sparked and glowed all shades of blues between my thighs. Could he see it? Any minute now he'd be calling to me. And he'd ask me why I was hiding, what I was writing...

Leaves fluttered as his boots disturbed their rest. The sounds grew faint as he trudged off, back towards the campsite.

My lungs hurt from lack of breathing. My left arm ached. My back cramped from leaning against the tree trunk. When the sounds of the night overtook the figure's rambling, I opened the journal again. Some of the ink from the quill had pooled on the page. My father's latest message was written with a hasty hand.

Hurry. The Eastern forces are occupying the city. Some Northerners too. The Freetors and the poor are being slaughtered in the streets. More die every day that the prince is not found. Our magic is limited. I know you have the Orb. Bring the Spear and the Orb back so we can save our people.

King Leszek ordered a search party to find Keegan. There is a reward for your head.

So it was true then. I laid a hand on the Orb. Lady Sylvia would stop at nothing to have the throne. All she needed was Keegan. And me, dead.

Yet I was sure that Lady Dominique had wanted me alive. Perhaps that was no longer her choice to make.

My people were dying because I wasn't there to save them.

I dug my fingernails into my palms, swallowed over the lump in my throat, and began my descent.

* * *

If Keegan had seen me hiding up in the tree last night, he didn't admit it. He ate some bluesberries I had foraged without acknowledging my presence, despite my best efforts to engage him. His silent dismissals gnawed away at my insides. One mouthful of berries, and I was full. He must know I was gone last night. Did he think I'd abandoned him? Was he angry at me for wanting to go to the edge of the world, instead of to safety with him? My fingertips brushed his hand but he pulled away.

"Must move quickly," Monju said. He pointed at the sun, still half hidden by the pink clouds of the horizon. The rays made his dark skin light up like gold. "Bandits strike most often when the sun is high in the sky, and when the sun begins to set. The prince and the lady ride towards her, the sun, and sight will be blinded, making it easy for the bandits to rob and kill. The lady and the prince must ride mornings to avoid the thieves."

We didn't argue. Because we wanted to preserve the horses for as long as possible, Monju would guide Winnie by the reins as he rode Song Spirit, and I'd saddle with Keegan on Lord Beauty. Monju boosted me up. I wrapped my arms around Keegan's middle and winced—my shoulder burned.

"The lady is all right?" Monju asked.

"I'm...I'm fine," I said, touching the place where the North's blade had pierced me.

"More herbs for tonight's rest. Soon the lady will feel no pain," he assured me.

Keegan muttered something inaudible as Monju leapt onto his horse. I leaned into the warmth of his back and willed for him to be calm, to trust in me. Instead, he snapped the reins and our horse trotted between the thick tree trunks.

"Shouldn't we wait for—?"

"I'm sure he's capable enough to catch up," Keegan said.

I glanced behind us and sure enough, Monju was manoeuvring the mares between the trees. Lord Beauty wasn't used to travelling in such tight spaces. He was spooked when Song Spirit burst from a collection of bushes to the right. One hand went to my pack and the other held onto Keegan as the stallion reared, which also sent Winnie into a tizzy and startled Song Spirit as well. Winnie snorted and looked wildly around, as if she were being attacked.

Quick and agile, Monju stopped Song Spirit, dismounted, and slipped through the chaos of the forest to appear at Lord Beauty's side. He uttered a slew of words in the native Southern tongue, creating a melodious up-and-down, singsong tune. The stallion fell under Monju's spell, which eventually calmed the horse's natural instinct to revolt.

"How did you do that?" Keegan asked, with an underlining tone of suspicion.

"Am good with horses. Skills fostered when Monju was a child," he replied, stroking the horse's muzzle. "Was also very good at *relieving* rich lords of their animals when Monju thought that they were being mistreated."

Keegan tensed beside me. Why would Monju volunteer that information? Even though Keegan was now his liege, to confess his past wrongdoings to a monarch was asking for punishment, even if we were in the middle of the forest. Monju glanced between me and Keegan with a hopeful look on his face. Maybe he was just asking for forgiveness. After all, I had done very similar things when I was the Violet Fox.

I was still the Violet Fox.

"Thank you," Keegan said. "You think it would be best for us to lead the horses on foot?"

"Through this part of the forest, that might be very wise, Prince," Monju replied respectfully.

"Let's do that then."

After retrieving Winnie, who had fortunately only wandered a few paces away, we pressed on. The sunbeams shining between the trees became progressively brighter as we trudged slowly through the untamed growth. Noon was fast approaching, and our window for safe travel, like the forest, narrowing. Eventually the growth thinned somewhat, and we were able to travel more freely. The horses were more cooperative and easier to manoeuvre. My feet grew tired, but I did not complain. Keegan breathed harder than normal, but he seemed to be taking the journey in stride. To ask him if he was tired would be an insult.

Monju scouted ahead, and when he returned to us, his expression was deeply unsettled. "Found something."

Wordlessly, he led us ahead, and tied Song Spirit to a nearby tree. He crouched, and brushed aside stray leaves and fallen twigs. My insides twisted with fear. We were not alone in the forest. Someone had tried to hide the evidence of their existence, and had done a poor job at that.

"Tracks," I said, kneeling beside them.

"Not made by the lady or the prince," Monju said solemnly. "But fresh."

Keegan bent down to examine them as well. He looked to me, and then to Monju. "Can you tell who made them?"

Monju looked nervous. That wasn't a good sign. "The lady and her prince should move quickly."

"Do you think they were made by the shadow killers?" I asked him. The owner had small feet and rounded shoes, but the heel was deeply indented. What unsettled me was that they were clear and unaltered: an expert tracker would've done more than cover them with leaves and forest debris. It was as if Monju was meant to find them.

"Perhaps." He returned to the horses. "Should ride, now that the forest allows. The forest becomes thicker again about a half hour ahead. Can camp there and catch some rest."

Neither Keegan nor I brooked an argument. As the three of us made our way through the uneven, unsure paths of the forest, a nagging voice in the back of my mind kept returning my attentions to the print. If the assassins were closing in on us, what were they waiting for? Surely our horses were not moving much faster than the shadow killers were on their nimble feet through the thicket. They could have overtaken us by now. What were they waiting for? Why play these games? I was missing something here, and I couldn't put my finger on it. I didn't know about Keegan and Monju, but I didn't want to die in my sleep just because I couldn't put two and two together.

No assassin jumped out at us during our ride to our potential camp, and I was somewhat disappointed. The hairs on the back of my neck rose. As we secured the horses, and settled down to rest, I couldn't shake the feeling that we were being watched. We were rats in a tunnel maze, guided by schemers to the tasty but poisoned cheese.

I refused to be someone's pawn. Not again.

Keegan noted my quiet frustration, and when Monju went to relieve himself in the woods, he broke the silence between us. "Are you all right?"

"Fine," I replied, more forcefully than I meant to, before sighing angrily. "I just—"

Monju tore into the clearing with an eerily silent and unsettling speed. "Lady. Prince. Must—"

Behind him, the bushes shook with great fervour. Monju spun and drew back between Keegan and me, holding out a shaking hand at the disturbance.

"Don't. Move," he whispered to us.

I frowned as I moved to unsheathe my weapon. "Assassins?"

"Shh," Monju said quickly.

The thing that slinked from the darkness was so black that it was the absence of space. Nostrils attached to a narrow snout protruded from the bushes first. Then its eyes: soulless and shiny, gleaming with the promise of a meal. Only a pinpoint of white in the centre gave away its gaze in the otherwise dark, sleek face.

"No. It can't be," I whispered.

The story that tugged at the edge of my mind was ridiculous, but I clung to it, for I could offer no other rational explanation. During the few precious days I'd had to learn everything there was to know about Lady Dominique and the North, one of the apprentices had told me a folk tale about the beatag: creatures sleek and dark like the large wild cats, but with antlers and teeth like the sabre-toothed tigers. They once made their home in the North but had been driven out by High King

Ciborno and his brave soldiers. The creatures had supposedly settled in the West, though there had not been a true sighting for hundreds of years.

I recalled my father's warning about the creatures of the forest. I should have heeded it.

The beatag padded out of the bushes. The antlers rose an arm-length from the top of its head. Curled fangs descended from its mouth. A tail twitched silently, long and spindly like a rat's. Deceptively strong leg muscles supported its large head, making up for its seemingly weak frame.

In the stories, they were famous for pouncing on their prey and making a swift kill. Staring at us, assessing our strength—this was far worse.

Behind us, the three horses whinnied and snorted. They were the easiest targets, as they were tied to the trees. If we lost them, it would be a long way to the nearest town on foot.

Monju was quick to draw. "Stay back, Lady Kiera."

My blade was already in hand. "I'm all right. Keegan?"

He didn't reply. I glanced over my shoulder, and he stared fiercely at the beast. His sword gleamed in the precious sun rays that had fought to reach the forest floor. No fear lived on his face. So practiced was he at hiding his emotions that even when faced with a creature of legend, he did not betray his true self.

"We shouldn't provoke it," I whispered, glancing between the two men.

"In his territory," Monju replied carefully without taking his gaze from the beast. "Cannot be helped."

"Can we kill it, if needs be?" Keegan asked.

The creature twitched and opened its mouth, revealing a set of small sharp teeth. Grinning, or contemplating us as dinner? I gritted my teeth to keep from shaking. Of all of the threats I'd faced in the past few months—intelligent schemers, power-hungry leaders, and daft women who listened only to their hearts—dying beneath the jaws of something that wasn't supposed to be real seemed cruelly unfair. "It can't understand us, right?"

It threw back its head and let out a screeching howl.

A beastly battle cry.

If I could escape up a tree, I could use height to my advantage. As Keegan and Monju charged the beast, I turned and grabbed the nearest tree branch, hoping to pull myself up with my good arm. Searing pain ran from my shoulder down my body. Rats. I must have done something to it last night during my late-night climb.

The beatag was sleek and fast, weaving between Keegan and Monju like an eel propelled by a strong river current. When Keegan swung, the beatag silently leapt out of reach, and snapped its fearsome jaw at Monju. The bard attempted to return the blow, but the beatag proved too slippery, even for our shadowy defender. Monju's small guitar thumped gently in time with his movements against his strong back.

Behind us, a thunderous roar of hooves and frightened noises cascaded right, and then left. I whirled around, steeling myself for more beatag. But no: it was Winnie and Song Spirit, fleeing the scene in fright. Our knots hadn't been as secure as we'd thought. Their reins dangled behind them and occasionally snagged on the spindly branches; only by dumb luck did the horses free themselves when they happened to jerk the right way.

Lord Beauty was not so lucky. Whether it was his size, or an inner knowledge that he was the prince's favourite, he remained. His tail swished in warning, his ears pressed firmly back, and he reared in the beatag's direction.

The promise of easy prey caught the beatag's attention.

I dove out of the way of the beatag as it rushed Lord Beauty. Keegan caught the beast with his knife on its backside, but made barely a scratch. I rolled and curled to avoid being caught under the stallion and the beatag. By the time I righted myself, the beatag had pounced on Lord Beauty.

Keegan cried out, attempting to distract the beatag. Lord Beauty reared just as the beatag came down on the stallion's neck. The force snapped the reins holding Lord Beauty to the tree and sent both creatures tumbling to the root-infested forest floor. The beatag sunk its sabre teeth into the horse's neck, and ripped deep gashes into his torso. The stallion thrashed and cried out in pain.

"Now, while it's distracted!" I ordered.

Grim-faced, Keegan caught wind of my idea, and raced to his suffering stallion's side. Angry that Keegan was interrupting its dinner, the beatag lashed out at the prince. Keegan managed to nick the beast in the face, drawing a quill-thin line between the beatag's eyes. It squealed and growled; in the distance, similar cries replied, closer now.

I leapt into the fray as it lunged more aggressively for Keegan. Seizing the opportunity, Monju and I attacked as one, driving our blades into the beast's back.

Like a horse, it reared in distress. Keegan cried just as loudly and swung his sword at the beatag's neck. The swing wasn't strong enough to chop off its head completely. Instead the blade sunk into the thick neck muscle, like a bread knife into hardened butter.

The beatag collapsed to the ground beside Lord Beauty. Keegan wrenched his blade free. The stallion took one last wheezing breath, and expired. Keegan bowed his head at his horse and closed his eyes in silent prayer. The wet, ragged breathing of the beatag permeated the air, punctuated by the loud, squealing cries of its pack off in the east, as the beast seemed to beg for death's release.

"Let it be," Monju said quickly. His feet twitched, eager to move from this place. "The lady and her prince must go, before other beasts show!"

Keegan furrowed his brows and loomed over Monju. "You would allow the creature to suffer in agony?"

"It is not innocent—the creature plays with its food for two hours before devouring the vital organs!" Monju exclaimed, and then seemed to realize that he was arguing with a prince. He lowered his gaze. "Apologies, Prince. Killing creatures, even if suffering, is wrong to Monju. Death is not the only way, not by human hands. But when the other beasts arrive, they will feast on their brother's and the horse's flesh, before coming after the prince. Prefers fresh kill. Will give the prince more time to put more distance between him and the beasts."

The beast squealed and whined again. I covered my ears just before hearing two answering calls close by. As sad as it was, maybe the other beatag would find Winnie and Song Spirit a tastier proposition, and opt to leave us be. The horses had already disappeared into the forest. "Kill it or don't, we have to leave," I said.

Keegan lifted his sword and without further delay, drove it into the creature's neck. The beast shuddered, and then quickly became still. No death cry; just silence.

Within several minutes, the three of us had sighted a mythical creature, and seen it die. I couldn't tear away my gaze as Keegan withdrew his blade from the creature. Blood as thick as syrup and dark as the night dripped from Keegan's sword, and from the beatag's wound.

The man who regarded me then was not the Keegan I once knew. Blood and compassion had transformed him into the ruler of Marlenia, holy in his will to act swiftly and without regret.

Monju regarded the prince with quiet disdain. An assassin who would not kill, and who wouldn't show mercy? Had he not quickly slain the shadow killers who'd attacked us, and the man in the alley who'd tried to kill me? He clenched and unclenched his free hand, wiped his sword on the grass, and then glanced to the south, where Winnie and Song Spirit had fled. "Will try to track down the horses."

The task was likely futile, but it gave him something to focus on. "Hurry," Keegan said.

Monju made his way through the trees, away from us.

I remained planted in the soil, watching Keegan clean his sword of the thick blood on his pants and the grass. He glanced nervously towards where we'd last heard the other beatag, which had gone suspiciously silent. He noticed me staring.

"What?" he asked. He wiped some of the dark beastly blood spray from his forehead.

It took me a moment to find the answer. "I don't think I've ever seen you kill something before."

"I killed a man at the stables."

"That was different. He would have killed you otherwise. This was a beast, suffering. You chose to kill it instead of walking away."

He frowned. "Does that...bother you?"

I stepped forward and clasped his hand. "No."

The change in his expression was subtle. A slight furrowing of the brow. A hint of confusion in his multicoloured eyes. He glanced at my hand grasping his, and brought his right hand, bloodied from the battle, over mine. The thick dark liquid dripped onto my skin, as if sealing us in a secret pact. I squeezed his tired fingers, and he pulled me against him.

It didn't matter whether I approved or disapproved of the kill. It was the decisiveness of the act. No hesitation, no thinking, only doing. It was how I had been trained, as a Fighter. And in that moment, I felt closer to him than I had ever felt before, knowing that there was a part of him that was like a part of me.

Nine

FEARING THE ONCE-MYTHICAL beatag, we didn't sleep during our next rest stop.

The horses were a lost cause. Without them, travelling was easier. We no longer had to worry about spooking or feeding them. Yet it made our journey unbearably long. Feenagh Forest stretched for endless leagues. The map noted it was at least a hundred leagues, though both Keegan and Monju thought that wasn't a generous enough estimate.

We made our camps close to the edge of the forest, as the large evergreens offered the only shelter from the frequent but brutal rains that plagued this part of the province. Several stone-throws away, grassy plains stretched for leagues. The main road that led from Marlenia City to Iar Bunsula was also dangerously close, and sometimes branched to the north or the south, leading to the larger towns of the West.

Soon, the road would fork towards Baile Gareth, and Keegan and I would part ways on our separate missions. I hated thinking of it.

For two days, we scavenged and focussed on putting one foot in front of the other. Like my father before me, I felt as though I was returning to a more basic self. Find food. Move. Sleep. Feenagh Forest was muggy during the day, cold during the evenings. The thick tops of the trees sometimes blocked the sun, and left the forest in near-perpetual night. That worried me more than the dampness: if the forest was frequently dark, predators might also hunt during the day. Every time wings fluttered, a branch fell, or a far-off wolf howled, the three of us drew our weapons and froze, counting the seconds until we'd feel teeth sinking into our necks. Sometimes there'd be a faint squeal far behind us, which would spur us to move faster, yet when we turned, there was nothing but more greenery beginning its descent into the reds and yellows of the new season.

A tricky balancing act ensued: while wolves and the beatag hunted in the forest, the bandits and the Eastern forces hunted in the plains near the road. At least two merchant caravans travelled the road each day, and when they disappeared, we snuck out of the forest and made up for lost time by traversing the plains. The mountains presented themselves in the distance; a looming reminder that the edge of the world lay beyond them.

By the second day after the beatag attack, the East seemed to have given up their pursuit: only one platoon had made it this far, and even their search of the area was lacklustre before they gave up and rode back towards Marlenia City.

"May believe the lady and the prince to be dead," Monju said thoughtfully, as we camped that night. "May not dare to venture too far into Feenagh Forest."

"Perhaps they won't think to travel as far as Baile Gareth," Keegan said, the hope plain in his voice.

"Will reach that road soon," Monju replied, casting a glance at me.

I sighed and warmed my hands over the tiny fire. For Keegan to leave me for the safety of Baile Gareth was the right thing to do, while I travelled on to find the Spear. Right now though, neither of us could stand to be out of each other's sight. He showed few signs of growing weary of the constant alertness required to survive in the wild, the lack of proper baths, and the perpetual hunting and foraging.

As far as food gathering and hunting went, Monju threw himself into the task. He would leave the camp for fifteen minutes at a time, and just when I thought he might have been captured or killed, he'd return with a rabbit, or a bird—a luxury. Apparently his *no killing* rule didn't extend to creatures we ate. My body was used to going for long stretches without proper food, but Keegan's was not. Campfires would scare away the beasts of the forest, Monju reasoned, but attract human attention. They had to be brief: long enough to dry our clothes or to roast his kills.

It was only during these absences that Keegan and I had any time alone together. Bringing up our imminent departure from each other was hard enough, and whenever either of us worked up enough courage to broach the subject, Monju conveniently appeared once again. We couldn't bring ourselves to say anything meaningful in Monju's omnipresence. Ever since Keegan killed the beatag, Monju had kept his distance from the prince, preferring to confer with me to pass the time.

Keegan seemed fine with this at first; his taste for the Southern man was limited, though he kept an open ear to our conversations. Monju wasn't brave enough to break his sense of decorum and ask about the ancient artefact supposedly located at Driscoll's End, so he filled the air with questions about my life as the Violet Fox. The more Monju and I talked, the more uneasy Keegan seemed.

On the fifth day of our journey, the impending separation loomed thickly. When Monju went to forage more disciple daisies in the woods for my rapidly healing shoulder wound, Keegan drew me close to him and spoke in a hushed, hurried tone:

"I don't trust him."

I sighed. It was potentially our last day together, and he wanted to discuss the bard? "Keegan..."

"He's far too eager to accompany us when so much is uncertain. How do we know he's not after the Spear? All he'd need you for is to decode your father's expedition notes, and steal your pack. He already admitted to being a thief."

I placed a protective hand over the bulging fabric. There were far too many powerful items in there. "He doesn't seem interested in the Spear. Only in my life story, probably for another song."

"He wants us to trust him," Keegan said. "He's saved our lives too many times now, without asking for anything for himself. Someone must be putting silver in his pocket."

I sighed. "He's a fighting bard. He's doing it for the glory. Maybe that's better than silver. Or maybe he expects a payment once you retake the throne."

Keegan looked unconvinced. His gaze slid to where Monju had disappeared. "The other night, before the beatag attack...when you left the campsite with your sack...he got up and followed you."

The man in the forest, who I thought was Keegan...that was Monju? But his movements had been so untrained. Loud. I had not snuck away to write to my father since that night. "How do you know? Did you follow him?"

"No," Keegan replied. "But he was gone for at least twenty minutes."

"Maybe he was just relieving himself." That was getting harder to do with any sort of privacy.

"That's what I thought, but I saw blinking lights off in the distance, in the direction he'd headed."

"Some sort of signal?" I asked.

"Maybe." I hadn't seen any lights—I'd been focussed on my journal.

Keegan leaned in closer, brushing his lips against my ears. "You know it's possible he's working with the North or the East."

"It's possible, but I don't think he is. He could have killed us, or conspired with our enemies to lead us back to Tramore lands by now. That would have been easier to do two days ago. But now we're well into Western territory."

Keegan drew away from me, looking grim. "I know. He just...he doesn't sit well with me. He is far too cultured and mannered, even for a bard. And his fighting skills...someone trained him. His movements are just as refined as the shadow killers', if not more so. There's something off about him, and I intend to find out what it is."

I raised my eyebrows. "Well you'd be better off doing that by making friends with him instead of casting dark looks his way every time he speaks, no?"

"Dark looks?"

"Yes, *my prince*," I said teasingly.

A small smile threatened to overtake his serious expression. "You are enjoying yourself far too much, Violet Fox." His brow furrowed as he allowed the silence to hang between us. "We'll soon be upon Lord Ansel's lands."

I crossed my arms. "I know."

"Kiera," he implored. "Won't you reconsider coming with me? At least there, I can order guards to keep an eye on Monju and limit his movements."

"Won't you reconsider coming with *me*? For all we know, Baile Gareth is an Eastern trap!"

Keegan slammed his fist into a nearby tree, though in his face I saw that he had thought of that. "Dammit, Kiera, if you aren't the most stubborn woman on the flat face of Marlenia!"

"At least going to Driscoll's End is doing something. At Baile Gareth, I would be a sitting mouse!"

"You'd be helping *me* rally forces against the East."

"The only way I can truly help is to find the Silver Spear for the apprentices. Until then, they'll only defend the underground. They won't go on the offensive."

Keegan was about to retort when Monju reappeared through the greenery. The bard cleared his throat, looking troubled as he held out a bouquet of purple disciple daisies, and a handful of mimberries. He plopped a berry in his mouth, and gave me a quizzical look. How much had he overheard?

"Spotted more tracks back there," Monju said, pointing behind him. "Same as before. Deep heel, rounded toe. Should stick close to the road. According to the stories, beatag don't like direct sunlight."

The promise of sunlight shone between the trees. It was likely that the good weather wouldn't last for long.

"Good idea," I replied, trying to keep my tone cheery.

Keegan's eyebrows quirked, but he did not argue.

I chewed on the disciple daisies as we trudged the open road. My hand went occasionally to my left shoulder. The daisies had done wonders in speeding the healing of the wound; it was already scabbing, and no longer required a bandage. It still throbbed, especially at night, and when it was about to rain. Keegan noted my pain, and touched my hand. He hated to see me suffer.

The longer we traversed the plains, the more on edge I felt. Even Keegan's gaze darted about uneasily. The hair on the back of my neck rose. We were so vulnerable everywhere. In the forest, beatag. On the road, bandits. In the shadows, assassins. I touched my pack for reassurance. The Orb was still there, at the bottom, hidden beneath my books and my cloak. If I had to, I'd use it again—though Keegan had a point. Exposing too much information to Monju, no matter how friendly and congenial he seemed, was a risk.

A sound from off in the distance behind us brought me out of my thoughts. I glanced behind me, seeing only the sprawling forests from which we had come, and the endless blue sky partially shrouded in clouds.

"I hear something," I said, urging Keegan to stop. "Wheels, on dirt."

Beside us, Monju listened intently. "Also hear, Lady."

"I don't...?" Keegan asked. And then, frowning, he caught wind of the sound. "Sounds like we have company."

In silent agreement, we hurried for cover nearby, on the perimeter of the forest. Keegan and I remained within the safety of the bushes that offered full view of the road. Monju hid two stone-throws from us, his alert dark eyes watching the approaching caravan carefully. My hand went immediately to my sack. I silently prayed that I wouldn't have to use the Orb—although part of me was itching for action.

A large carriage rolled into view on the flat terrain, led by two horses. I stiffened and gritted my teeth. The ornate large cursive *f* on the door meant the carriage could only belong to one family: the Frostfires. One or more members of the royal family must be in there. What would King Leszek be doing out this far west?

Unless he knew of Keegan's plan to escape to Baile Gareth.

More disturbing than the Frostfire presence was the parade behind the carriage. Other than the dozen or so armed soldiers on horseback tasked with carrying the ration supply for this seemingly elaborate expedition, one Eastern soldier—marked by his bright red chestplate bearing his rank—rode behind the entire entourage, and was in charge of two prisoners. One rode backwards on the horse with the soldier. The other had a noose tied around her neck, attached to the back of one of the saddles, and was forced to keep up with the trotting horses in her heavy skirts or be choked to death. A sack covered her face, but I feared the worst.

Monju appeared behind us without making a sound. "Easterners?"

"Sylvia," Keegan said through gritted teeth.

My eyes widened. The note in Keegan's study. Everything that had happened at the castle felt decades old. If she had found it...

Keegan's guess proved right when the carriage stopped and out sprang a young blonde woman in a large, poofy red dress that barely fit through the slender door. She squinted against the sun, ran her hands over her frizzy hair, and addressed the soldier in charge of the prisoners with her screechy voice.

"We're breaking for a quick moment. Tell the men to search the area while I have a private moment with my chamber pot. And if *one* of you dares to follow me again, I shall leave you for the wolves and whatever other nasty creatures dwell in the forest. Understand?"

"Yes, my lady." The soldier gestured to the men bringing up the rear, and they broke into organized groups of three and fanned out across the plains and into the forest.

My mind transported me to a time when I had to avoid Marlenian patrols. "Split up. Meet back here in fifteen minutes."

Monju nodded wordlessly, and he dashed into the bushes. Keegan grabbed me roughly by the arm, silently urging us to move out of their search path. I tried to wrench from his grip—did he not understand that we had a better chance at surviving if we split up?—but he pulled me close to him.

"This is our chance," Keegan whispered. "We could continue without coming back here. Leave Monju to think we've been captured."

"What if Monju gets captured? If tortured, he might spill our plan to them!"

"He will anyway without torture, if he's a spy."

Sounds of a struggle ten stone-throws away interrupted our argument.

"My lady, we found this rat in the forest!"

The Frostfire men burst from the bushes with a struggling Monju in tow. He must have hid his pack and his guitar, for he had nothing but the clothes on his back. One of the soldiers punched Monju hard in the stomach. The bard gasped for breath and doubled over, muttering in his native tongue. I cursed under my breath, torn between leaving him in Sylvia's hands, or running.

No Freetor would come to the rescue if another happened to be captured. Only my brother would do such a thing for me if I were in trouble. Monju had no one. Even if he were an Eastern spy, he didn't deserve to suffer at Sylvia's hand. Not after all he'd done for us.

I reached for my dagger. Keegan stayed my arm.

"We're outnumbered. We don't know what she's doing out here."

"We can't just leave him!" I wrenched my arm from his grip. "Stay here if you want. Continue on to Baile Gareth. But I'm going to save him. He's helped us get this far."

"Kiera, wait—"

Rushing into things headfirst because it felt right was something Rordan had always criticized me for. The moment I stepped from the bushes, and Sylvia turned her plump head to fix her beady stare on me, I regretted not listening to Keegan.

Especially since I'd forgotten to hide my sack first.

"It must be my lucky day," Sylvia said dryly. "Look who decided to crawl from the filthy woods and grace us with her presence. The false Princess of Marlenia."

"At least I'm not a usurper," I replied.

I quickly took stock of the enemy. My initial quick count had been accurate. Twelve men in the rear, the man on the horse, and the carriage driver. Sorely outnumbered was an understatement. My pack weighed heavily on my shoulder. All I had to do was take out the Orb, and somehow call upon its lightning, and then all of our problems would disappear.

"Usurper? You accuse me of usurping the Marlenian throne when you were the one who interrupted *my* wedding to Prince Keegan?" Sylvia's full, lush lips pouted as she gestured to her small army. "This is what we've been waiting for. Arrest this pretender!"

Monju's face lit up in alarm. I swung my sack around and prepared to withdraw the Orb when Keegan bounded out of the woods. I cursed inwardly. No, Keegan, that was what she wanted you to do!

Sylvia's face lit up with excitement. "My prince! So you *are* here." Again, she gestured to her men. "See? Didn't I tell you he'd be out here?"

They exchanged tired, awkward glances before mumbling in the affirmative to their monarch. Monju no longer struggled in their grip: he seemed just as surprised as I was that Keegan had revealed himself.

"Stop this foolishness, Sylvia," Keegan commanded, pushing back his shoulders as he joined me at my side.

"What are you doing?" I whispered to him.

"It's all right," he muttered. "Sooner or later, she would have found us." Then, louder, to Sylvia: "I'm here. You have something you'd like to say to me?"

"I want us to pick up where we left off, of course," she replied in a sickening sing-song voice. "I thought you'd want the same?"

It was as I'd feared. She'd found the letter in Keegan's study, thought it real, and had dragged a small platoon to the middle of the west just to find her precious prince.

Keegan stared at his former fiancée, unblinking, yet without malice. The longer he concentrated on her perfect, round cheeks, her bright eyes, and her button nose, the more impatient I became. It would be hard to prove to Sylvia that the letter was not real; that Keegan's affection for her was about as warm as pie on top of a mountain. Better to let her be blinded by turbulent lust.

"How did you know to come this way?" Keegan asked carefully.

Of course; he was trying to see if the East knew of his plan to escape to Baile Gareth.

Sylvia smiled and ran her fingers through her curled, frizzed locks. The damp climate of the West was not agreeing with her; the East was far drier. "Some of your less-than-loyal servants divulged some very intriguing information about the Violet Fox traipsing off in search of a weapon to fight our brave troops. Father thought it was poppycock but I figured that it was stupid enough to be true. And when no one could find you"—she hovered a finger over Keegan's chest, and looked up at him through hooded lids—"I knew she had tricked you into following her."

"So you came all the way out here. Are you looking for some kind of reward for braving the wilderness?" I asked dryly.

Thankfully, she shifted her flirty attention away from Keegan and fixed me with a potent glare. "The only reward I'll receive is Father's blessing to raid the Freetor underground. Once he sees how I've handled you, the queen of the rats, swaying him to agree to my extermination plan should be a breeze. And of course, he'll agree to my marrying Keegan. That one will be—"

Extermination plan? "Your people would never make it. Freetor magic—"

"Largely gone, thanks to your own incompetent Elders, so I hear." She smiled slyly. "Information flows freely in Marlenia City, now that it has been liberated."

"Liberated. Is that what you're calling it." Keegan's tone did not betray his anger, but one hand clenched into a fist, while the other hovered above the hilt of his sword.

My father had said that the apprentices were guarding all entrances to the Undercity! Granted, the ratio of secret holes and trap doors to apprentices in Marlenia City alone was at least two to one. I had been too sure that the underground would stand against the East. Fear or ignorance of magic had been an effective shield for so long. If they managed to breach the magical defences, and capture even one apprentice…I couldn't bear to think of what secrets they might unravel and exploit.

With a shrug, Sylvia ignored Keegan. "I didn't come unprepared, in any case. I figured if I spent some time out here, I might attract your attention and convince you to return to the city."

"That so. How might you go about convincing us to do anything for you?" I demanded.

Sylvia gestured grandiosely to the guard on the horse with the two prisoners. "I'm *so* glad you asked. Lieutenant."

The Frostfire soldier turned to the prisoner beside him and yanked off the hood. My chest tightened. Laoise! She looked bewildered, then afraid as she adjusted to the harsh sunlight, but she did not cry out. I didn't know what was worse: the fact that she'd been caught, or that she'd had to endure who knew how many days on the back of that horse, in Sylvia's company.

"I have it on fairly good authority that you know this filthy Freetor rat," Sylvia said. "This other one has been a Freetor informant for years."

The mud-soaked prisoner with a noose about her neck did not stir, and now I knew for certain who was showing such resilience in the face of the Marlenian threat. The solider removed the hood from Bidelia's head. Her face was a mask of deep lines, as if she'd aged ten years since her capture. I wondered how many years she'd been waiting for a day like this, a day when the Marlenians would find out where she was really from and punish her for her years of hard labour and whispering royal secrets into Freetor ears.

"And to think I let you in my *bedroom*," Sylvia spat.

Bidelia said nothing, as we were all told to do when we are captured. Words would often make things worse when you were dealing with ignorant Marlenians.

"If you don't comply with my demands, I will have these two executed in front of your eyes," Sylvia said simply.

Hiding my true feelings in any situation took immense focus. Despite Sylvia's ridiculous dress and misplaced confidence, I stirred at her threat to kill the two women I had always considered family. Catching the two of them would've been no small feat, and barely anyone knew of Bidelia's true origins. Regardless of her girly, childish behaviour and motives, Sylvia's sources and methods must have been ruthless and cunning.

"You dragged these two innocents out here, with the purpose of having them murdered if *we* don't listen to *you*?" Keegan asked, bewildered. "That's madness, and you should know that, Sylvia." His right hand tightened around his blade. "Seizing my family's home. Terrorizing the capital. Capturing and torturing citizens loyal to the Tramore Crown. The list of your crimes grows longer by the second. You and your father will rot in the dungeons for the rest of your lives if you do not release these innocents and stop your attack on the city."

"This *attack* is your fault," Sylvia said with a sneer. "Rejecting me as your wife. Humiliating me in front of the four kingdoms. But we can meet your demands easily, as long as you meet mine." She quirked an eyebrow. "I'm giving you one more chance, because I know in our shared hearts that you deserve one. Formally retract this ridiculous engagement to the Violet Fox and return with me to Marlenia City. The East can offer you so much more than that Freetor traitor ever could."

"You are the traitor," Keegan said. Anger seeped into his voice. "My father is on his deathbed, and your army has decimated my city! You think that after all that, I would consent to marry you?"

A curious, cruel smile slid across Sylvia's face. "My father thought that holding the Holy One and the city hostage would be a very effective way of convincing you, yes."

Keegan swallowed. Sylvia had neither confirmed nor denied whether the Holy One had died. Frown lines creased his forehead, and suddenly he looked so much older than his eighteen years.

He drew his sword. "Call off your soldiers, my lady."

Sylvia eyed her men, and they started laughing. So did she, snorting with every second breath. "Oh, Your Grace, you have such a sense of humour! You think that the two of you can defeat my fourteen men here? They are the best rough-terrain combatants we could spare for my little mission to find you, out here in the wilderness."

"What are you doing?" I asked under my breath as the laughter raged.

"I had hoped to scare her off..." Keegan hissed.

One by one, Sylvia's men freed their weapons. Over half of them remained on horseback. This was not good. They could easily cut us down.

"Wait." Monju's foreign accent echoed across the plain. Sylvia's men were no longer holding him captive; I supposed attacking Keegan and me was more important, and he was unarmed. Monju held up a hand as if he were a noble in court, commanding the attention of his subjects. "The golden lady need not draw blood just yet. Not before knowing the true risk to her men."

Sylvia hesitated. "What are you talking about, foreigner? My men are the *best* at running through cowards and Freetors like you."

"That may be so," Monju admitted, bowing his head slightly, not bothering to point out that he wasn't a Freetor. "However, the Lady Kiera is more apt with calling lightning from the sky. With her bare hands."

My eyes widened. That was definitely not true. Did Monju know I had the Orb with me? Revealing that I had it now would save our skins—if I could call upon its magic one more time. I had no choice now. It was this, or die by the Frostfires' hands. And I had no intention of giving Lady Sylvia that satisfaction.

Laoise shifted awkwardly on the horse, as if trying to tell me something.

"Yes," I said loudly, stepping into my new role. "You remember that day, Lady Sylvia, when I called lightning from the sky. You wouldn't want to make me angry, would you."

Sylvia scoffed and worried her lower lip. "I don't believe you."

The men around her exchanged glances. They looked less than certain.

This plan wasn't going to work. I couldn't give them the display they wanted. I wasn't my father. I wasn't an Elder, or an apprentice. My fingers dug into the strap of my bag. I had to use the Orb...

Laoise's fidgeted again, and this time I noticed that the ropes binding her hands had loosened. I realized Monju's plan: buy enough time to allow Laoise to free herself and her mother from their bonds, so they could launch a surprise attack. She looked almost free.

I had to keep talking. Distract them. Just like the old days.

"I don't care if you don't believe," I shouted. Make as much noise, as much commotion as possible: I had to keep their attention. I waved my hands, hoping their gaze would follow. It did. "But if you care for a demonstration, I will have no choice but to oblige. After all, you are a daughter of the East, a *guest* on these great Western lands."

"These are *my* lands—"

"Ah, ah. *Lucindous, Maxima, Strika!*" The words themselves were gibberish, but I suspected the lady would believe them to be Freetor magic words. "*Guardians of Lightning, hear my cries…*"

Three guards slid off their horses and advanced. I took a step back and chanted my nonsense louder. Each man bore a longsword: two-handed, cumbersome, yet deadly when used effectively. Another two stayed near the prisoners and Sylvia. The lady bunched her skirts and looked as if she was about to pee herself with fright.

I grinned. "Just a few more words, Sylvia, and my spell will be complete. I had no idea how much you wanted to be a pile of ash. Very well, then. *Flashica*—"

The rope around Laoise's wrists flew through the air as she spun around, stole a knife from the closest guard's belt, and cut her mother free. Monju ran into the fray. The Eastern guard closest to him swung his blade; Monju ducked, fell to his hands and knees, pulled a knife from inside the Easterner's boot, and stabbed him in the foot. The other two guards around him swung their swords at the lithe Southern bard, but he was more agile. He rolled out of the way, grabbing the sword from the stabbed Frostfire man, and took on the two healthy guards. Startled by the sudden commotion, some of the horses galloped across the grassy plains.

Blurs of red ran for me and Keegan. Fighting was instinct. Very little room to think. The three men attacked at once; I ducked to evade their triple threat, and caught one of them in the shins beneath his protective plates. He fell. The remaining two swung their heavy longswords. Keegan distracted one by catching him in the left side, where he was weakest: he could not raise his bracer in time. Where they were slow and clunky, I was fast and light—so long as I stayed out of their reach.

As I danced between the two men, signs of fatigue crept into my movement. My shoulder ached. Keegan was my second body in the fight: complementing my weak side, yelling *duck!* when I didn't see the blade coming, and ensuring that the men didn't get too close. I scooted from one blade's path. While Keegan met the soldier head on, I stabbed the man in the side, where his armour didn't cover his flesh. When he fell, I sliced the leather bonds holding his bracer in place. Angered by my evasive manoeuvres, my remaining opponent shouted for help as he attacked. I jumped out of the way, picked up the bracer, and whacked it against the side of the soldier's head. He tumbled to the ground, dazed and bleeding from the ear.

Blue lightning struck in the corner of my eye. Yet the Orb was still in my pack...

Where did Keegan go?

No time to think. Two more Eastern men came at me, and my comrades were too busy with their own opponents to help.

These men had shorter swords and buckler shields, with leather chest armour. Not as senior in Lady Sylvia's army, then. Yelling with the thrust, I stabbed at the nearest one. The lightning flash had left dancing blotches in my vision. Did the man just swing his sword? Yes—duck!

Then, another flash of light, a rush of heat over my front, and the smell of burning flesh.

Rordan.

I recoiled from the sensation as escaping tears dried immediately on my face. Pieces of black ash fluttered in the grass where the attacking soldier had been.

What...?

More movement, to my left. I dove and rolled out of the attacker's path. The thought of my burning brother invaded my concentration once more as I narrowly evaded my opponent's blade, earning me a thin, faint red line across my right side.

"Help!" Sylvia cried over the sounds of clanging swords and felled men moaning for life.

Monju had cornered the lady against the carriage. His blade just inches from her face was enough of an attack in her mind—Monju merely threatened her with his presence. He grinned at the soldiers who gallantly came to their lady's aid, and cut them down accordingly.

Five, perhaps six men had rushed to "save" their precious princess. While my opponent was distracted by Sylvia's distress, I pushed him to the ground and kicked him in the head. The Frostfires had more silver quid than anyone, yet they had failed to invest in proper head armour. Perhaps they'd thought we didn't stand a chance.

Sylvia continued to scream at the top of her lungs—even stoic Monju could only take so much. He grabbed her by the neck and threw her to the muddy underfoot of the horses and the carriage, and abandoned her to slay the rest of the Eastern men.

Bosom heaving in her bright red dress, anger distorting her puffy face, Sylvia glared at Monju. Her blonde curls, dishevelled enough from days of travel, were now streaked with the thick brown substance. A high-pitched wail ripped from her pouting lips. "You!" she screamed.

She tried to get up but her dress was so large and laden with mud that it dragged her down.

Laoise and I snorted with laughter. Monju's solemn expression did not break, but I did see a sparkle of amusement in his eyes as he and Keegan (there he was, thank goodness he hadn't been cut down) finished off another Eastern soldier.

Sylvia screamed again.

Only three of her men remained, scattered across the field. They gathered their wits and prepared to engage when Sylvia screeched a final command. "Enough!"

Was this a surrender? I didn't let down my guard; neither did Keegan or Monju.

Sylvia turned her venomous glare to Keegan. Her cruel smile from earlier returned in full force as she released her most lethal weapon.

"Your father is *dead*."

The news, so callous from her retched lips, settled upon us as heavy as a smoke bomb. Keegan's eyes glazed over as he relived a distant memory. He parted his lips to speak and breathed shallow, long breaths instead. Even the Eastern soldiers didn't use the opportunity to strike, unsure how to handle this information.

With Eamon Tramore dead, that made Keegan the last of his line, and the ruling High King of the Western Province of Marlenia. The Holy One.

I took one step towards him, and he immediately held up his hand: *I can do this myself*. Even though I was three stone-throws from him, his trembling fingers were painfully apparent.

Realizing the impact she'd made, Sylvia continued the attack. "Happened three days ago, just before I left. My father was thinking of killing him, but the old man was raving mad anyway. So he told the servants to let him be, to let nature take its course. Not that it matters, now that my father is the new *emperor* of the realm." She smirked. "The title *Holy One* is a bit outdated, don't you think?"

I looked to Laoise, who was also battle weary and exhausted, for confirmation. She pursed her lips, and then nodded.

Keegan remained perfectly still, labouring to breathe. "You will never be High Queen," he whispered.

Sylvia's rage flared once more. "I *will*, with or without you!"

"Without," Keegan replied vehemently, and raised his sword once more.

Sylvia cowered near her carriage as bits of mud dripped from her arms and onto her dress. She shook with fury and fear as she re-evaluated the odds. Had she also noticed the flashes of light? The smell of cooked flesh?

"Protect me, you idiots!" Sylvia shrieked to her remaining men.

She disappeared into her carriage, and I ran after her. One of the men blocked my way. I swung, and he caught my arm. He brought down his sword and I wrenched myself from his grip to avoid becoming an amputee.

A shrill whistle filled the air, originating from a tired, desperate soldier sitting on the top seat. The reins were already in his trembling hands, and the horses were anxious to flee.

My opponent gave me the once-over, and decided he wanted to leave the fight unscathed. He ran towards the carriage, which was already in motion. I squinted and ran after it. Besides the fleeing soldier, and the nervous driver, I thought I saw the silhouettes of two people in the carriage. Three Eastern soldiers and Lady Sylvia escaping the fight.

If she escaped, and brought reinforcements...

I ran for the nearest horse: an older gelding munching grass just stone-throws away. The carriage became smaller and smaller as it disappeared into the horizon. If I rode fast enough, I might be able to catch her.

"Wait, Kiera!" Keegan caught up with me and grabbed my arm. "Let her go."

"Why?" I demanded. "After what she—?"

"Because having a dead Eastern princess will only complicate things. It's at least three, maybe four days' ride back to the castle." He sighed and wiped his brow. "Taking her prisoner would be more trouble than it's worth."

I conceded the point and reluctantly relaxed. How could he be so collected, so calm? His father was *dead*.

He averted his gaze; one crisis at a time.

I suddenly remembered Bidelia. Where was she? Had she survived? Panicking and thinking the worst, my gaze darted about the field until I saw her lying flat on her back in the grass. Laoise was running towards her mother, but my heart slowed its tremulous pace when Bidelia's chest rose and fell. I didn't know what I would have done if she'd died.

Laoise helped her sit up as I arrived at their sides. Bidelia rubbed her neck absently, and immediately covered the red rope burns with her dirtied collar.

"I'm all right," Bidelia said warily. "Scrapes and bruises."

Her eyes told me a different story, but I only nodded. Bidelia was a tough woman, and likely not used to being humiliated. Though her body might be beaten, wounded pride would have a far longer-lasting effect. If she wanted help, she'd ask for it—or Laoise would.

A swirl of wind swept through the open plains. The black ash swarmed like flies and invaded my mouth and my nose. The battlefield, once filled with men loyal to the Frostfire family, meaning to capture or kill us, was now littered with the stuff. While I counted six bodies in the grass, it was not hard to guess the fates of the remaining five. The smell of burning meat lingered in the air, and the bright flashes of light had left purple and green spots dancing before my vision.

Keegan knelt beside a large clump of the ash, and gave me the barest of glances as I approached. "Fried," he said. "Freetor magic?"

"Keegan," I said gently, dropping to my knees beside him. "Your father—"

"Is dead. Thank you. For your...sentiment. But we can't think about it right now." In his gaze, I saw the torment of setting aside grief in favour of serving the realm—of doing what was right for the people. It was a look and a feeling I knew all too well. A swell of emotion rose into my throat as I thought of Rordan.

If my prince could set aside his father's recent passing for the realm, then I had to be strong as well. My hand wandered to my pack briefly. "I don't see how it could be Freetor magic. I didn't use the Orb."

His gaze flitted to the edge of the forest, searching for any magical influence hiding between the mess of trees and brush. For all I knew, an invisible pair of eyes was staring back at me. The full range of magical abilities of one who had mastered the craft was unknown—the Elders liked to keep it that way.

Keegan shared my expression. "Who could have had the power to do this?"

"All the Elders are dead," I replied. I lowered my voice—Laoise and Bidelia were some distance away, and Monju was examining the dead Eastern soldiers. "My father, to my knowledge, doesn't have the power to do this. The apprentices are in Marlenia City, guarding the underground. No one else I know can wield magic."

He looked grim. "What about the shadow killers?"

A seed of dread bloomed in my stomach. "I don't know."

Keegan took my hands and squeezed them. "Kiera…this is beyond any kind of destruction I've ever seen."

I pressed my forehead against his, afraid. "If it was the shadow killers, why would they slay Frostfire men? Aren't they on the East's side?"

"Yes, but maybe they're free agents. The North has many secrets that we don't understand."

He could say that again.

"Although," He furrowed his brow. "Sylvia coming all the way out here reeks of desperation. High King Leszek is not a desperate man. He's patient. Organized. This plan was reckless."

"You don't think Sylvia had her father's approval to bring those men here."

He nodded. "Exactly."

"I don't see how that matters," I admitted, staring down at the ash.

"If I'm right," Keegan said, "it means that retrieving me alive was not part of the East's plan. If none of the Tramore family live, it makes Leszek Frostfire and his sons more appealing successors to the throne."

"Meaning Sylvia would be cut off from being a High Queen completely, unless she married a prince in another province." Like the North, or the South. Lady Dominique did have a much younger brother named Marin. With Keegan presumed dead, and High King Leszek managing the realm, marrying his only daughter off to the North would secure a stronger alliance with the Castillo family.

"If she wanted anyone else," Keegan muttered.

A sharp wind picked up, carrying the scent of the horses and the battle into the sky. Soon the vultures would be here. Sylvia's hasty exit and the exodus of the majority of the horses had left supplies strewn across the road and in the grass. I rifled through the nearest dead soldier's pack, revealing half-eaten wrapped dried meat and stale bread. Keegan frowned, disapproving of my scavenging, but then shrugged. Our supplies were limited, and we had to do what was necessary to survive.

"We should take what we can carry," I said. "And then we should get as far away as possible from here."

No one argued.

Ten

We stole the horses that hadn't run from the battle and rode along the road as fast as they would allow until the sun began to set. That evening, we camped among the trees again. Keegan created the fire—Monju had shown him how to use his pocket flint, and Keegan was getting quite good at striking it the right way—while Bidelia napped beside him. The rest of us hunted for food. Though three of Sylvia's men had escaped the fight, it was unlikely they'd return with reinforcements tonight.

Laoise and I headed side by side deeper into the forest. Just like old times. Our weapons were ready in our hands, and her face paled when I told her about the beatag.

"We ran into bandits once on the road," she told me. "But Sylvia's men cut them down. They don't mess around."

And yet the five of us managed to defeat a small army of them.

"I'm surprised Lady Sylvia came at all," I admitted.

"She complained the whole way," Laoise said. "There were a lot of stops."

The image of Sylvia, in her poofy dresses and uptight demeanour, running through the forest made me smile. Laoise looked distant, and for good reason: Bidelia had been forced to travel the whole way on foot, noosed to a horse.

"She really wanted to find you and the prince. She's obsessed. Besides grumbling about her father and her brothers, and how she felt unfavoured, Prince Keegan was the only thing on her mind," Laoise said. She stooped, and coaxed a handful of tart dark mimberries from beneath a small bush of heart-shaped leaves.

"Do you think she was acting on her own, without her father's approval?"

Laoise frowned. "Maybe...sorry. I just...I don't know. But you don't have to worry. She doesn't know anything about the Spear. At least I don't think she does."

I glanced at Laoise, shocked. "How did you...?"

"Mother overheard you speaking with your...father...about it." She twisted her lips at the mention of the Advisor. "And when we couldn't find you after the attack, and your father seemed so distraught, he told us what you wanted to do..."

"Distraught? The Advisor?"

"Kiera. He's your *father*."

Now it was my turn to look disgusted. "Yeah, I know, but that doesn't mean that he acts like one."

"He was worried about you. That's why he told us about the Spear, and your insane idea that you could find it."

"*My* insane idea? He's the one—look, let me show you."

Glancing over my shoulder and listening for signs that Monju was eavesdropping, I dug my father's expedition notes from my pack and presented them to Laoise. She leaned against a nearby evergreen tree and flipped through them. "And these notes belonged to...?"

"The Advisor. My father. Yes."

Her eyes roamed the pages of Freetor code as I briefly filled her in on my father's past expedition to the cave of the Silver Spear. "These last few pages are missing," I said, feeling the torn edges. "But this proves it exists. And if I find it for the apprentices, they have given their word that they will join the fight against the East."

Laoise sighed, long and low, through her nose. "They should already be fighting against them. They shouldn't need you to go through all this."

I snapped the book shut. "Are you saying you think this is pointless?"

"No," Laoise said firmly. "The Spear is powerful. It's Alastar's symbol. Having it isn't pointless." She looked sympathetic. "I haven't seen your father since, but I'd heard he was trying to rally some of the apprentices to fight the Eastern occupation. I don't think he's gaining much traction there."

"The apprentices wouldn't listen to him, I bet. They already made it clear they wouldn't help fight any surface wars without the Spear," I muttered. "Has he openly declared himself a Freetor?"

"I'm not sure it crossed his mind to distinguish himself," Laoise admitted. "Though Lady Sylvia was scheming a massive campaign against Freetors, contriving to undo all of the work you and Keegan have done to secure our freedoms. If she knew that your father was a Freetor, he would be more of a target than he currently is." She sighed again. "I just wish there was an easier way than this. It's dangerous, and long, and so much could go wrong."

"I know. I'm sorry I got angry at you." I cleared my throat. I wasn't so good at apologies. "I..." I clenched my left hand into a fist, feeling stiffness in my still-healing shoulder. "I'm afraid that Keegan thinks this whole journey is pointless. He wants me to go to Baile Gareth with him to establish a resistance there."

"The Gareth lands haven't been taken by anyone. It isn't a bad plan," she replied slowly. "But he would leave you to find the Spear alone?"

"Monju would accompany me," I said, trying to say the words with the certainty of a queen. "I just don't know if Keegan *wants* to come with me."

"Have you asked him?"

"Of course I have! But I can't force him. And even if he does come with me, it's not because he wants to. It's because he feels he has to protect me. I...I don't want to make him have that role. And besides, what happens if the unthinkable is true, that we've crossed the world for nothing?" I leaned against the nearest birch tree, and crossed my arms. "I don't want to take him away from his duties as the future Holy One of Marlenia. Starting the resistance in Baile Gareth is the best thing he can do for the realm."

Laoise nodded understandingly. "You're afraid he'll put the realm before you. And yet, that's what you love about him. Your shared concern for the people. He'll stand behind you, no matter what. He chose you."

I lifted my gaze to my best friend. "I do love him, don't I."

She smirked. "I think it's pretty obvious that you do."

My cheeks heated and we continued stepping lightly through the forest. "I guess I'm afraid he doesn't love me enough to accept that this is something that I have to do for the Freetor people."

"He's come with you this far," Laoise said. "Would you accept him if he went to Baile Gareth because that's what he has to do for all Marlenians?"

"I'd be mad at him," I admitted. "But I'd know that he was doing the right thing."

"Then he probably feels the same way about you going for the Spear. Just talk to him about it. You two are the future rulers of Marlenia. You have to communicate."

Now I smiled. "Maybe I should make you my personal advisor."

"If it comes with a raise, you know I'm in," she replied with a grin.

We scavenged for mimberries, disciple daisies, chicory plants, and young clovers for another twenty minutes with few words between us. I walked most of the way back to camp to ensure Laoise's safety, and then turned around. "I just need a minute of privacy, I'll be right back."

Gripping the strap of my bag, I headed deeper into the woods until I could no longer hear the sounds of camp. It was getting dark, and although the creatures could be lurking, I had a score to settle with my father.

The journal felt heavy in my lap as I opened it and settled against a tree with rough bark. I went to our last interaction: my father had added nothing new for me. Probably too busy wasting time with the apprentices. I started with the obvious: *Laoise and Bidelia are safe with us.*

The ink dried quickly on the parchment. It could be some time before a reply. Despite myself, I kept writing.

Lady Sylvia, defeated. She's rushing back to Marlenia City with her tail between her legs. I hope.

I took a deep breath. Still no reply. Of course not—he was running for his life from the East.

Or...

My mind returned to the Eastern soldiers who had become ash, blowing in the wind. He wasn't powerful enough to do that. If he were, we wouldn't need the apprentices' help, and I wouldn't be halfway to the edge of the world looking for an ancient weapon that he happened to covet.

Still, my father *was* the Advisor. He had more secrets than anyone.

The book warmed, and golden ink flew across the page beneath my messages and glowed a faint blue.

I was wondering when she'd catch up with you.

I pressed my lips together. *Why didn't you tell me she was coming?*

He replied: *Thought you would have heard her a league away with the circus she had in tow.*

I thought about asking him about Keegan's theory that Sylvia was acting in her own interests, but wrote instead: *And Bidelia, and Laoise? Did you know she had them as prisoners?*

A pause, and then: *I didn't know she had them with her. Though I knew Bidelia had been taken. Where are you?*

Why do you want to know, I wrote. *Are you following me?*

The reply was immediate. *Why would you ask that?*

Suspicious answer to a yes-or-no question. I tried a different approach. *Pretty aggressive of you to fry Sylvia's soldiers like that. I didn't know you were that powerful.*

An ink blot bloomed on the parchment, growing wider with each passing second. Eventually, in slow, sweeping cursive, he wrote:

That wasn't me.

A black pang of dread spread through my body like the dark ink on the page.

"Lady Kiera?"

Startled, I snapped the journal shut and drew my knees up to my chest. Monju stepped through the bushes cautiously, his outline a dark shadow in the twilight. "The prince was looking for the lady. Friends, too. Wanted to know if the lady was hungry."

"Oh." I relaxed, letting out a tension-filled sigh and then a laugh. I suppose I'd been gone a while now. "Yes. I'm coming."

With the slightest quirk of his thick brows, he turned, and disappeared suddenly into the brush.

***

My return to camp was greeted by laughter.

Bidelia, now awake, was propped against a tree with a blanket around her legs. We'd stolen it from one of the horse packs. Laoise leaned against her mother, resting her head on her shoulder. I smiled at them, and they offered warm returns. It wasn't often that I saw them this affectionate towards each other. Bidelia had spent long parts of our childhood away in the castle while Rordan kept an eye on Laoise and me. I looked away from them suddenly, not wishing to dwell on my confused feelings for Rordan, not tonight on this happy reunion.

A small fire burned between them. "Wind points west, away from the road and the castle," Monju explained. "Will not keep it for long."

"Good for drying my feet," Bidelia said.

I nodded, and sat beside Keegan. A wide smile blessed his handsome face—he was in good spirits for someone who just found out his father was dead, and had narrowly escaped death himself. He was even engaging Monju in conversation. A smile found my face at that. It was about time we all got along.

Monju sat diagonally across from me, his hands resting comfortably on his knees as he stared into the fire. He was the odd one out here, I realized.

We shared the food we'd foraged from the forest along with two packs of dried, cured meat we'd nicked from the abandoned Eastern supply. Fortunately, one of the horse packs had had a small pot, which Monju had filled with water at a nearby stream. The fire was far too small to construct a proper surface for the pot, so he laid it next to the fire. Although it wasn't necessary to boil the chicory and the clovers, they tasted better after a warm soak. The mimberries we ate raw, and even the bitter taste of the disciple daisies eased our battle wounds. Laoise and Bidelia ate quickly, and quietly; they had the biggest share. Sylvia's men had given them almost nothing during their imprisonment.

"Tell me what happened," I said to Bidelia as I finished the meagre meal. "How did you get captured?"

Bidelia sighed in her impatient, maternal way, rubbing her neck where she was once bound. "Everything was in disarray. We escaped with the rest of the castle staff through the underground tunnels. Many Easterners occupied the castle, the streets, the city. Many Freetors on the surface ran back to the Undercity, as it was suddenly the safest place to be. I don't blame them. Perhaps we should have gone too. But I couldn't. My mission, even without an Elder to guide it, still stood: uncover intriguing, useful information within the castle, and report it to Freetor authorities. The East had brought some of their own servants to tend to them, but clearly not enough. So I made the hasty decision to commit myself to the Frostfire family, with the hope of gleaning some information about their inner workings. Barely a day later, I was summoned by one of their barristers, accused of being a Freetor spy, and promptly arrested. Hours later, they found Laoise and dragged her in."

"Everyone always said that the Easterners were better listeners than thinkers. Better doers, too," Laoise added. "One minute I'm sneaking around the merchant district, the next minute, I'm surrounded. Gave them a good chase, but..." She gave me a sympathetic look, and then shrugged.

I pursed my lips. "What about the people in the city? Surely there must be a resistance?"

Bidelia looked especially grim in the shadows cast by the fire. "On the first day, many of the remaining guards in the Western Army formally announced their opposition in the Grand Square.

Ten minutes later, eight hundred bodies lay bloody on the stone. No one spoke out against the Frostfires after that."

Keegan hung his head and mumbled a prayer—or perhaps an oath.

"They were also offering a reward for information that would lead to your capture," Laoise said. She glanced at Monju, attempting to read his motivations. "And the Eastern soldiers—"

"Hush, that's enough," Bidelia interrupted.

"I will hear it," Keegan said.

Laoise flicked her gaze to me. "They were rounding up people sympathetic to the Tramore family and...executing them."

I offered Keegan my hand, and he took it, and squeezed hard. I hadn't told Keegan what I'd learned from my father about the goings-on in Marlenia City. I hadn't wanted to burden him with that. A part of me was afraid he'd turn around and launch a foolish campaign to reclaim the throne by himself. He would never do such a thing. But what if he had gone back...even if he'd been able to save just one person...?

"I see," Keegan said. He pressed his lips together, forcing all emotion from his face.

"I heard that some managed to flee. I heard that some Freetors took in some Marlenian families and slipped them through the tunnels, and beyond the city walls. But...those could just be stories." Laoise folded her hands in her lap.

"They could be true," I said, trying to infuse hope into my voice.

"The apprentices had the entrances to the Freetor underground locked up tight," Bidelia said. "Your father was able to slip in once or twice, but..." She stopped, remembering that Monju did not know that Advisor Ivor Ferguson was really Conal Driscoll.

"The lady's father?" Monju asked. "Not realize that she had family. Thought that her bloodline lives only in her."

Keegan and I shared a worried glance. I took a deep breath. "No, he's alive."

"The lady is always fortunate."

I curled my lip and stretched the silence. "No, Monju. I'm not, not really. My father is the Advisor."

Monju looked up with a start. "The lady is half Marlenian?"

"No. Um..." I glanced at Keegan, and he offered no resistance. We owed Monju the truth at least, after he had saved our lives today once again. Laoise nodded encouragingly. There was nothing my father could do about it out here in the middle of the West—unless he was closer than I thought. "Advisor Ferguson isn't a Marlenian. He's a Freetor. Was a Freetor, I guess. Until last month I thought he was dead. Turns out, he's just been living on the surface. In the castle." I smirked. "Kinda funny when you say it like that, I guess."

To my surprise, Monju didn't look horrified. He nodded, his face hungry with curiosity. "The song is wrong, then? He matched his daughter to the prince?"

"No, no," I said quickly. "Your song...it was accurate."

"Then fortune brought the lady and her father back together again."

I shrugged. "I guess. I don't really believe in that."

"Am sure he missed the lady very much."

I pressed my lips together and said nothing. Laoise lifted her eyebrows, as if to say, *It's true, why don't you believe me?*

"Our relationship has a long way to go before I can consider him a father again," I said quietly, to no one in particular.

Keegan laid a hand on my knee. Had I said too much? No.

Monju stared into the fire. "Monju's father, he is...ill."

"Sorry," I said.

"Monju thanks the lady for her sorry. But he has been sick for many years. The Race is catching up with him."

Race was a drug made from a certain flower in the South. It sped up your mind and your body, for a while. The more you took it, the more your body slowed, until it stopped working completely. Rordan told me once that you could tell a Race addict by how slowly he moved.

"Tried to get Peta to stop taking it. But the drug, it spoke to his mind. Poisoned him. Made him strange." Monju shook his head and smiled sadly. "He would not listen."

"And that's why you're not at his side," Keegan said. "He disowned you."

"No, the prince misunderstands. The West is rich with coin. The Southerners are a people of song and dance. Came to the West to make a fortune, and find some way to...to..." He trailed off and waved the thought away. "It was a foolish dream. Thought that maybe the songs could coax coin from the nobles, so Monju could make Peta better."

"I don't think our healers can cure the effects of Race," Keegan said. "No one can."

"Yes," Monju said softly. "Fear nothing can help him now."

I curled my knees into my chest. Monju sat on the other side of the fire, alone. He'd sworn his loyalty to us, holding onto a kernel of hope that we'd be able to help his dying father. If I were still the Violet Fox, living underground, I would have allowed him to stay in our cavern what with all he'd done for us. He'd sacrificed his precious last moments with his father to travel across the world, to seek out a cure for the addiction that plagued him.

As Monju stoked the fire, I realized he was the young man my brother would never become: romantic, not idealistic; reflective instead of rash, and far better in a fight than either of us could've hoped to be.

I had to find a way to help him—I would not fail him like I failed Rordan.

Even Keegan looked sympathetic. "The first chance I get," he said, "I'll send my best healer to care for your father, if he still lives."

Monju looked up. "Would do this for Monju, Prince?"

Keegan nodded. "My father, there was no hope for him. But maybe..."

A wide grin spread across Monju's face as he leapt up. "Many thanks to the blessed prince!" He collapsed again to his knees before Keegan and pressed his forehead to the dirt. "This...this is a great burden lifted from Monju's shoulders..."

My heart swelled. I grabbed Keegan and kissed his cheek. "You are wonderful."

A blush filled his cheeks. He brought me in closer. "Well. Without Monju, we'd both be dead."

Maybe, I thought, rubbing my sore shoulder. I was a pretty good fighter, but Monju had had more practice. I was used to running away and hiding most of the time.

Bidelia yawned and shifted her position against the tree. "We best sleep. We have a long ride tomorrow. Don't want to stay in one place for too long."

"What are your plans, now that you've escaped the East?" Keegan asked.

"We could return to the nearest underground tunnel," Laoise replied, glancing sideways at her mother. "Though the nearest noble family loyal to you would be the Gareths."

Keegan cast a glance at me. "You were thinking of heading that way?"

"Maybe," Laoise said evenly.

"The road forks half a league to the west," Monju said helpfully.

I stared into the flickering flames. The conversation had been going so well. And now, once again, I was reminded that I was going to lose Keegan to the realm.

"The two of you would be able to manage on your own?" Keegan asked.

"There are six horses," Bidelia said. "If His Highness allowed, we would take two."

"Yes, of course." Again, I felt Keegan's gaze on me, as hot and piercing as the fire. Then: "Well, I might ask you to deliver a message to Lord Ansel for me."

My heart nearly stopped. "What sort of message? Wouldn't you want to...?" I looked up at him finally, to see his face lit by the warm light of the fire, and those golden-green irises containing such passion, such joy. My confusion reflected in them.

"I think it would be in my interest to go further west," he said to the group, but he didn't take his gaze from me. He took my hand.

"Baile Gareth is supposedly safe," I said. "You *can* go."

His lips twitched, but he said nothing more.

"The further west, the fewer populations," Monju said, nodding sagely at Keegan's decision. "But more must the prince and the lady disguise themselves. More thieves, many Roamers, and cutpurses, searching for lost targets."

Keegan smiled and pulled me closer to him. "I'm sure the Violet Fox will come up with some convincing disguises and backstories."

I leaned into his shoulder, elated that he would hold me in such intimate company, but when my lips parted to ask him why, he shook his head. *Later.*

Fine. I would put his reasons out of my mind, for now. How could I not be happy about his decision? Keegan was coming with me to the end of the world.

But what if the Spear wasn't real? Would he still have faith in me then? Would he still love me?

I was overthinking it. This was a victory. I wasn't going to lose him. I breathed in the comforting smell of the fire as Monju conjured a tale of romance and adventure with his soothing voice, holding Keegan, Laoise, and Bidelia rapt with attention. My mind drifted in and out of the story as I savoured the warmth on my face, and Keegan's arm around me.

The apprentices weren't powerful enough to turn a man to ash. That was Elder-level magic. Come to think of it—even if my father *was* strong enough to pull off powerful fry-a-man-to-a-crisp lightning, he hadn't said that he was anywhere near me. If he were following us, he'd have shown himself by now, unless we had a few days on him.

A deep-seated fear bloomed in me as I rubbed my sore shoulder. What if Keegan was right? The Northern assassins had been trained in dangerous acrobatic killing arts. What if they also dabbled in Freetor magic?

No. Impossible. The Northerners hated Freetors. They had the largest Freetor slave trade in the world. I doubted an Elder or an apprentice would have been able to confess any magic skills before King Matís ordered his or her tongue removed for insolence.

Yet that did not change the piles of ash blowing in the wind. Whoever had killed those men seemed to be on our side. I should be grateful. That did nothing to alleviate the ever-present concern that somewhere in the shadows of the forest, someone powerful was watching our every move.

Eleven

I WOKE WITH the dawn to see Bidelia and Laoise off. The sad truth was that the more people there were in our expedition, the slower we went, and we didn't have the time or the resources to be encumbered when assassins closed in from sights unseen. Bidelia seemed confident that given her connections in Baile Gareth, she could raise some awareness of the attack in Marlenia City within the underground and servant communities and hopefully find some allies to prepare for Keegan's return.

Laoise enveloped me in a strong, fierce hug as we stood on the rocky road that stretched far in both directions. "Find the Spear," she whispered, squeezing me tight. "Bring it back. Make us proud."

"I will," I replied, holding back a sob. I drew away from her grip.

Bidelia set her lips in a disciplined line that seemed to be suppressing a smile. She was never much for overt emotion, preferring to be stern rather than sanguine. She cast a wary gaze over my shoulder, back towards the trees where our campsite lay hidden. "Though, a word of advice. Be careful of the foreigner."

"I trust him. And so should you. He saved all of our lives yesterday."

"That may be so, Kiera," Bidelia said stiffly, "but there were other men in our lives who earned our trust, and broke it all the same. We cannot be too careful. The future High Queen of Marlenia must be the most cautious of all of us."

Other men. Like my brother. Like my father.

I turned to my best friend. "Laoise? You agree?"

She failed to hide a pained expression. "He seems charming. But I'm...not the best judge of character."

Another sad reference to my brother. "If he were going to kill me, he would have done so already. And he doesn't know that we're searching for the Spear." I ran my fingernails across my palm. Already they were becoming long.

"Do you have a message for your father that you'd like us to pass along?" Bidelia asked.

"Oh. No." They didn't know about my journal.

Laoise narrowed her gaze at me. "Kiera."

I sighed. "Just...if you happen to contact him, just tell him we're fine. That Keegan is in good hands. That...I'll try not to let him down."

"That's better," Laoise said with a hint of a smile.

We helped Bidelia onto her horse, and then Laoise hoisted herself up into her own ill-fitting saddle. With few words of goodbye, they took off down the straight plains of the West, heading towards the fork that would lead to Baile Gareth. It was a day's ride along the road, and I hoped that whatever beasts or bandits were out there would find me a better target than them.

Trudging back to the treeline, I heard a faint snapping of twigs underfoot—someone else's foot.

"Keegan?" I said, hopeful.

I stepped through the brush, and Monju's dark eyes met mine with an inquisitive intensity. One hand gripped a tree trunk, his knees were dirty, and he was slightly bent over, as if he were coming out of hiding from beneath the ground.

"What are you doing?" I asked.

"Foraging," he replied.

I glanced at the road. The thick brush obscured much of the sightline, but any conversation likely could've carried. After his confession last night, I hated to assume the worst of him, though Bidelia's warning had brought forth Rordan's old betrayal.

"Were you doing anything *else* while foraging?"

Monju looked somewhat guilty. "Not meant to hear the lady's farewells."

"Or what they said about you." Regret settled in my stomach. "I'm sorry. I'm sure if they had more time to get to know you, they'd see just how"—my face heated—"how helpful and devoted and...how much of a friend you've been to us."

He dropped his gaze to the forest floor. "A friend?"

"Yeah."

"Monju has not had many friends."

"Neither have I, really."

A pregnant pause, and then he said, "The lady is gracious to consider Monju so near to her heart."

The intimate wording startled me. It was nothing personal, I told myself. The Southern language had many nuances that the Western tongue did not. That didn't stop it from taking root and germinating a host of awkward scenarios in my mind.

He seemed oblivious to my preoccupation, and only focussed on the overheard conversation with Bidelia and Laoise. "The lady should know that Monju would not hurt her," he said emphatically. "Finds it hard to hurt any living thing, especially if there is another way."

"But what about self-defence? In the alley, when you saved me, or...yesterday?"

He shook his head. "Precise blows, made carefully, to the right organs. Might die eventually, if the men do not seek help, but then that death would be on them, not Monju."

I wasn't sure if I agreed, but I nodded anyway. "I should make sure Keegan's awake."

"Good idea. Will collect more berries and herbs." He met my gaze with a small smile. "Monju...enjoyed this chat."

Turning too quickly to see my surprise, he slipped into the depths of the forest once more.

Stop overthinking it, I told myself as I hurried back to our campsite. Handsome and charming as the bard was, Keegan was my intended. I had fought hard, sacrificing nearly everything, to be with him. The bard probably treated every lady with the same courtesy. Even if Monju had affections for me, I could not allow myself to become entranced with him.

Even if Monju and I had more in common.

"Ugh! Stop!" I muttered, just as I burst into the camp. Monju was a brother-in-arms, not someone to be ogled.

Keegan, huddled over a small fire, looked up in surprise. "There you are. You're all right, there?"

"Yeah." I smiled a little. Keegan was coming with me to the edge of the world. Even if Monju failed me, Keegan would always have my back. I hoped. My thoughts of Monju disappeared as I realized what Keegan was doing. "Where did you get that fish?"

It was almost unrecognizable, impaled on a stake and roasting over the fire. He'd gutted it properly as far as I could tell, which would have been no small feat. The fish was half an arm's length.

"Caught it in a stream, just that way." He pointed into the woods, away from the road. "It's almost done, I think. Did you want some breakfast?"

"Yes." I sat on the edge of a rock across from him. Keegan hummed a tune as he slowly turned the fish. The meat was white, and small bits fell off into the fire as he turned the homemade spear. "So who taught the Prince of Marlenia how to catch and prepare fish?"

"Captain Murdock. Your father. Books in the library." He gave me an incredulous look as I reacted. "What, just because I grew up in a castle, you think I don't know how to hunt and kill an animal?"

Yes. That was exactly what I thought. But when I considered it, it made sense. There was an entire sanctuary behind the castle populated with game. Of course the Holy One wouldn't have confined his son to the castle all day and night. Monju had done much of the hunting so far—perhaps my skilled intended could show the bard assassin a trick or two.

I grinned as he removed the fish bit by bit from the spear, and handed me a piece. It was somewhat underdone, but it had been a while since I'd had fish. I gobbled it up without ceremony. Keegan laughed, and I covered my mouth as I chewed, embarrassed and proud of my decidedly unladylike behaviour.

"How are you feeling this morning?" I asked cautiously.

Keegan's lips twitched as his good humour soured. "I'm managing."

"I was a mess after Rordan," I said quietly. Saying his name hurt. I looked down at my feet. "If you wanted to talk about it...I'm here."

He ate the rest of the fish meat and absently wiped the remnants from the spear. "It's been a long time coming. He's finally at peace now."

"That doesn't mean it's any easier. I just want to make sure you have what I didn't—someone you can trust, and...lean on." I took a deep breath. I felt like an idiot expressing my feelings. It was so much easier to write them down and not be judged.

"Thank you," he said. The barest of smiles touched his face. "I'll just take it one day at a time, like you told me before."

I made a noise of approval. "You know..." I fidgeted, digging my fingernails into my dirt-stained palms. "You could have gone with them to Baile Gareth."

He nodded solemnly. "I know."

I slipped off the rock and knelt before him on the cold ground. "Thank you. For staying. It really means a lot."

His fingers splayed through my tangled curls, and in one swift, desperate motion, he tossed aside the spear, slid down from his seat, and pulled me close against him.

"You're not alone here, Kiera," he whispered. "I could never leave you."

"We have a realm to serve," I replied, nuzzling into his chest. His tunic smelled like pine and smoke. "I would have understood."

Keegan drew back, and ran light fingers over my high cheekbones. "Yes, but I wouldn't have forgiven myself. I believe in your judgment. Together, we will find the Spear, and take it to Baile Gareth, and show the East just how strong a united Marlenia can be."

I pulled his face to mine and kissed him. It had been a while since

I felt his lips. Castle life, the dangers in the forest, and the constant running from our enemies had left us exhausted, and never alone. We were unable to appreciate and know each other the way we should.

Monju conveniently announced his arrival from a distance, giving Keegan and me time to disentangle ourselves as the bard entered the camp. He was eating berries from a stuffed coin purse.

"Found breakfast?" Monju said.

"Yes," Keegan said. He rose and stomped out the fire. "Let's prep the horses, if you're ready." He looked up at the sun's position, and then to the west. "There is a sizeable town, Amardeas, within Baile Paddon, not too far from here."

I retrieved my father's notes from my bag and studied the map. "Yes, but it's way off the road. We'd have to double back to make it to the Throat. Even then, we're still going to have to go through Iar Bunsula to get to the pass, but at least we don't have to stay there. The town of Traddale is closer, and on the main road. We should only go there if we must. Staying in a town is too dangerous—and we don't have that much silver."

"A few pieces from the dead Easterners," Monju replied. "Enough for one room in a roadside inn."

The three of us, in one room. It wasn't as scandalous as my mind wanted to make it. As a Freetor, there had been times—not many—that I'd had to sleep in a cavern with others. It hadn't been such a fuss. Everyone needed a place to rest after a long day of running from the enemy. So why did I feel so uncomfortable with the notion now?

"Kiera could use a decent bed to sleep in," Keegan said, giving me the once-over.

I raised my eyebrows. "Me? I'm fine."

"Your arm, Kiera."

"My arm is fine. A lot better, thanks to all the herbs." I smiled appreciatively at Monju. "I've slept on stone for most of my life. If you want a real bed you can just say so. Don't need to pin that on me."

"I wasn't, I was only thinking of you and your comfort."

I heaved a sigh. "All right then. Monju, what do you suggest? Are there any nearby inns that you know of, not in towns?"

"Perhaps. But another solution, much better, presented itself in the woods." A knowing smile crossed his face. "Saw the markings for a Roamer camp on the trees. A large, moving camp. It will be safer to hide among their numbers."

The Roamers had existed for hundreds of years, though they had flourished in the past century. Because of the harsh laws that had forbidden Freetors to live and roam the surface, many Freetors—especially Forest Freetors—had chosen to relinquish their duties and run away with the Roamers. Roamers had a carefree lifestyle, romanticized by Freetor spoken-word poets and some Marlenian artists. They travelled across Marlenia and settled their caravans where they pleased, bringing foreign wares, entertainment, and often petty crime to the area. Old surface folklore said it was good luck to have Roamers settle near your land, as they kept away worse evils in exchange for gossip, food, and stories.

Despite their attractive lifestyle, I could never abandon my people, so I had never been tempted to run away. But they were the perfect example of Marlenians and Freetors living in perfect harmony. It didn't matter where you were from with the Roamers. You were born anew when you joined their caravans.

Keegan looked sceptical. "Sounds...risky. What if there are Northern and Eastern ears among them?"

"People come and go from the camps; it would not be unusual for three poor peasants to arrive as one. Word spreads quickly about new faces, yes, but the prince and the lady can change their faces. Monju is trusted there. Friends of Monju are friends of the Roamers. Talk to the Roamers, allow them to fill stomachs with drink and song, and they will soon forget that the prince and the lady are strangers from the unmoving cities."

Keegan fixed me with an indecisive stare. Although Roamers were different from Freetors, their unconventional way of living was my domain more than it was his. "What do you think?"

"Sounds like a good idea," I said, nodding to Monju. "Are you sure we'll be able to find them? That they won't be too far off our course? We still need to go through the Throat. Beyond Iar Bunsula, there aren't any towns or civilizations that we know of. This could be our last chance to resupply."

"Monju is certain the Roamers will be just before the pass—the markings signified that would be the case. Fortunate if they are, for the Roamer bandits will not rob those who come to trade and attend their festivities."

"Bandits as well, are they?" Keegan asked dryly.

Monju's smile returned. "They have to make a living somehow, Prince. Songs are not so profitable this far west, when there are no ears to hear them."

"Let's go then, so we can make good use of the sun," I said.

Keegan took the lead and Monju held up the rear as we took to the road. I stole a glance at the foreign man. To my surprise, he was looking at me. I guess that wasn't so much a surprise. He winked and my stomach lurched—there was something far too bold there.

I spurred the horse into a gallop and soared to meet Keegan's pace.

* * *

Feenagh Forest tapered out, and the vast plains sloped into rockier, rougher terrain. The mountains loomed, suddenly much closer than before. Groupings of trees dotted the road, which winded in and out of thick brush, up steep hills, and down into nearby streams.

"We're in Baile Macant," Monju said.

"Owned by the Macant family," Keegan explained to me. "And the Jerrolds own some land just south of here. Lesser lords. Not much farmland this way, or towns. Only bailes, and small ones at that. Hunting and fishing are their mainstays."

"If the prince continued along the road, would come to Traddale.

But the Roamer camp is that way." Monju pointed off into a cluster of trees, closer to the mountains. "A tricky ride, but should be there by sundown."

Sundown seemed ever nearer now. The mountains took up more of the sky than I had ever thought possible from rock and stone. Even the Marlenia City castle, embedded for hundreds of years upon the steep precipice, paled in comparison to the Shoulder Mountains. The snow-tipped giants were so wide that they conquered much of the horizon. Somewhere, through the windy pass and beyond those steep monstrosities of nature, was the land of my ancestors.

As per Monju's instructions, we veered from the road and into the trees. Unlike in Feenagh Forest, the trees here were thinner, and easier for our horses to navigate through. Monju stopped every so often to venture out of sight and check the secret marks that designated the camp's movements and latest location. Keegan asked about my father's map. When I drew it out to estimate our progress, I noted that my journal was glowing. A message from my father? I'd have to check it later, if I got a chance to be alone.

The map said we were another day's ride from Iar Bunsula and the Throat. Unfortunately this was where my father's notes turned loopy, as he was suffering from hunger, exhaustion, and a near-fatal wound. I stuffed the book back in my sack and sighed. We might be on our own from this point on.

The sun drew closer to the mountain tips and cast a yellow and red glow over us. We shielded our eyes from the harsh light.

"The prince and his lady will need a story. A few stories, to be believable. Roamers trade not only with the material, but also with memories," Monju warned us. "Cannot be noble. Too suspicious."

"Well, I could be a Freetor. That's easy enough," I said.

Monju nodded. "Not the Violet Fox, though."

"No." I glanced at Keegan. It would be hard for him to pass as a Freetor. His skin had been too blessed by the sun, and his mannerisms were too refined. It was possible he could change his accent, but changing the way one walked *and* behaved was trickier. "How would you feel about being a Marlenian peasant? Maybe a shopkeeper's or healer's son."

"I suppose I don't have much choice in the matter," Keegan replied dryly. "But these stories we're supposed to have...?"

"A humorous event about the prince when he was small, or a love lost, or unscrupulous deals that benefit the less fortunate. Roamers enjoy those stories especially." Monju squinted through the trees. "They are also hungry for gossip of the capital, but keep stories of the attack to a minimum. Eastern ears may be listening, even among the most forgotten of Western Marlenians—the Roamers would do anything to earn a quick piece of silver."

An hour or so later, we passed strips of bright green cloth tied around tree trunks, and the sounds of revelry filtered from somewhere below us. As the trees cleared, I hastily pulled the horse to a stop.

A large basin, at least three hundred stone-throws wide in its circumference, lay before us. It was as if Dashiell himself had punched a hole in the earth. Patches of water lay here and there, but the entire lakebed was populated with a distracting, dazzling display of coloured fabric and wooden caravans.

"The Roamers," Monju said grandiosely, gesturing downward. "More than usual. A meeting of several camps." He grinned at me. "Do not get lost."

I peered down, wondering how we were going to get there, when Monju clucked to his horse and directed it around the left side to a worn path. Rocks let loose and tumbled down the sharp slope as he fearlessly descended deep into the sea of chaos and colour.

"I've only seen portraits of Roamer camps," Keegan said, unable to hide the fascination in his voice. "Sometimes they'd come to the city. More before the wall was built. I've never seen so many gathered in one place."

We followed Monju, passing a wooden sign worn by weather and the sword, nailed to a tall pine. It was still legible: *Toram Lake.*

"Must have dried up," Keegan said. "Almost."

As Monju rode hastily down, I quickly drew out my father's map. Sure enough, the words *Toram Lake* were scrawled just south of the mountain pass, with a rough illustration. Near it, he'd noted: *Water safe to drink. Black berries in nearby bushes toxic. Lake fills greedily with rain.*

Glancing at the clouds, I noted that precipitation didn't seem likely, so this would be as good a place as any to stay for the night. My stomach lurched and I leaned back as the horse expertly navigated down into the basin.

Perhaps as many as five hundred people of all ages scurried underfoot. Many of the children under five years of age were naked, and happily so. Laughter, singing, and shouting created a lively, chaotic environment. Many people spoke the common Western tongue and the native Southern language, and a song drifted into my ears that sounded Northern—a language that hadn't been spoken in near four hundred years, at least.

Men and women dressed in shabby, bright rags greeted us with smiles as we approached. We had horses, which meant we probably had silver—but our clothes suggested we weren't rich. I was a Freetor pretending to be a queen, pretending to be a Freetor.

Tents of every colour and size were pitched wherever the Roamers felt they'd like to sleep or sell wares, creating a disorganized array of vendors. Eventually Keegan and I had to dismount and guide our horses around a sea of fabric.

"A silver for your shoes, good sir!"

"The story of your mother, in exchange for shiny beads!"

"I can't see how that would be valuable to them, to know about my mother," Keegan remarked as we spotted Monju and his horse up ahead.

"The beads are probably fake, or stolen, and best gotten rid of while they're still hot," I explained. "Or, they're looking for a convincing backstory to change their own history."

"I suppose a convincing story from a charming weaver of words is all it takes nowadays."

My hand found my bag as I thought about my storyweaving father. He'd better be all right, and far from here.

Monju saw us approach, and waved us excitedly over. A tall, jovial man with a curly, untrimmed beard and a balding head also lumbered towards our Southern bard. He looked like a man who had lost a great deal of weight quickly. His stained red tunic went to his navel, and flabs of loose skin peeked from beneath the fabric. Like most of the Roamers, he was barefoot. His facial features—a strong, beaky nose and high cheekbones—suggested a Western heritage.

"Ah! Monju Farin!" he said excitedly. "Come sing us a song! The fire is just up there." He pointed further into the mess of tents to a column of grey smoke ascending into the sky.

"Pascal Antony. Good to see the general is still roaming."

"Could never stop." He smiled at Keegan and me cautiously, evaluating us the same way a fox evaluates its prey. "I haven't seen your faces here before."

"New friends. Jon, and Bree."

I nodded curtly, falling into my new role. Keegan shifted uncomfortably beside me. He almost offered his hand to shake but I grabbed it, taking it excitedly in my own. A handshake would be a mistake here—it could be too easily mistaken as a noble demanding a lesser man to kiss his ring. Fortunately Keegan had not thought to slip on his jewelry before leaving the castle. I grinned and pressed my head into Keegan's shoulder, and stared up at him as if I were lost in a dream.

"Ah, new lovers," said Antony. "Thought the Roaming life might give you a little adventure, did you?"

"Yes," Keegan replied. He returned my love-soaked smile and squeezed me tightly to his side. "I always wanted to see the world."

That much was truth, at least.

"You always attract the romantics, Monju Farin," he said, shaking his head at the Southern bard. "Got to stop writing those sappy songs and start regaling people with tales of my victory, no?" He slapped his giant hand on Monju's shoulder, bellowing with laughter. Monju joined in.

"Someday, Antony," he promised.

"You're a fighter then, are you?" Keegan asked, intrigued.

Antony's eyes lit up. "Oh, aye!" He ribbed Monju again, much to the bard's quiet distaste. "Used to belong to the Western Army. That was twenty years ago, though. Had some run-ins with the Freetors, and then fought freelance for the High King Leszek Frostfire during the trade war. But his pockets weren't as deep as they all say. Came here to the Roamers, where I still see some action when the Holy One says don't settle here, don't pitch a tent there. Well, I'll pitch where I like, thank you, old man!"

He rumbled again with laughter, and I joined in superficially. So news of the Holy One's death hadn't reached Roamer ears yet. Keegan's smile was haunted. Too haunted. So I grabbed his face and kissed him.

"I know it hurts," I whispered as I kissed his cheeks, and nibbled his ears. "You have to pretend."

Keegan mumbled something in reply but I shut him up with another kiss.

"Miss the battles, I do, but my body ain't what it used to be," Antony continued, but now he was looking curiously at Keegan. "Say, I don't know you from somewhere, do I?"

"Unlikely," Keegan replied evenly, and shrugged with just enough nonchalance.

"You're from the capital, did you say?" Antony asked.

I matched Keegan's expression while digging my fingernails into his arms. We did *not* say, but that was a clever tactic to get us to reveal our origins all the same.

"My family comes from there, yes," Keegan said slowly. "But—"

"I'm a Freetor," I interrupted. I blushed and gazed lovingly up at Keegan. "His mum and father didn't exactly approve, you see, so, now we're here."

"Ah." Antony nodded. "Classic tale. We got a coupla mixed bloods here too. You'll fit right in!"

Phew. Before Antony could make any more inquiries about

Keegan's familiar-looking face, Monju jumped in. "Monju and his friends would like a tent."

"I see that," he said, good-naturedly. "Someone told me fifteen minutes ago there were two extra tents available up that way." He pointed close to the fire. "If they're not claimed now, they could be yours for a price. And for a quid, Teddy the stable boy will care for your horses. May buy them from you, or trade as well."

"Many thanks, friend," Monju said. "Will join the fire festivities shortly."

"You'd better!" Antony called after us as we disappeared into the crowds.

I breathed a sigh of relief as we wove between the many tents and caravans. Holding tight to Keegan, afraid I'd lose him, I leaned closer to his ear and squeezed his hand. "People are going to say things about the Holy One here. I know it's hard, but—"

"I know. I'm sorry, I'll do better," he said quietly. He glanced back at the former general and then tapped Monju on the shoulder. "He might be out of shape, but if this Pascal Antony is as experienced a fighter as he claims, perhaps he could be of some use. Is he in charge here?"

"No one is really in charge, but Antony is well liked, and people listen when he speaks and makes orders. There are some retired soldiers among the Roamers. Some more talented than others," Monju said. "The prince would have to have much silver to convince them to leave their carefree ways and fight against the large, better-paid armies of the East." He pulled five silver coins from his pocket and tossed them in the air, catching each in turn. "A silver can only buy so much loyalty."

Seven silver quid later, we had two tents, and our horses cared for, at least for the night. That was all we could afford. The tents were within shouting distance apart, and looked much like all the other tents. I tore off a piece of purple fabric from my cloak and wrapped it around the top post of the nearest tent so that I could tell it apart from its neighbour.

"Is it all right that we...share?" Keegan asked.

Oh. Right. Two tents, three people. Keegan and I hadn't slept in the same bed since the masquarade at the Gathering. Being in an enclosed space with him was far different from sleeping under the stars with him. My cheeks heated.

Monju answered for me. "Better that the lady not sleep alone. Monju will take the other, but will likely be by the fire until late in the morning."

Keegan nodded, satisfied. "Well, what do we do now?"

"Whatever you want," Monju said with a smile. "Socialize, trade. When the sun sets, food will be available near the fire. Don't leave anything of value in the tents." He glanced at my sack hanging at my hip. "The lady does not carry precious items, does she?"

I gulped and tried to stay calm. Everything I'd ever owned was slung over my shoulder. "I'll keep it close."

"Many Roamers here have good hearts, but better fingers."

I put on my best fearless face. "Then I'll just have to be better."

"It's just for one night," Keegan said, more to himself than to us. "We should try to sleep early if we can."

Monju laughed. "Not possible. And more suspicious. The Roamers will party until the tiny hours of the morning. Watch Antony. Stay as late as him, and then leave ten minutes after. No earlier. Much disrespect, otherwise, especially since he welcomed the prince personally, and the prince and the lady are new faces."

Keegan heaved a sigh. "All right, then." He glanced at me. "You're going to have to ensure I don't fall asleep."

"I'm pretty sure that's one of my roles as High Queen, isn't it?"

* * *

While Monju joined the other musicians at the fire, and Keegan went to make water, I removed my journal. Sure enough, my father had left me a message.

Eastern riders headed your way. The city is buzzing with the rumour that the prince still lives. Wherever you are, keep moving.

No chance of that. My heart chilled momentarily. I drew a deep breath and tried to be warm. I glanced around the excitement of the Roamer camp. I didn't see anyone particularly interested in me. Still, I ducked in the tent to reply, as many Freetors couldn't read much less write. The top of the tent brushed against my head, and it was barely wide enough for Keegan and me to lie side by side in, but it was safer than sleeping beneath a tree. There was even a blanket to sit on—better than lying on rocks.

We're safe.

The reply was hastily scrawled:

No, you're not. Keep moving west. You're not in Baile Gareth, are you?

My thoughts went to Bidelia and Laoise. *Is it in danger?*

Baile Gareth, well defended—for now.

I wrote: *Is the Holy One really dead?*

Yes, he replied. *For days now. So are many others. Leszek and his sons won't stop until everyone bends the knee to them. Don't stop. Everyone is looking for you now.*

His sons?

Keegan opened the flap, and I scooted back, startled. He smiled in apology and crawled in next to me. I snapped the journal shut and threw it into the sack. It was highly unlikely anyone would find us here, in the sea of Roamer tents, at the bottom of a drained lake near the mountain pass.

"They're starting to serve food," he said. "I tried to get some, but I'm afraid I'm not the best storyteller, and I don't think we have any silver left."

"Good thing I'm here to provide for you."

Smirking, he drew the tent flap shut and lay down next to me. Side by side, face to face, we held each other, listening to the distant music and the sounds of revelry. We'd have to join them soon, but not yet, not yet.

I leaned closer to Keegan's ear. "So. How is His Highness

enjoying his time with the common folk?"

Keegan threw me a disapproving look as I called him by his title—the tent walls were as thin as parchment—but he smiled and took my hand. "It certainly smells a lot more than a Gathering."

"I bet I smelled just as pungent when you met me."

"I was too busy focusing on your knife at my throat instead of how you looked or smelled."

"How romantic."

He kissed me again, tenderly this time.

"You know, I think you're starting to like this," I said teasingly.

"Kissing?"

I laughed. "No. Well, yes. But being in the woods. With the common folk."

"I can see how the lifestyle would be appealing." He traced my fingers as he pondered. "Would you want to stay here?"

"It's certainly nicer than the underground," I admitted. "But you know I'm committed to seeing you back on the throne."

"I just..." He shifted, sitting up. "I don't want to force you away. If you really did find a better life—"

"I *have*. With you."

He looked unconvinced. "Just don't marry me just because you feel you have to, just because you think it'll keep your people free. That's all... that's all I meant." He gaze fell upon my sack. "If you were in love with someone else, or if being a queen wasn't what you wanted to do, but you *felt* you had to do it, because of an obligation to the promise, or because you felt your people expected it of you—just, don't. I don't want to hold you back. From anything."

"Keegan..." If I were in love with someone else? Did he think there was something between Monju and me? I tried to think of something to say to counter his point. *Of course I want to be queen. Of course I have feelings for you. I am not doing this for my people, I am doing this for me.*

But...

The Violet Fox was not a queen. She fought for her people. She had very little. Above all, she loved her people. Adventure was her spouse. Fighting for freedom was her purpose. Doing something because *I* wanted it, it was a foreign concept. Every major thing I had ever done—stealing food and silver, freeing my people, opposing the Marlenians—I had done for the greater good of the Freetors.

"I already made my decision. Just like you did," I said finally. "Uniting Marlenia is important to both of us. Being with you is important to me. It's what I want."

"All right," he said, unable to hide the relief in his voice. He pulled me close. "As long as it's what you want. I just hope that we find what we're looking for."

My stomach clenched. "And if we don't?"

"I don't know," he said quietly, after a moment of silence. "We can't search forever."

He stroked my hair and my thoughts wandered. All I'd ever wanted was for my people to be free, to live under the sun as equals. I'd never considered joining with the Roamers as a solution because they were a constantly moving, unorganized mass spread across the world.

Yet it certainly sounded more appealing than arriving at Driscoll's End to find an empty cave. I pursed my lips. Perhaps Keegan's faith in me only went so far.

The task ahead of us was as daunting as the mountains. Looming, ever-present, unmovable. I closed my eyes, and thought of climbing.

* * *

I'd fallen asleep with one hand clutching the sack and the other splayed on the cold blanket.

Keegan?

I sat up as my eyes adjusted to the darkness. One blessing of the journey was regaining my acute night vision. Grabbing my bag and slinging it over my shoulder, I crawled for the tent exit.

The moon was nearing its highest point in the sky. I'd slept longer

The Silver Spear

than I'd intended. Where was Keegan, and Monju? I cursed my laziness, though my nap in the tent had been better than nights and days of my worried, fitful sleep. I called Keegan's name, and then his false name, but my cries were drowned out by the flurry of people revelling and dancing around me.

Every face was adorned with a mask. Most were made of cloth and string, but others glittered alluringly in the light of the moon and the fire. I wished I'd known about the proper Roamer dress code before leaving the tent. I dug out the fabric Violet Fox mask from my bag and strung it around my eyes. Much better. Without my cloak to match, it was doubtful anyone would recognize me here. At best, this far from the capital, I was an aspiring lookalike.

Fast-paced, cheery music originated from around the fire, but it seemed omnipresent. I tried to spot Monju among the musicians, but it was almost impossible to focus on anything. Every colour, every mask, every detail seemed to demand equal attention, and strained my eyes.

The figures danced gaily, twirling their arms. Some sang along with the tune, which didn't seem to have a beginning or end, while others swigged from their flasks and made up their own lyrics. A smile lit my face without my realizing. This was what a celebration truly was. This—the cloudless sky, the warmth of the fire, the readily available drink and food shared equally among equals—this was what life was supposed to be.

The Freetors in the underground didn't have celebrations such as this—not as long as I'd been alive. There was so much colour, so much life to this camp, that did not exist in the depths of the earth and between the unmoving stone of the castle.

I could live in this place. Lady Kiera of the Camp. High Queen of the Wandering Souls.

It was in the midst of this freedom that a figure, hooded and masked, shrouded in a dark cloak, weaved through the crowd towards me. Normally I would have adopted a defensive stance and reached for my knife, but in my altered state, he was not a threat. Just a spot of darkness among the colours. He approached me, making no sound between the notes of the fervent music, and took me by the arm and drew my lips to his. He smelled of the woods, of smoke and pine.

Keegan.

No—this was someone different.

I leapt backwards, startled by my own realization, but the man just smiled—he was youthful—and then fled into the crowd of dancing bodies.

Who was he? How dare he steal a kiss from me, the Violet Fox?

How dare I...enjoy it?

I wiped my mouth and tore after the shrouded figure, but a shrill scream broke through the revelry. The music died and the screaming continued to pierce the air.

Then, an explosion, off to my left. And another, to my right: a caravan burst to pieces, sending deadly projectiles soaring. Men and women dashed about—some crying for their loved ones, others screaming nonsense.

Red chestplates with blue trimmings caught my eye.

The Frostfires were here.

"Father," I said, and went for my sack.

Suddenly, someone grabbed me roughly by the arm and threw me to the ground. My cheek sunk into the wet mud.

A figure stood over me, and then many more, and then a violent *thump* sent me into a confused sleep.

Twelve

"Lady Kiera. Kiera. Please, wake..."

Blurry vision gave way to large dark eyes and a desperate face. Rough bark dug into my back and my head throbbed mercilessly. A bump the size of a small egg protruded from my tangled hair.

"Good, the lady is awake. Can understand?"

I nodded as the mind fog receded. The basin was a few stone-throws away. The celebratory, smooth music had been replaced by shouting and the clanging of steel on steel. Up here, the grass was dry and cold and so far removed from the warm mud of the ongoing battle below.

"Drink," Monju said, pushing a flask in my face.

When my lips found the spout, Monju tipped the fresh warm water into my mouth. My throat was parched and I welcomed the water eagerly. Though I thirsted for more, he pulled the flask away. "Not too much. Breathe."

"There was an explosion." I gripped Monju's tunic, desperate for answers. "Where's Keegan?"

Startled, he glanced down at my grip, but made no move to remove me. "What's the last thing the lady remembers?"

"The explosion," I said again. I touched my lips. "Someone kissed me. There was also a scream, and then I was knocked out."

Monju threw a nervous glance to the commotion in the dried-up lake. "Should leave."

"Not without Keegan. Where is he?"

"Not sure. Disappeared into the madness."

I released my grip and braced myself against the rough bark of the tree, took a deep breath of fresh forest air, and climbed to my feet. "We'll find him, and then we'll make ourselves scarce."

"Too dangerous!" He stopped me from approaching the edge of the basin. "Can meet in Iar Bunsula, yes? Splitting up may be the only chance of survival."

"I won't say this again. I'm not leaving without Keegan."

The moon had disappeared behind thick clouds. Most of the lights in the Roamer camp below had been extinguished, but the fire where the musicians had played burned low and menacing, lending blood-red light to the squalling Roamers, and the few who were facing off with swords. Smoke rose from a burned caravan—perhaps one that had exploded. The sounds had painted a bigger picture of battle and bloodshed, yet all I saw below was darkness and confusion.

"I thought there was an attack," I said. "Did the Roamers fight the East? Were the shadow killers?" I turned to Monju, determined to squeeze the answers from his lithe, dangerous body. "Tell me what happened."

He drew a deep breath. "Saw suspicious men in the shadows, slipping between the dancers, not allowing the fabric to touch them. Masterful. Dangerous. Monju had to act. The lady was in their line of sight, and too recognizable, even with her Violet Fox mask. The prince, nowhere in sight. Had to shield the lady's face. To save her."

I took a step back as his words peeled away into meaning. "You...kissed me?"

"Had to save the Lady Kiera," Monju said softly. Desperation made his eyes round and shiny in the moonlight.

My father had been right, and I had been foolish. Staying with the Roamers had been a mistake. And trusting Monju...

"Why kiss me?" I asked, trying to keep my emotions in check. "You could have pulled me to the ground or pushed me into the nearest tent!"

"She looked radiant by the fire, in the glow of the dance," he said.

My face flushed, even in the cool night breeze. "You could have let me fight my enemies."

"Swore to protect the lady!" Monju said, flustered. "It was the first thing that came to mind. Did not want to resort to violence unless necessary."

I was taken aback. Again, his restraint surprised me. "How did I get up here?"

He closed his eyes, and opened them again as he looked up at the full, bright moon overhanging the basin. "Carried."

"Did you knock me unconscious too?"

"No, the lady was knocked to the ground, struck by accident."

My head throbbed, and the sounds below only made me feel worse. I reached for my sack, but nothing hung on my shoulder.

"My bag. Where's my bag?" Possessions were nothing to Freetors, but I'd never forgive myself if the Orb of Dashiell and my magical journal fell into the wrong hands. Gripped by fear and desperation, I rounded on Monju. "Where—?"

"Did not have a bag!" Monju replied. "Only thought of saving the lady."

I couldn't blame him for not thinking of it. He didn't know the value of its contents. My fingernails sunk into my palms. First Keegan, now *another* magical artefact from Dashiell I had to find...

Monju's boots made no sound on the grass as he ventured closer. "Calm, Kiera, calm," he said, and began whispering in his native tongue. His hand trailed down my mess of curls with the lightest of touches and the heaviest of intentions. "Will find Keegan, will find the bag, but must do quickly. Yes?"

I wrenched myself from his grip. "I am not a horse that you can calm with soothing words."

"Sorry." He looked truly hurt, which frustrated and wounded me more. Of all people, he must understand what I had gone through to be with Keegan. He had written the song that would undoubtedly immortalize my relationship with the prince. Monju might not have been born of dirt, but he lived in it as I had, and that made us brothers, not lovers.

He was a brother I had to trust, as I no longer had a brother to lean on.

I rubbed my face with my dirt-ridden hands. One thing at a time. My priority was to find Keegan and ensure his safety. Then, find the Orb. Then...then I'd deal with Monju. "You're right. Let's be quick."

Even without much light, Monju managed to follow me into the camp and through the throng of people gathered near the fire. The smell of smoke was heavy in the air, and familiar to my senses. Not the typical smell of a campfire, or of a torch, but the elusive, earthy-sweet smell of Freetor magic.

The faces in the crowd were angry, desperate, and afraid. People whispered and speculated about the attack. I pieced together a narrative from overheard conversations as I kept my head down and quietly weaved through the crowd. I hadn't been the only one who'd seen the flashes of red and bright blue. From the way they were talking, dozens of Eastern soldiers had washed over the camp like a wave over a rock, frantically grabbing and beating on every young woman with dark hair—searching for someone.

Me.

Several of the well-armed Roamers were trying to decide what to do. There was no sign of the Eastern men now, yet the chatter was that some Roamers had struck out on their own to search the surrounding forest to seek justice for the unwelcome interruption. I caught a glimpse of General Antony, strapping on a battle-worn breastplate.

I swiftly made my way towards him when Monju's hand caught my arm. "I found him."

One of the caravans was parked near the edge of the lake basin, fewer than ten stone-throws from the fire. Tall barrels and crates occupied much of the space behind the caravan, and as I blindly followed Monju into this dark, narrow place, I was dimly aware that this was the perfect spot for an ambush.

Keegan lay on his back in the dirt, his left cheek in the mud and his arms splayed. I fell to his side and cupped his still-warm face.

"Keegan! Wake up!"

No response. Warm breath exited his nostrils and tickled my fingertips. Some of my worry melted away. I patted him down, searching for blood or fatal wounds—a bump on his head, like mine, and some scratches, but nothing fatal.

I glanced over my shoulder. We were well hidden, and the commotion by the fire was far louder than any noise we could make at present. My hand rested on the firm mud, feeling an unusual, long indent. At first I dismissed it as our footprints, but the marks were as wide as Keegan's body, and as I investigated further, I came to a chilling conclusion.

"He was dragged here," I said. "But he's still alive."

Monju appeared concerned. "Someone wanted to protect the sleeping prince."

Unamused by the moniker, I crept around the secluded area. The caravan was pushed almost to the edge of the basin, creating a storage space with access from around the left and right sides. Keegan had been dragged here from the right—the same way Monju and I had entered. Natural light here was a memory; he'd be undetectable for the night, though in the morning he'd be discovered easily.

As I explored the storage alcove, a crunch beneath my feet threw me off guard. The dirt and mud of the dried-up lake occasionally gave me pause in my flats, but this texture was unusual. I took a step backwards, knelt before the substance, and ran tentative fingers through the grittiness.

The smell hit me first, awaking the memory I needed: the fight with Sylvia's men. Freetor magic wielded by an unknown assassin had turned breathing, fighting men into dust.

Two more piles rested a stone-throw away, still warm and undisturbed, unsettlingly close to Keegan's unconscious form. While Keegan breathed evenly, the remains of three dead men surrounded him.

My father had warned me not to stay here.

"This is the lady's bag?" Monju asked, holding it up.

A protective urge struck me. I leapt over the ash and snatched the bag from him. It still felt heavy. That was a good sign. I stuck my hand inside—yes, the Orb was still there, and my journal, and the expedition notes, and my cloak and even my Violet Fox mask.

How did Keegan come to have it?

Who had taken it off my body?

Someone with Freetor magic had killed three people, left Keegan vulnerable and unconscious, *and* failed to notice a magical Freetor artefact?

The commotion at the fire grew louder. People chanted angrily, demanding justice and blood. Time to leave.

Monju leaned against the caravan with his weapon drawn as I knelt by Keegan again and tapped his shoulders and his cheeks. "C'mon, Keegan, please wake up..."

His eyelids twitched and he batted my efforts away with a heavy hand.

"It's all right. You're with me."

Groaning, he struggled to sit up. His flailing hand hit one of the barrels and knocked it over on top of an ash pile. That seemed to bring him to his senses. "Kiera?"

"Here." I took his hand. "There was an attack. We need to get out of here." Best not to mention the part where Monju kissed me. Not now.

Using the caravan and my grip for purchase, he climbed to wobbly feet.

"What's the last thing you remember?" Monju asked.

Frowning, Keegan's gaze darted about. "It...must have been a dream..."

A cry from a hundred voices resonated in the night. Men and women shouted: *Make them pay! Blood for blood!* Another voice, which sounded like Antony's, was egging them on, though I couldn't make out the particulars. If they had captured Eastern soldiers or even a shadow killer, that was one less enemy we had to worry about.

"Will not make it far on foot," Monju muttered. "Better to have horses."

"Can you find some?" I asked.

With a curt nod, he rose and silently sidestepped the ash piles to disappear around the caravan, and into the Roamer crowd.

Once the bard was out of sight, Keegan took my hand and brought me close. He brushed the bump on my head and I winced.

"I couldn't find you," he said.

I drew away. Sentiment would have to wait. "We need to leave."

"We do." His tone didn't match my urgency. A conflicted expression twisted his face, and gave me pause, even though I itched to run.

"I saw you..." He gathered more resolve. "You kissed someone."

There was no point in denying it, even though I was unnerved by his accusation. "*He* kissed *me*. And everyone was wearing masks. For all I knew, it was you."

"You knew it wasn't me."

True. "I'm not an Elder. I don't have magic. I can't read minds. I know how this looks, but why are you mad at me for this?"

Keegan was silent. Riding and walking for days with fitful sleep had taken its toll on both of us. We'd come so far, and we were so close to the Spear—now was not the time for us to question our loyalties.

"Was it Monju?"

Blood rushed to my face. I took a step back, furious. "Why would you ask that?"

"I've seen the way he looks at you," Keegan replied. "The way you look at him. You have a lot in common."

I gritted my teeth. "Of course we do. That's not a reason for me to...to..." The word sounded suddenly disgusting. "I fought every day to be fed. You had anything you ever wanted. Why would you be jealous of a connection between two once-hungry people? I thought that *we* had many things in common. Like saving our people. A sense of honour, and duty. And..." Our physical attraction did not need to be expressed in words. It pained me to stand this far from him and spout hateful things, even though they needed to be said.

He held out his hands to take mine, and then seemed to think better of it. "It's not that I don't believe you." Retrieving my sack from the ground, he pulled out my journal. "The camp was chaos, and I couldn't find you. I was wandering around, and there were so many people, but then I saw your sack on the ground. You'd never go anywhere without it, so I figured you'd been taken. I was knocked unconscious soon afterwards, but not before I'd gotten a chance to see this."

"You went through my journal?" Although he knew the significance of the tome, he couldn't read it as it was written completely in Freetor code.

The pages flipped quickly under Keegan's deft hand and rested upon the latest conversation I'd had with my father. But scrawled in what looked like my handwriting, in the common tongue, dripping with the ink of the quill, was:

I think I'm falling in love with Monju.

"I didn't write that." I wouldn't write in the common tongue for everyone to read. Rereading the false confession conjured Monju's hurt face from when I'd brushed him aside earlier. The writing was so like mine, it was uncanny. And frightening.

"That letter to Sylvia in your study—you said you didn't write that. Well, I didn't write this. Maybe they're connected. Someone is trying to drive us apart."

It was a flimsy idea, but the memory of how the letter had driven a wedge between us burned brightly, and seemed to give Keegan pause.

"Does Monju know what you have in your pack?" Keegan asked. "He would be the only other one with opportunity, and motive."

He had been eager to abandon Keegan earlier. To get me alone. Monju could have separated me from my bag when he carried me from the lakebed, to leave me helpless and dependent on him. Yet a quick glance inside would have made him realize the value of the contents. Would he know enough about the relations between the West and the East, Keegan's handwriting, and the location of Keegan's study to write and plant a false letter? I frowned. He might have misplaced feelings for me, his muse, but he didn't seem the malevolent sort, and it pained me to think that Keegan would think Monju so manipulative.

"You keep the journal on you at all times," Keegan said suspiciously, closing the tome and offering it to me.

"And yet, here you are with it."

I took it from him and replaced it in the sack, wishing I could crawl in there myself. The bag seemed heavier than ever as I slung it over my shoulder once more. Who would dare defile the sanctity of my journal, in *my* handwriting no less?

"I cannot be the daring, dark stranger that he is. I am sorry if that is what you want. I am sorry that I cannot offer you more than a kingdom—when I'm able to take it back from our enemies. There is a special kind of pain that comes with being a ruler, but you wouldn't know the physical pains of surviving it day to day."

"You think I want more than that? Luxury beyond imagination?"

"I think you want *this*." He gestured to the forest. "The adventure. No responsibilities. No people to worry about, but yourself."

I opened my mouth to protest but the Violet Fox silenced me. She wanted the adventure. She wanted to draw the blood of those who had wronged the Freetors. She wanted to travel with the bards and the adventurers and seek justice for those who had no voice.

"If that is what you want," Keegan continued, "say so. And I will free you from our engagement. I . . . I do not want to force you into a position you do not want, in your heart."

"I didn't say I didn't want it. I told you, before—"

"Before was different. Before there was a castle, and you were living under a different name, and we were swept into the excitement of a forbidden romance. Now there is no castle, no secrets, nothing stopping us from being together. Nothing but your own heart."

A seed of doubt burrowed into my mind and grated along my memories of the past few days. Monju had always been kind to me. More than kind. And I'd been kind to him.

No. I wouldn't let anyone undermine my feelings—especially the deep feelings I had for Keegan. I would never write such a thing. And if Keegan felt for me what I felt for him, I knew with certainty that he could not have written that letter to Sylvia. Whoever our guardians in the shadows were, they were willing to kill for us, but they also didn't want me and Keegan to be together. Unless there were more shadows than we'd previously thought.

Having to prove myself to Keegan was the cruellest punishment.

I grabbed his hands and had composed an apology when movement from the left startled us both. Monju returned with two horses noisily *clomping* in the mud. I cringed as the hooves dug into the piles of ash, mixing the remains with the mud and dirt.

"Must go quickly," Monju said, gesturing for us to hurry.

Pulled by the bard's urgency, I almost released Keegan's hands and bolted for the horses. My desperation kept me anchored, and my voice low. "Do you trust me?"

Keegan squeezed my hands. "Kiera..."

"Come now!" Monju hissed.

The horses snorted. The storage area was barely large enough for the two of them to manoeuvre, and Monju was getting impatient. One horse bumped into a crate, knocking it over.

"Where do you think you're going?"

Antony appeared beside the horses, wearing his dark, stained breastplate and a long, thin sword at his hip. His quick gaze didn't miss Keegan and me conspiring some distance away. Keegan's expression said, *We should run*, and my tensed body was inclined to agree.

"It is time to depart," Monju said. He tried to guide his horse around Antony, and was stopped by three intimidating, well-muscled men.

"No, it's time to seek justice," Antony said. His torch cast eerie shadows on his face. One by one, more Roamers gathered behind him, and at the other side of the caravan, blocking our convenient exits. Behind and above us, I heard the telltale scrapes of flats against dirt. We were completely surrounded.

"What is the general saying?" Monju asked. He released the horses' reins, and lowered his right hand to the hilt of his curved sword. Keegan tensed beside me, also preparing for a fight.

Antony curled his lip. "A Roamer has been murdered."

I was surprised there had been only one death—the scream I'd heard before passing out? "We're sorry to hear that," I said.

"The murder was in your tent," Antony said, pointing at me. "You must answer for your crimes."

My breath caught, and my confidence wavered. "I didn't murder anyone. None of us did. Just because someone died in *our* tent—"

"There was an attack less than an hour ago by well-armed men from the East, wearing Frostfire family crests. You three were the only outsiders to come tonight, and no one else has a large bounty on their heads that would attract combatmen. It follows then that you brought them here." He scoffed at Monju. "Thought you said you weren't being followed by nothin'."

"Said, weren't being followed by anyone who would dare attack," Monju said diplomatically.

"Same thing," Antony replied gruffly, and sneered. "Now a woman is dead, and many more injured, and afraid. She looked just like you." He gestured to me, almost as an afterthought. He held the torch close enough to my face that the flames licked my hair and heated my skin unpleasantly.

The East had killed a woman matching my description. An innocent woman was dead because of me, just because she'd crawled into my empty tent at the wrong time. Keegan's hand wrapped around my forearm, though I barely felt it. We should never have come here.

The crowd built around Antony, and his booming voice took on a sinister quality. "The punishment for murdering a fellow Roamer is public stoning, and if the criminal survives after three hours, he or she is forgiven." The surprise must have shown on our faces. "Most don't survive. Our life is hard, and we must show the forgiveness that life never showed us." He cleared his throat. "As you three are guests of the Roamers, the punishment is more severe. You come to our camp, and eat our food, and drink our wine, and sing with our brothers and sisters"—the crowd buzzed with anticipation, and a fury of righteous justice I knew all too well from the underground swelled among them—"so not only are you responsible for the death of one of our own, but you have also taken our hospitality, and spat in our face."

"Kill them!" someone yelled.

"We haven't had a stoning in a long time!" roared another.

The faces in the torchlight grew ugly and more insistent. A public punishment was a form of entertainment for many Marlenians, but these Roamers did not live by the Crown's justice, try as the Crown might to place restrictions and rules upon them. With no formal leader, they were ruled by the loudest voices, and at the moment, they all looked to Antony to guide their voices to act as one.

"The woman's throat was slit, was it not? The East come blazing in, while the shadow killers commit tragedy," Monju protested.

Antony laughed dryly. "Shadow killers, indeed! No one sees them and lives—unless they are collaborators." He threw a distrustful look at Monju. Seemed as though their friendship only went so deep. "You brought this trouble here, and several people are injured, and someone has died. Which of you will take responsibility for her life?"

Blaming it on mysterious killers who by description could hide and murder easily seemed childish. It was my tent, and a woman who matched my likeness was now dead because of my foolish pride and inability to listen to my father's warning. From the corner of my eye, Monju looked ready to step forward as well.

"I am responsible," Keegan said, raising his hand to silence us both. "Whatever the punishment is, I'll bear it."

A few hushed gasps echoed among the Roamers, but most of them nodded emphatically, happy to have a scapegoat.

I clasped my bag tightly. The Orb. I could use it to save us.

Noting my gesture, Keegan shook his head, which stayed my hand. Withdrawing the Orb meant revealing our identities—and would sow more distrust between the Crown and the Roamers. With so many of them surrounding us, there was no guarantee magic would save our skins.

Antony grinned—already an unpleasant sight with his rotten teeth, it was more terrifying in the circumstances. "Set up a platform."

Immediately we were surrounded by tough Roamers—men several heads taller than me with broad forearms—and Monju and I were shoved aside. They grabbed Keegan, and although he struggled in their grasp, he did not attempt escape as they led him from the enclosed area out into the sea of tents.

I wouldn't give up on him that easily. I grabbed for his tunic and it tore in my hands. As they dragged him away, his gaze found mine. "A king takes responsibility for his actions. I have run away from my people. I will not turn my back on them again."

His words were lost in the cheers and the chants for justice. A caravan slowly wheeled through the crowd and settled before us. The wood was painted in green and purple flourishes—a carnival caravan, one made for pop-up performances. The side opened up and became a stage, complete with a flowing curtain in the background. The Roamer people enjoyed a performance, and tonight's entertainment was no exception. Roughly, the muscled men dragged Keegan up onto the caravan stage as the crowd swarmed, eager for the best view.

"If we tell them who he is, he might be spared," I said as Monju caught up with me.

Monju stayed my arm. "Do that and you may further endanger his life."

Antony's men released Keegan, and the prince faced the Roamer audience stoically. My heart tore as someone passed Antony a long black whip.

"Twenty lashings, one for each year of the dead woman's life," Antony said.

This didn't satisfy the swelling crowd. The torches seemed to multiply their numbers. "More for the outsider!"

Their bloodlust could not be quenched. The crowd at Rordan's burning had been the same.

Keegan stared off to the left, past the Roamer muscle, into the dark forest. The moon peeked through the clouds and the torches cast gloomy shadows on his face, cold and warm, making him impossible to read.

If Keegan had stayed at the castle, Sylvia would have imprisoned him, or her father would have had him killed. Senseless deaths in the Grand Square would have been prevented.

He would have been able to see his father one last time.

Antony placed his muddy, grimy boot on Keegan's back and forced the prince to his knees. Keegan didn't resist. He barely flinched as Antony cracked the whip before him, testing the strength and speed of the punishment, looking for a reaction from Keegan. Barely a flinch. The general looked perplexed; perhaps he was used to more resistance from his prisoners. He gestured to one of his men, and one removed his belt. Keegan frowned as the man held the leather to Keegan's face.

"Does the criminal refuse our small mercy?" Antony asked. His voice echoed in the dead lake and awakened a roar within the crowd. He didn't use Keegan's false name when referring to him—that would have humanized him.

"Take the belt!" I shouted, knowing my voice would be lost. It would save his teeth, and his tongue—if he survived the whipping itself.

The man with the belt stepped away, shrugging with a slight grin on his face. Either he was impressed with Keegan's stupid bravery, or he believed it would be Keegan's downfall.

I fidgeted beside Monju, willing Keegan to look at me. In Keegan's gaze, I saw the kind of sorrow that came with commitment to a lost cause, which awakened a horrifying thought within me.

What if he thought I didn't love him?

What if he died believing I didn't care deeply?

"I have to stop this," I said.

"They won't stop the punishment until it's done." Monju looked uncertain. "Usually."

"What do you mean, usually?"

"Twenty lashings is...generous for one accepting punishment for murder."

My eyes widened. "They'll kill him?"

"Perhaps. To the Roamers, justice will have been served, and the burden of allowing a murderer to be free will not exist."

I wrenched myself from Monju's grip, unable to bear the thought of this perverted sense of justice any longer. Antony tore Keegan's filthy tunic and exposed his bare, royal back to the moon.

"Twenty lashes," Antony reminded the audience.

The noise from the Roamers died—or perhaps I tuned it out. My breathing, the sound of my footfalls on dirt and mud, the surprised gasps and rude utterances as I pushed my way through the crowd: these things dominated my senses. The crack of the whip sent a jolt of fear as potent as Freetor magic through my body. Cheers and shouts of lude encouragement exploded upon the whip's contact with Keegan's bare skin. One red mark—a scar he'd carry for the rest of his life.

As I approached the front, Antony struck again, and this time Keegan cried out with the rest of the crowd. His teeth ground together. I hoisted myself deftly up on the platform, minding my sack, and drew my knife, suddenly confronted by three muscular Roamers.

"Stay back," I warned, swinging my knife wildly.

Wary but determined, they stayed out of reach of my short blade as I scampered towards Keegan. Antony seemed unconcerned that I had joined them onstage. The whip drew back as I rushed forward to shield my prince with my body. The whip snapped in the air and connected with my back. I cried out and gripped Keegan tightly for support. The hot burning pain spread across my skin—but I refused to let them turn my pain into entertainment.

"That one won't count," Antony warned. "The sooner you move, the sooner this gets done."

While the crowd shouted things like *Punish her too!* and *They're both guilty!* and *Only a criminal defends a criminal!* I gripped Keegan's head and forced him to look at me. His eyes were shut and his cheeks were wet. Although the whip had struck him only three times, his back glistened red.

"I won't let you bear this alone," I said. "Do you hear me?"

Keegan groaned and muttered something inaudible. Strong arms gripped me and attempted to take me away; I swung my knife and slashed at the offending, exposed flesh. The men roared. The whip came down again, this time on Keegan's left side, where my flesh was not guarding his. Keegan squirmed in my grip while the wounded men surrounded me.

"He must pay the price," Antony said simply.

"He's already paid it! He *will* pay it. Please . . . stay with me," I said, stroking his face.

"Kiera . . . get away . . ."

"No, my prince," I whispered. "Listen to me. You need to live so you can rule. Don't give up on me now."

"They . . . have to be shown . . ."

Crack! The strike hit a previous wound, breaking the skin and deepening the gash. Dark blood pooled and dripped freely.

"That you're strong? Not like this." I shook my head violently and gripped his chin as his head lolled with the pain once more. "Their support for your name will mean nothing if you die here on this stage."

"That's enough. You're prolonging his suffering," Antony said.

"I won't stand around and do nothing while another person I love dies because the people have cried for blood!" I snapped. "Has there not been enough violence tonight?"

"Justice demands the punishment be seen to its conclusion. You are interfering with our right to dole our justice."

I held Keegan tight to my chest and spoke only to him. "You are still a citizen of this land and bound by its laws. This is not justice."

"If a ruler cannot respect the laws of the people in his domain," Keegan said hoarsely, "then how can he expect his people to follow the laws he makes?"

"They don't know you're a prince," I hissed in his ear. "Your sacrifice is pointless!"

"I am not above the law. This is not a sacrifice. This is a punishment. Their laws allow this," Keegan sputtered. "No exceptions."

No exceptions, not even for a king.

The men had finally had enough of our posturing. One grabbed my legs and yanked me away. As my body slammed onto the platform, a man clutching his middle desperately in pain sank his foot onto my knife-wielding hand. Fearing he would break the delicate bones, I released my weapon immediately. There were other ways I could hurt them, if it came to it. Briefly I searched the crowd for Monju. His face had melted into the sea of uncaring Roamers.

"Hold her still," Antony commanded.

It took both men to hold me back from Keegan as Antony resumed his torture. The impact of the whip became less apparent on his face as it cracked and landed on his bare back. With each stroke his face hardened, his eyes softened, and his entire state of being seemed to hinge on my unblinking gaze.

I had watched my brother burn to death, and did nothing.

This time nothing would not be done.

I counted twelve more strokes until Antony, sweating with exersion, paused. He drew back the whip and grimly surveyed Keegan's raw, ripped back. Keegan's head lolled to the side as his eyes drooped. If he went unconscious, I feared Antony would not hold back, and would send Keegan to wherever it was that Marlenians went when they died.

As the crowd cheered and encouraged Antony to continue, the general circled around Keegan, curious—and perhaps concerned—about his prisoner's status.

"Hasn't he had enough?" I shouted. My voice was raw from screaming. "Let me take his place, if I must!"

Antony threw me a confused gaze, and shrugged off the idea, returning to Keegan. My struggling began anew as Antony grabbed a fistful of Keegan's long, now-stringy dark hair, and lifted the prince's face up. Keegan struggled to focus, and muttered something fierce, but inaudible.

As Antony peered closely at Keegan's features, the knowledge of his identity clouded the general's gaze. He released Keegan's hair as though it had suddenly transformed into a handful of snakes. "I thought I knew your face."

Hope glimmered inside me. Surely it was a crime to torture a member of the royal family, whether or not they sat on the throne.

Instead of cowering, Keegan cleared his throat, and slowly sat up, balancing on his knees. Sweat dripped from him and pooled on the platform. Void of fear, he said to Antony, "If you know my face, then you know how important it is that I bear this."

The crowd was deaf to the exchange as they roared for more violence. Two men with wills of silver and iron, staring each other down. Finally, Antony averted his gaze, and returned to his position just behind Keegan.

"Five more," Antony announced, holding up a weary palm.

Keegan braced himself. Antony sighed, steeled himself, and swung.

One. Keegan grimaced and squeezed his eyes shut.

Two. I struggled against my attackers, knowing it to be futile.

Three. Monju's face appeared and then disappeared just as quickly near the front.

Four. Blood dripped from Keegan's mouth onto the wooden stage while his arms shook with exhaustion.

Five. The last *crack* summoned whoops and cheers from the crowd.

Antony took a deep breath and stepped back, concluding his reluctant performance.

"The sentence is complete," Antony said, casting the whip aside, as though it no longer held meaning or interest.

Roamers shouted in opposition, demanding more justice, but more than half of them seemed satisfied with Keegan's near-death pale face, bloodied back, and slumped form. Torches fled slowly from the scene, making their way across the vast carved-out lake, back to their nomad existence.

I struggled, and the men holding me released their grip. I rushed to Keegan's side and covered my body with his. He hissed in pain, and I recoiled—I'd touched his back.

"Keegan," I whispered, stroking his hair, desperately trying to think of something to do that would save him. "Keegan."

He groaned. I looked up to Antony, but he just shook his head, unwilling to sacrifice his position of power to help the young prince.

My extra tunic, dirty from travel, was all I had for bandages within reach. I withdrew it from my sack and pressed it against his bloodied back. A whimpered grunt ripped from him, but I had to apply pressure to stop the bleeding. I glanced around for a sympathetic soul, and only Monju looked on from the dissipating crowd. The rest of the Roamers turned their backs to us, willfully blind. A sudden cold wind ushered away the remaining bystanders. I held Keegan as close as I dared for warmth, and comfort.

"It's over," I said. "Don't pass out, please, Keegan. I..."

He stared up at me with unfocussed eyes, and said my name wistfully before passing into unconsciousness.

Thirteen

FOR THE REST of the night, I didn't sleep.

One by one, the caravans littering the emptied lake wheeled up and out of the basin and into the dark forest, scattering into the night. Removing Keegan from the platform proved difficult as he wavered between fitful sleep and confused wakefulness. I dragged him to the edge, and Monju appeared wordlessly by my side, eager to redeem himself. I couldn't turn him down. Together we extracted Keegan from the platform, eliciting feral howls from the wounded prince. The caravan drove off a few minutes later, pulled by two strong workhorses.

It was no longer safe for us to linger in the remains of Toram Lake. The remaining Roamers kept their distance as we tended to Keegan's wounds, but they made it clear that we were no longer welcome, and that we needed to leave. Some hissed at us. Others shouted rude comments. I slung my sack over my shoulder like a bulky shield, as if that would protect us. I ignored them, unwilling to leave Keegan's side, using the few supplies that Monju had lifted from the camp to care for the wounded prince: a needle, a vial of potent liquor, and thread. Keegan moaned as we applied what little herbs Monju had left and cleaned the wounds with liquor. Three of the twenty gashes were deep enough to require stitches. My hands shook at first, but habit overtook me as soon as I punctured his skin. Monju held a torch to guide my work until the sun filtered through the trees and spilled into the basin.

"It could've been worse."

Antony approached us slowly as we finished bandaging Keegan's back. His shadow loomed over us and I gritted my teeth; I hated being watched while working.

"You should leave as soon as you're done," he continued. "Justice has been served, but Roamers don't want bringers of mayhem sticking around."

"We're almost done," I said flatly. The Roamer camp had shrunk to about a tenth of its original size since last night, and they'd already moved the supplies that had been near us to the other side of the lake. Yet Antony remained—the only one besides Monju and me to know Keegan's identity.

"He didn't deserve this," I added, stroking the off-white bandages wrapped around his torso. He stirred.

"No one deserves anythin' in this life," he replied, not unkindly. "For what it's worth, he's a tough lad. Taking responsibility for the crimes of his enemies when he knows there's no alternative. Not many kings or princes would show that sort of vulnerability—to take the burden of the whip because some Roamer girl got murdered."

"The Roamers are my subjects too," Keegan said warily. He blinked away sleep, and turned his head to look up at the general.

"We are, by the law of the Crown. It does not change the fact that you brought the East and whoever else hunts you here. Many will not be so forgiving of that, bravery or no. I, however, not so easily impressed, am struck by your tenacity, and"—he gave us an opportunistic smile—"am not so keen to obey an Eastern High King, especially when he cheated me in the past."

Keegan nodded, understanding his underlying meaning. "Help me stand."

I gripped his arms. He grimaced as he climbed to his feet. Blood spotted through the bandages, but the places where I had stitched him seemed to hold. He shrugged off Monju's help, leaning on me for support.

"You know that I have nothing with which to pay you in exchange for your help," Keegan said.

I fought every instinct to touch the sack. I could not let this opportunity go to waste. "But if you go to Baile Gareth," I said, jumping in before Keegan could continue, "find Ivor Ferguson. The Advisor for the Holy One. He may be able to help you with your *debt collection* problem."

My father was a far better negotiator. We had no gold, nothing to bargain with save our lives, and the Orb, which was out of the question—I would not allow Freetor magic to be bartered with just anyone. Keegan and I had primed him to help us, but my father could seal the deal.

"I may find myself that way soon," he said, lifting his eyebrows and inclining his head, intrigued. "It doesn't sound like you are headed in that direction yourself. Why would a prince not be in his safe haven with his advisor?"

A tricky question: telling him we were on the run would ruin his impression of Keegan's bravery. Telling him about the Spear was also out of the question—though it was possible the rumour of my travelling to the land of my ancestors had reached this far west.

"We are seeking the help of an ally near Iar Bunsula," Keegan said evenly.

"Not much love for the Crown near there, nor the surrounding bailes," Antony said, suspicion belying his words. "Though there isn't much love for the East, either. Drumming up support for your cause will not be easy."

"I don't do things because they're easy," I replied, matching his expression.

"No, Violet Fox, I suppose you don't. Many Roamers admire you for that. They'd admire you further if you were as good as your word about giving Freetors land."

"I *was* working on it," I said bitterly. "But know this: the East has no intention to give the Freetors anything. They will slaughter us. And anyone who opposes them. They've already done so in the capital. The safest place for anyone with a grudge against the Frostfire family is Baile Gareth. The Roamers are just as vulnerable. If you care about your people"—I gestured to those who remained on the other side of the basin—"then you'll help us."

Antony chuckled at my passion. "I don't doubt your tenacity. East, we will go. But our help doesn't come free. Until we meet again."

He dipped his head in respect to Keegan, and then returned to his people. The weight that we had the support of some of the Roamers was overshadowed by the knowledge that everything had a cost.

"Do you think we can trust him? After what he did to you?"

"I suppose we'll have to see," Keegan said.

He was in pain; I could tell he was trying to hide it from me. "Look, what happened last night—"

"It's all right," he said. "I just...I don't want to think about it now. Antony was right. We should put as much distance as we can between us and here. Do you...uh..." His torso was bare except for his bandages, secured tightly around his middle. In the midst of the torture and the patching him up, I'd barely had time to realize that he was half-naked.

Despite myself, my cheeks heated as I reached into my sack and withdrew my Violet Fox cloak. My spare tunic, which had been used as Keegan's initial bandage, lay on the lakebed, soaked with blood. "It's a little torn, but with a little manoeuvring, we could..."

"Thank you." He grasped my hands and the cloak. "You never left my side."

"I would never abandon you," I whispered.

Keegan leaned towards me when movement from behind him caught my eye.

"Traded songs for horses. These suit the lady and her prince?"

I jumped, startled by Monju's sudden intrusion of our moment. I hadn't even realized he was gone.

"Yes. Thank you, Monju," I replied, taking the reins and stroking the horse's nose fondly. It snuffed but did not object to my petting. "How did you get them to trust you? Don't they know that you're with us?"

"Some too hungover to realize, and eager to give anything to make loud, out-of-tune noises stop." He grinned, gestured to the guitar strapped to his back, and flashed his silver tooth before his smile disappeared into solemnness. "Got a look at the dead girl last night."

I grimaced. "And?"

"Looked as though there was very little struggle. Full of drink, she stumbled into the lady's tent before the attack and passed out. Died choking on her blood, waking from sleep to her attacker's face." He looked away, seemingly haunted by the image. "An intimate way to kill, but a coward's kill, to attack while the victim sleeps. Was a knife mark on her throat, but not the cause of death. Thought initially was the shadow killers, but . . . now, not so sure."

Monju's analysis of the murder sent rippling chills up and down my body. A coward's kill. Were the assassins that afraid of us? It seemed unlikely—unless they knew I possessed a magical artefact that would subdue them. Killing us in the forest would have been not too difficult, but if they thought we had partaken in the wine, and let our guard down during the chaos of the raid, slipping into the camp and taking our lives would have been easy. Not to mention, it fit the profile of the other murders in the capital.

Once again, I had been spared a ghastly fate, and Keegan had paid the terrible price. We were dangerously low on supplies. Driscoll's End and the Spear couldn't seem further away.

* * *

Keegan managed to ride with me for three leagues before his strength waned. We had hoped to ride through Iar Bunsula without stopping, but now that was impossible. The wrap-shirt we'd fashioned from my cloak was holding, and his back had stopped bleeding, but he'd need fresh bandages soon, and he couldn't keep wearing my bright violet cloak forever. In it, he looked more like a prince than ever.

The forest broke once again into hilly meadows dusted with brown. Before us, the mountains protected the west from the edge of the world. My neck strained as I looked up. Their tips disappeared into the clouds. Once, I overheard a scholar in the castle call them the

Shoulders of Dashiell—fitting, as it was the Throat that led to the end of the world, Driscoll's End, and the rocky cliff that dropped off into the Forever Sea.

The Shoulders were so close, so immediate to our surroundings, it was unsettling. Especially as we entered the outskirts of the town. First one, then two houses, then more clusters huddled closer to the rocky inclines. The sun was already descending behind the mountains, creating silky reds, blues, and purples in the sky. The road widened as it met with cobblestone, which was a rare sight in a town so small. This road led right for and connected with the pass, and was thus considered a holy path to Dashiell.

The gap between the unforgiving, steep slope of the Shoulders looked as if it had been carved by magic hands; the smoothness of the walls inside reminded me of the Great Cavern. The space looked narrow. It would be impossible to travel on horseback side by side—though our horses would be needed, as my father was unclear in his notes how long the Throat stretched.

Out of habit, I touched my sack. I had to let him know we were still alive.

Houses and shops dotted the wide road. For a town resting before the throat of the world, it was a highly trafficked area. Many men and women wore robes of dark blue, white, and black and walked with their hands clasped about their middle.

"Monks and pilgrims," Keegan explained. "The only true devotees of Dashiell left. Here to study and worship at the Throat, and beyond that, specifically, the Tears."

I had read about the God Tears. Some hot springs were muddy, and some were made of the sweetest water ever to be tasted, but the God Tears, the hot spring beyond the Throat, was a dark purple colour, and thus revered. Scholars explained away the colour by citing the various minerals embedded in the mountains. Monks cited divine providence. When it rained, water ran down the sides of the basin-cavern that enclosed and flooded the pool—thus its name.

"The monks bless water, and pour it down the sides of the basin,"

Keegan said, dipping his head in respect as we passed. "Thus the tears are maintained even when the sun is shining, to remind us of the suffering of others, even when we ourselves are fulfilled."

The religion of Dashiell had waned in the past several decades, even though many traditions from previous generations remained with the people. Much of the Tramore family history was steeped in this tradition—just as we Freetors had a code of honour above and below the ground, the Marlenians had their man-god. Keegan rarely spoke of his religion, though given our location, and his father's passing, it was hardly a surprise that it was on his mind.

"Have you ever been here before?" I asked.

He shook his head. "It's tradition for new High Kings—and especially the Holy One—to make a pilgrimage to Iar Bunsula and the God Tears, and spend a full day in meditation there."

I touched his shoulder gently. "Do you need to go to the God Tears?"

He looked surprised. "I...I don't know. I suppose I never considered it. I've been so focussed on everything else."

"It's not far. A trail leads up from the Throat, and winds to the site," Monju interjected. "May be a welcome break. The Throat winds are treacherous."

"Well, I've dragged you this far," I muttered. "We should stop at the God Tears. If you want to uphold your family tradition."

"It would mean a lot," he admitted quietly. "We still need to get past the guards at the Throat."

"Can disguise as scholars on a pilgrimage," Monju suggested. "Though best the lady make herself look as a man does—the Frostfires are looking for two men and one lady, not three men."

I supposed that was easy enough, so long as they didn't require me to remove my clothing. Through the sea of robes, I spotted two guards lounging by the large, dark pass. They looked extremely bored. Likely they were not expecting trouble in the form of a Freetor princess, a wronged prince, and a skilled bard assassin.

Keegan frowned and rubbed his temples. The cloak covering his back was dark with sweat, and possibly blood. I hunched closer against him to cover the evidence of his wounds, afraid to touch him. "Going through at this time of day may be unusual. Many traverse during the day. We'd blend in better if we waited until morning."

Good way to save face, Keegan. Even though he was right, he shouldn't feel like he needed to make that excuse.

"Could get a room in an inn for the evening, rest, and head for the Throat before the sunrise," Monju suggested.

"We have no silver," I said.

He raised his eyebrows. "Lady Kiera thinks this. What does the Violet Fox think?"

I sighed. Selling the horses wasn't an option—we'd need those to travel quickly through the Throat. My thieving fingers were out of practice, and my moral compass didn't like the idea of stealing from innocent civilians. Monju had *borrowed* a substantial number of things since our journey began, but stealing silver quid wasn't like stealing items. Coins were kept in purses, in sacks, and were sewn into trouser pockets or skirts. And I was not a card player like my brother—I could not win money fairly.

Monju explained the plan, leaning to cross the gap between our horses. "Will play for a while," he said. "Bards do not travel this far; not as much silver in these parts, but there may be some nobles visiting, some monks with poverty vows that happen to come into quid when desperate families wish to buy prayers. Watch the people who stop to listen, pick a target. The lady can do this. She must."

I nodded. "And Keegan?"

"Can find monk robes, take the first silver earned, and have a drink in the tavern. Not uncommon for monks to stop for libation. The prince may hear gossip about the East, the North, and their movements."

If he could stay upright for that long. "Let's be quick about this."

Monju and I slid off our horses. He took the lead against the crashing tide in the sea of robes and travellers. Keegan slid from the horse as well; the road was mainly populated with those travelling on foot, and sitting atop the animal, he was exposed. With my free hand, I found his fingers, and gripped them tightly, fearing that I'd lose him again.

From my left, a blur of violet filled my vision as it waded through the passersby, heading for us. Not Keegan; he was behind me. This person was hooded, like the scholars, but strode slowly and was jostled by the annoyed, apathetic crowd.

I stopped in alarm, recognizing her immediately.

It was the Violet Fox.

Or rather, a poor imitation of my costumed identity.

She wore bells on her ankles and around her wrists, which attempted to hide the sight and sound of the shackles binding her. Only the determination in her face was familiar as she shuffled around our horse. Her dark hair was long and dirty, and it was only when she stumbled and landed in the dust that I noticed the freshly burned *s* blazing on her left cheek.

Slavery was illegal. And yet, here my shadow danced, mocking us.

I leaned forward to help her up but she drew back, avoiding my gaze. Was this a cry for help? Who had done this to her?

They would not get away with it.

A crowd gathered, pushing to surround the girl. Instead of shouting for the guards, they clapped and dealt sarcastic remarks to the entertainer. They'd seen this before. I glanced around for Roamer carts, but political satire wasn't usually their style, and there was no sign of a collection hat.

"Don't mind it," Keegan whispered. "We should continue with Monju's plan."

It was one thing to heed his words and another to tell my stomach nerves to stop fluttering. I couldn't move, not when one of my kin was being forced to make a mockery of everything we stood for. Men with red chestplates decorated with blue surrounded the entertained: I counted at least seven armed Frostfires. No matter what we did, they were always one step ahead of us.

Fingernails dug into my palm as I pushed my way through the

crowd. Keegan and Monju grabbed me just as a silky voice boomed above the cheers and jeers.

"Good to see so many of you back," he said, pointing and smiling at some of the faces familiar to him. The man looked to be in his early to midtwenties, a few years older than Keegan. His red chestplate, decorated with a blue belt, was adorned with the Frostfire crest—a white hunting bird with a crooked beak hovering over red and blue flames. Sandy blond hair, curled by the climate, framed his round face. His strong nose and determined gaze made him a sadly familiar sight.

"A cousin of Sylvia?" I whispered to Keegan. Many of the Frostfires shared fair complexions.

Keegan looked down and scratched his head; his face, even covered in dirt as it was, could still be recognized by the keen. "I could be wrong but...I think that's Leon Frostfire. Her older brother. Second-born son."

I pursed my lips. He was a long way from home. Could he be doing his father's bidding, or did he, like his younger sister, have an agenda of his own?

"Last night we had such a response," Lord Leon Frostfire said grandiosely. "Many of you told us that you'd written to your Holy One, to your prince, about the Freetor blight in your land. And what have you heard in response?"

A murmur from the crowd confirmed that they had heard nothing, to very little.

"Placations. Empty promises." He stepped upon a wooden crate to rise above the crowd and looked down at the dancing pretender. Her movements faltered under his gaze, though her bells inevitably cut the silence with high-pitched jingles.

"But because of your inherent helpful nature, we have rooted out a nest of ten Freetors, ones who were raiding Farmer Arron's lands by moonlight." He gestured to a man in the crowd, who was nodding emphatically. "Did you know, since yesterday, the Frostfires have rewarded three families of peasant birth with fertile land? One family was from this baile."

My breath caught. If it was true, how had they managed that? Likely their murdering spree of families loyal to the Tramores had left some vacancies. We'd spent the past month negotiating land agreements and had gotten nowhere. The East was known for efficiency.

Although much of Iar Bunsula was made of monks and scholars, it was also populated with the lost, the hopeful, and the devious. Just as the Freetors travelled to the Great Cavern of the underground to pray to the ray of sunlight for salvation, the surface folk journeyed here and bowed before the shoulders of their man-god, asking nature for a miracle. The Frostfire men, strolling into the dusty town with their red and blue colours blazing, were likely taken as an omen from Dashiell by the faithful, and a shrewd opportunity by the starving.

"We will be buying information about the whereabouts of stray Freetors until tomorrow afternoon," Leon continued.

The crowd erupted, with several people shouting their tales at the men in uniform, and the slave girl's bells jostled as she jumped, startled by the sudden reaction.

The Frostfires called for silence, and Leon said, "We will hear all of you. You know where to find us. I just wanted to stand up here and say that I have a *message* for any of those Freetors hiding in the crowd today. You idolize Kiera Driscoll, your Violet Fox, as if she is a heroine. She is no such thing. She's not even a Freetor."

I gasped sharply, my reaction blending in with the rest of the crowd's. Had my true relationship with the Advisor been revealed, and misconstrued? I touched my sack.

"The Violet Fox, the *Freetor* known as Kiera Driscoll, was a lie of the Tramore family," he continued. "She wasn't even a Freetor at all. She was an abomination. Half Freetor, half Marlenian. Paid handsomely by the Tramore family to play dress-up on the streets to *inspire* the Freetor people to rebel against their betters, to give the fat guards at the castle someone to fight.

"Now what do we have? Chaos. Disorder. A criminal, calling herself a queen. That is not the kind of blood we want sitting on our throne, now is it?"

The crowd murmured in agreement.

"And," said Leon, holding out his right hand, "if she truly wanted to be a queen, would she not be in the capital, at least *attempting* to fight for her crown?" The Frostfire guards shared a private chuckle, as if they had fought me and thought me a poor opponent. Leon snorted, and one of the guards handed him a brass crown, embedded with round glittery stones. "Instead, she's off trying to find a magical artefact, trying to cater to good folk of this land so that they will believe her lies, and sully the Frostfire reign. Rumour has it that she's travelling through this way. If any of you fine people see a young man and a young woman travelling towards the Throat, you let us know. We are offering payment in silver in exchange for verifiable information on her whereabouts."

Eyebrows rose. Opportunists made interested grunts, and mothers with large broods thought about the food they'd be able to afford.

"In the meantime," he said, "enjoy the show."

He threw the brass crown at the Violet Fox impersonator, and it hit her in the side of the head. A flash of old pain painted her face before she donned the mask of a wobbly smile, and bowed to retrieve the crown. She shoved it down on her head and proceeded to clap and dance for the laughing crowd.

"Stop it!" I shouted, twisting in Keegan and Monju's impossible grip. No one turned to look at me. I was no one. My cries were drowned out by the bells and the laughter, and the shouting of the Frostfire men for her to perform lewd dance moves to entertain the local men.

"Do you know her?" Keegan asked.

I shook my head. "We need to free her."

"Likely she does this for her family," Monju murmured, not unkindly. "Dance, or see them dead."

That stayed my hand. It was a familiar situation for some of us.

"We can't stay here now. We have to keep moving," Keegan said.

"You'll die if you don't get a proper place to sleep," I hissed.

"Grass is as good as any bed—isn't that what you'd say?"

"Yes, but I've never been flogged into unconsciousness before."

"I can sleep on my stomach."

I pressed my lips firmly together. "Since we can't save her, we're saving you. We're staying. And"—I glanced at Monju—"we don't have to let her suffering be in vain."

He nodded, understanding me immediately. They eased their grip on my shoulders, and Keegan gave me a concerned look. Monju went one way, and I went the other, navigating the crowds with ease. We picked our targets carefully, avoiding the monks and the scholars and the poor, striking those with exposed and bulging purses. The jingling of the bells crushed my heart and covered my footsteps, and earned me ten silver quid from two men. As people lost interest in the spectacle, more gravitated towards the Frostfire guards. I curled my hands into fists around the silver, and caught the eye of the enslaved Violet Fox as the crowd parted.

I could spare a silver piece. Slip it to her as a sign. Tell her to not give up hope, that I'd come back for her, and use the Spear to set her free.

Sympathy was easy for us to spot; what was easier to see was my sack. *Freedom under the sun*, lettered small along the rim of the flap. Even if she couldn't read, a Freetor would recognize the code. She raised her eyebrows, and stumbled noisily forward.

Two Eastern men noted the slave's distracted movements. I recoiled, bringing the hidden silver to my chest with one hand, and gripping my sack with the other. The show was over anyway, and the attention of Iar Bunsula was elsewhere. The men grabbed her, forced her to the ground, and dragged her to a caravan parked across the road.

I never saw her again.

Fourteen

THERE WERE THREE inns in Iar Bunsula, and only one had vacancies. Unfortunately, it happened to be the same inn occupied by Leon Frostfire's travelling platoon. The pub below the rooms crawled with them. The stench of several bodies together filled the stuffy pub, and the three of us were more than happy to retire upstairs, to where it was quieter—but not cooler.

We could only afford one room, with one bed. I settled Keegan in it immediately, though it was likely ridden with fleas. How long had it been since I slept in a real bed? A luxury I once gave little thought to seemed too inviting, especially now.

He snored into the thick lumpy pillow and I sank to the floor beside him. My face pressed against the mattress. It smelled musty and used. I tugged at my collar, eager to undress in the heat, decorum be damned. Keegan stirred beneath the sheets and I blushed. I supposed someday I would see him naked too.

And see more of the scars I had inflicted upon him.

The door before me squeaked open and shut—Monju, returning from the latrine. I hadn't even reached for my knife; there was no lock on the door, and the intruder could have been anyone. I was getting soft. Perhaps I was finally getting used to the bard.

Bard assassin, I reminded myself. Yet another man who had broken my trust.

"The lady, she is all right?" His charming smile was back.

I averted my gaze. I was not in the mood for tricks tonight. Keeping Keegan alive was the only thing that mattered right now.

"I'm fine," I said flatly. "Just tired. I might try to get a few hours of sleep."

He slunk closer and sat beside me, two hand-widths away. I drew my knees closer to my chest. Although Keegan's gentle snores layered the room with a sense of calm, Monju acted as if the prince weren't in here at all. He leaned an elbow on the mattress and studied me.

Did I not just say I was going to sleep? I stood and sat on the bed instead. Although it had only happened yesterday, Monju's unwanted kiss felt fresh on my lips. Being closer to Keegan felt safer.

"What are you going to do?" I asked.

"Was hoping that the lady would want to talk," he replied.

Keegan's sleep was deep; our voices hadn't woken him yet. I sighed. "It's all right. I wish you hadn't kissed me, but that's done now. All I want to focus on is keeping Keegan safe, and retrieving the Spear."

Monju shifted, startled. He settled on the edge of the mattress and leaned forward, as if afraid to sit up and be taller than me. "Those were not...the words to be said. Will she take his sorry again?"

I stared at my lap and felt some of the tension leave my body. Truthfully, I could not sleep now even if I wanted. "Yes."

"The lady is always noble," he said quietly.

"I'm just trying to do the right thing for my people. Like Keegan."

Monju bristled. "It is not easy to know the right thing. Or the right one to trust."

I pursed my lips and cast a sympathetic glance his way. "Do you have someone special in your life? A lady of your own?"

He was silent for a few moments. "Once. She is...far away, now."

I waited for him to clarify, but he didn't. Maybe she was another Race victim, like his father. His imprecise method of speaking our tongue both fascinated and frustrated me.

"She had much faith in me," he said, almost to himself. "But then...lost faith in self, maybe. Did an unspeakable thing." He laid a hand on his chest.

I copied the gesture across my breast, thinking of Rordan. "I know what that feels like."

"The lady must not lose hope so easily. Monju believes. The prince believes in the lady, too."

"I hope he does," I found myself saying, as though my tongue had no will of its own tonight.

"He does," Monju replied, nodding sagely. "The way of thinking is different, though. The lady knows this, Monju thinks. Emotions cannot be expressed in the castle. Fear, and rules, and order on the faces of the royal, to give the people the same sense of calm."

"Yes," I agreed. I glanced at Monju, who, to my surprise, was staring at me.

"But you, you wear your feelings on your face like no other. Much passion. Would be difficult for you to hide your feelings." My heart jumped, because it was the first time he'd referred to me as *me* and not *the lady*.

I shouldn't be talking about this with him. This was too dangerous. Especially after what had happened with Keegan, and with Monju's kiss. I stood to pace when Monju caught my wrist. His hands were rough, like mine. He had known strife. Playing his instruments from dawn until dusk for silver had calloused the tips of his fingers, and his palms bore the marks of heavy lifting.

I didn't resist, and neither did he. The brother fighter and I, we were too alike.

"Forgiveness," he said quietly, and released my wrist. "Only wanted to say one more thing."

"What's that?"

Sadness pooled in his gaze. Loss. "The cost to save a life is high. Finding this artefact, the lady will use it to save the Freetor people?"

I drew a careful breath. That wasn't what I had been expecting him to ask. "It will help unite all Marlenians, above and below ground, in our cause."

"It unites... or the Violet Fox unites?"

"It does. And I will, when I wield it, and lead the charge against the East and the North. But I can't do it alone. If I don't get it, the apprentices..." I pursed my lips. I was already saying too much.

"But does the lady *need* it?"

My eyebrows knitted together. The heat was getting to me. "What is that supposed to mean?"

He shook his head. "Apologies. Only means that the lady needs to look inside herself to see the value there."

I was speechless. Angry, frustrated, exhausted... and yet none of these emotions would give me the words I needed to put Monju in his place. Unlike before, in the castle, he didn't back down from my gaze. Out here in the wild on the other side of the world, we were equals once more.

Monju patted my hand, and stood from the bed. "Will leave the lady alone with her prince."

"Why?" The question slipped out. He had been so keen to talk; what was he hiding now? Surely he wanted to monopolize my attention, now that Keegan was asleep?

"Because." Whatever was in Monju's face before, whatever whisper of an idea that could have transpired, was gone. "Worked hard on the song. *To free her people, she had to be strong. Hold her head high, and do no wrong.* The lady knows in her heart that being with the prince is not only the right thing to do, but also, it is what her heart wants, deep down."

He trudged towards the door. I went after him. "How do you presume to know what's in my heart when I..." When I barely knew myself.

Smirking, he waved me off. "As said before. The lady does not give herself enough credit."

***

I drifted in and out of an uneasy sleep, constantly aware of Keegan next to me. I startled awake each time he cried out, and lay there in the dark, heart pounding, realizing that he was still asleep on his stomach.

Nightmares. I wished there something I could do.

I rolled out of bed, aware of the noise downstairs, and of Monju's absence. Did the man never sleep? I was glad that he had given Keegan and me some privacy, but not knowing where the bard assassin was unnerved me.

I checked the journal for news from my father. Nothing. Just the last warning I'd received from him. *Everyone is looking for you now.*

"I'm trying to stay strong," I whispered.

The lie that I loved Monju lay accusingly beneath the message. I grimaced. My journal had been defiled by the enemy. It was now a liability.

I turned the page. The quill dripped ink onto the blank slate.

Still alive, I wrote. *Keegan too.*

How had my father survived by himself out here? His notes on Iar Bunsula were illegible and brief. Why would he give this to me with so little instruction? He must have had all the faith in the world that I'd make it.

Then why remove two critical pages?

"Did you sleep?"

Keegan startled me; he gave me a puzzled look as I snapped the journal shut and leapt to my feet.

"Some," I replied, unconcerned. "How do you feel?"

"Better." He rubbed his eyes. "Hungry."

I clutched my stomach. The feeling had snuck up on me like an old friend. "We have two silver coins left. Might be able to get bread and ale, or water, if you're up for that."

"I don't suppose they have attendants who will bring us our meal."

I frowned, ready to retort, when his face lit up with a boyish smirk.

"Don't expect me to go down there and get it for you," I said, unable to suppress a smile. "*Your Highness.*"

"Oh, I wouldn't dream of—*ugh.*" As he sat up, he grimaced. His hand went immediately to his back.

I rushed to his side. He was still wearing my dirty purple cloak. It needed to be changed. Shooting fitful glances at the door, I carefully unwrapped the cloak bandage to assess his wounds. The stitches seemed to be holding, and the herbs Monju had applied were speeding the healing, but the slashes Antony had delivered were angry and red. I couldn't say for sure how long it would take before the slashes became scars. Most of Rordan's wounds hadn't been as deep as these, and the castle healers who had treated Keegan's lip were far, far away. I felt alone and out of my depth.

Unwilling to part with my cloak, no matter how bloody and worn it was, I shoved it at the bottom of my pack. It would serve to hide the Orb. "We'll use the sheets as the new bandages."

"These sheets?" Keegan gave them a disgusted look, and then sighed. "I suppose we don't have a choice."

"No. After that I'll have to find you something better to wear."

Once again, Keegan set his lips in a hard line, looking as though he was going to object. He nodded, lifting his eyebrows to raise my spirits. "I suppose it would be too distracting to have the prince run around topless at the end of the world."

I sat down behind him, taking the top sheet and folding it appropriately in preparation for the wrap. "You seem to be in good spirits for someone who almost died yesterday."

"Yes. Well..." He shrugged and grimaced again. "I take my cues from a certain strong woman who's had it a lot worse off than me."

The confession shocked me. My hands trembled as I pressed the sheet against his wounded back. I supposed overall, my life had been harder than his. But never had I faced such torture—willingly. No, instead I was forced to watch my people and the ones I loved suffer.

"I'm glad you're here," he added quietly. He found my hand fumbling with the sheet bandage and squeezed. "If I were alone...I wouldn't know...I would have no skills."

"You're a trained fighter. You're not completely helpless."

"True, but I wouldn't have been able to steal silver to obtain this room. I wouldn't know which herbs to eat, or put on my back. My whole life things have been given to me. You were right about that. It's easy to forget that not everyone can open their hands and receive what they deserve, be they Freetor or Marlenian." He released my hand and I continued to dress the wound as he stared into the dark night behind the stark white windowpanes. "I'm sorry I'm not more useful. And I'm sorry for causing you grief."

I secured the bandage and repositioned myself beside him on the bed. "If you didn't cause me grief, you wouldn't be worth dragging along." Realizing that sounded harsher than intended, I rephrased: "I mean... I'm glad you're here too."

A sigh of relief escaped him, as if he had been holding onto it for a long time. "Good." He ran a hand down the makeshift bandage. "I don't suppose we'll find fresh bandages in the mountains. Should take as many supplies as we can before we head out in the morning."

"Yeah. I'll go see about finding new clothes."

It was past midnight, but the Frostfire soldiers were still drinking downstairs. While they seemed to occupy most of the inn—thirteen rooms in total—two of the rooms were occupied by monks. Soundlessly I slipped into one of their rooms, and was rewarded with two black robes and their belts hanging over a desk chair. Monk belts had satchels, handy for carrying food and other supplies. I counted five monks sleeping in this room, dead to the world. As praying at the God Tears was a wet business, monks often carried an extra robe. They might miss the robes when they woke, but we'd be long gone before they suspected foul play.

As I turned to leave, I caught myself in a looking glass hanging by the door. I was a shadowy form in the dark room, though my sharp Freetor vision could make out my basic features. I ran a hand through my curly, frizzy hair. It had grown so much in the past month. I thought briefly of cutting it with my knife to make me more unrecognizable, but truthfully I didn't want to give up the length. It made me feel older somehow. I stepped closer to the looking glass, realizing that I'd never had much of a choice before about how I styled my appearance. I rarely had the opportunity to look at myself, and when I'd arrived at the castle, Bidelia and her servants had been in charge of making me presentable.

Enough of that, I scolded myself. Being selfish and vain wouldn't help anyone.

The clanging of glasses and the revelry downstairs hid my footsteps as I hurried down the hallway and back into our tiny room. I hoped that the Frostfire men would sleep well into the morning and give us a chance to escape into the Throat without notice.

Keegan frowned disapprovingly when I presented him with my findings, but he shrugged into the monk robe. "When I get the throne back, I'll make some sort of donation to the Church."

At least he hadn't given up hope, I thought.

After making ourselves look suitably like monks, I grabbed my sack and we headed into the hallway to the top of the stairs that twisted down into the pub. We peeked between the railings. While I'd counted seven Frostfire men delivering propaganda, their numbers had seemingly multiplied while we were sleeping. At least twenty men bore the distinguishable red and blue colours of the Eastern house: twelve men, including Leon Frostfire, around the tables, some playing cards and others engaged in a drinking contest; one leaning against the only exit to the inn; and at least two outside, visible through the shaded window in the door. Four Frostfire men sat lazily at the bar, where Monju happened to be nursing an ale.

"Whether or not she knows it, Sylvia made good on her threat to find us," Keegan said in a low voice.

The Frostfires were the only patrons. The innkeeper, an old balding man behind the bar, looked exhausted. Leon Frostfire ordered another round of ale for his friends involved in the drinking contest. Looked like he and Sylvia shared a love of boisterous drinking. The Frostfires weren't going to bed anytime soon.

"We don't have to go down there," Keegan said, resting a reassuring hand on my upper arm. "I can last until sunrise. You should sleep."

"I'm fine. I got a few hours."

"You look tired."

"Of course I'm tired. That doesn't matter. I can sleep when we get the Spear."

He sighed again. "I'm just trying to help."

"I know."

Monju took another drink while the adjacent Frostfire man sloppily regaled him with a story. Monju nodded in all the right places, but I could tell that he was sizing them up, evaluating whether there was anything of value on the soldier that we could take with us through the Throat.

I was about to make my way down when Keegan's grip on me tightened. "Wait."

"For a man who is awfully hungry," I hissed, "you're not too keen on getting food."

"I just want to watch him for a minute."

"Leon Frostfire?"

"No, Monju. He could be working for the North," Keegan whispered.

I rolled my eyes and shot Keegan a frustrated look. "The North is working with the East. The shadow killers prove that. And they attacked all of us. Monju saved me from them, and he saved us from Sylvia's men."

Keegan looked unconvinced. "I suppose..."

A jolt of fear shot through me as I glanced down at the bar once more. Monju's gaze locked with mine and held me in place. It could have been the dim light of the lanterns, or my exhaustion finally settling in, but I could have sworn he nodded not just in acknowledgement of my presence, but to say that he'd heard everything we'd said.

"I'm going down," I said, wrenching myself from his grip. "If you want to fill your stomach, or at least ease your hunger, stay close to me."

"Like you said, I can protect myself."

True, I thought as I descended the creaky stairs. Though I wasn't entirely sure if he could keep himself out of trouble, especially with his suspicions surrounding Monju at an all-time high.

Keegan and I pulled our hoods close around our faces and entered the nest of drunken men. Some of them were so far in their cups that they yelled greetings to us, hailing us like old friends. If only they knew.

One of the men sitting next to Leon Frostfire at the table grabbed me as I passed. I stiffened. The hood obscured much of the top half of my face—I wasn't sure how the real monks managed to wear these bloody things all the time—though I believed my lips and my jawline to be distinctly feminine. All it would take was one curious soldier drawing back my hood, and then...

"Hey, listen," the man said, slurring his words, "put in a good word for me with the Man on your next trip through, eh?"

What did he—?

Keegan appeared in front of me and dipped his head reverently. "You can be sure that we will, brave soldier."

The Frostfire man furrowed his brow. I held my breath. My sack was exposed; any one of them could grab it.

The men erupted into ferocious laughter, and the inquiring man released me. I dipped my head as Keegan had, giving him a slight smile. And he thought that he wasn't useful?

Monju noticed us, and he tilted his head towards some empty seats on the other side of the blabbing Frostfire soldier. We grabbed them eagerly. Keegan took the seat nearest to the talkative, drunk man, sparing me. The sack sat on my lap, and I dug through it to find our precious two silver quid to pay the tired innkeeper for our meagre meal. He seemed relieved to serve two mugs of warm mountain water and half a loaf of yesterday's bread, and took our coins without a second thought.

Only moments after Keegan and I had devoured the bread did Leon Frostfire rise and stagger to the bar. He landed on Monju's left side, furthest from us. I tensed. It was bad enough that one sat to Keegan's left, blowing noisy bubbles in his ale while ranting on about the *Freetor problem*.

Leon wore the smirk of a man who knew something the rest

of the room didn't. He stared at Monju, running his teeth along his bottom lip, appraising our silent friend. My knife is in my sleeve, I told myself in an effort to remain calm.

"My friends over there have a wager," he said without preamble, spewing saliva everywhere. His voice boomed above the revelry. "In a town full of Westies, here at the Shoulder, you don't get many *prancers*."

Prancer was a derogatory term for Southerners; one of nicer words, too. Likely he was just getting started. The South prided itself on its carefree culture, rich with festivals and drawn-out gatherings, while the Eastern stereotype would find that wasteful and indulgent.

Monju maintained his calm demeanour. "If the man is asking about profession, am a bard."

"A bard?" Leon made an exaggerated look of amusement and then snickered with his friends at the table. Around us, the other men started to take interest. The man between Monju and Keegan laughed the hardest, swaying back and forth as he stewed in his drunkenness. I buried my face in the large mug while I ran over potential escape routes.

"Yes," Monju said evenly.

Leon leaned an arm against the bar and the laughter settled down. No amusement remained on the Eastern man's face. "We saw you out there today, sinking your dirty little hands in our things."

My insides ran cold. One by one, like predators at a watering hole, the soldiers quieted as they picked up the scent of nearby prey.

Monju didn't give him the satisfaction of his gaze. Beneath the bar, his right leg shifted, ready to spring from the stool if necessary. "Am just a bard passing through. Not a thief."

"A liar, then." Leon slammed his palm down hard on the bar, which rattled the mugs and startled the extremely drunken man beside Keegan. "Pay back the purse you stole, or I'll cut you open so fast you'll see your half-digested supper before your lunch comes out your—"

The men at the bar slammed their cups down and shouted obscenities and urged their lord on. Behind them, the door to the inn opened and three more Frostfires came inside, reeking of something herbal. The innkeeper made a disgusted face, but instead of putting a stop to anything, took leave of his post and hurried upstairs. No help to be found there.

Monju's tunic and instrument hid the bulk and shape of his sword, which he carried now on his back. To them, he was a thieving bard seeking his fortune at the end of the world. It chilled me to think that they could underestimate him so much.

Perhaps that didn't matter. Although drunk, the East still outnumbered us.

They *always* outnumbered us.

"Not wise, threats," Monju said when Leon finally quieted. The bard took another sip of his ale.

None of this was wise. I tugged on Keegan's sleeve, urging him to leave while we had the chance, but the prince remained firmly planted on his stool. Of course *now* he's throwing caution to the winds, when we're in the thick of a storm.

"No?" asked Leon, intrigued. "You think you can take me? You wanna fight, small man?"

No, Monju, no! I gripped Keegan so tightly that he turned towards me and put a finger to his lips. I grimaced. It was too late to leave now. The innkeeper might've been able to get away, as he had earned his goodwill by providing the liquid entertainment, but I doubted that even our robes would buy us much—not if they suspected Monju had an accomplice.

Monju's eyebrows twitched. "Likely the Eastern man would not win in such a fight."

"That so."

Leon Frostfire grabbed Monju's instrument and smashed it to splinters against the bar.

"How about now?"

Something snapped within Monju. The change in the air was

subtle. Even the men shifted uneasily in their seats as Monju's dominant hand twitched.

The drunk man between the prince and the bard fumbled for a knife.

Keegan and Monju acted as one. They drew their swords, crossing the blades in front of the drunk's neck. Startled, the man tipped and fell backwards onto the floor with a horrendous crash.

Monju turned his head slowly to look at the Frostfire lord who had destroyed his most precious possession. "Now the man pays."

The men at the tables cheered Leon on he unsheathed the knife at his waist. As Keegan shifted to rise without stepping on the fallen drunk, I moved to flank him. But caught up in the moment as I was, I'd forgotten about my own treasures, protected in my lap.

Although the strap hung around my left wrist, the sack was open from my earlier rummaging. All it took was one overeager swing as I withdrew my knife from my sleeve and a miscalculated step forward to send the contents of the sack flying across the floor.

Notably, the Orb.

It dropped onto the uneven boards and rolled to the centre of the pub. Flustered by the interruption of its magical slumber, it awoke to shine a brilliant, distinctive bright blue, and darkened the wood as it sizzled.

All twenty or so men leapt to their feet, forgetting their merriment. Steel escaped leather as the glow of the artefact illuminated their terrified faces.

"Freetors," Leon Frostfire hissed.

Fifteen

As they lunged, I dove.

The inn floor was bumpy, gnarled, and slanted towards the door. The heel of my palms scraped against the wood as I tried to make myself as small as possible while I crawled between the men's legs to gather the spilled contents. The drunken dance they made to avoid touching the Orb resulted in several fallen soldiers. The artefact rolled further from my grasp. I scuttled by their groping hands, and kicked at least one in the face as I saved my journal from being trampled.

Monju and Keegan provided ample distraction; they engaged the Eastern force, which was more than eager to meet their blades. Leon Frostfire especially. He cursed and loudly called Monju more unsavoury names as he attacked. Two bodies fell behind me and shook the tables. The Orb was to the right of the door. My father's notes, to the left near the bottom of the stairs.

A throwing knife landed a hair away from my right pinky finger, forcing me left.

A large, stocky man blocked my path. Knife still in hand, I raised it, preparing to strike. The space between the wall and the table was tight, and being impaired, he swung his large broadsword low. I scrambled to my feet and jumped over it. The blade sliced the monk's robe as my heels hit my bottom. Unprepared for the momentum, the soldier unwittingly slammed the sword into the wall.

My father's journey, driven by mad hope, lay in the notebook within reach. I bent to retrieve it when two monks appeared at the top of the stairs, mouths agape at the violence below. When they spotted me, an unfamiliar brother in their colours, their expressions soured. One raised his eyebrows. "You are not—"

Then: tightness about the neck, the sensation of falling backwards. My knife clattered to the ground as I struggled for air. A dank, rotten smell enveloped me as I struggled against the strong grip of the large man. He'd abandoned his sword in the wall, as trapping me in a chokehold became a more convenient way to kill. Flailing, kicking, desperate for something to latch onto, and short on air, I hooked my foot on a table leg. My vision darkened as the chaotic tableau of reds and blues fighting the darker colours of the prince and the bard melted together. The table scraped against the wood as the man moved left, trying to force me away from my salvation.

"Kiera!"

Keegan's voice was a flash of clarity. My chest burned for air and my other senses were rapidly failing me, but I was vaguely aware of his scooping something blue from the floor.

The Orb!

As the glowing magic artefact hurled across the room, the soldier released me. I crumpled to the floor in an exhausted heap, gulping all the air I could afford. My arms shot above my head purely by instinct, and grabbed the smooth Orb.

I pulled it against my chest and curled into the fetal position by the table. It would be easy to allow sleep to overtake me.

No. Get *up*.

Growling, I crawled to the wall and hoisted myself to unsteady feet. I rolled to face the room, counting the Frostfire men without thinking as I retrieved my knife, abandoned near my feet. At least twelve remained, Leon included. Monju was constantly in motion, fending off five with his curved blade and a second, smaller sword. Keegan faced two, and felled one with a quick jab to the lower stomach. There was no sign of the monks: I suspected they had fled upstairs. My former opponent hand abandoned me to fight my prince, thinking my Orb too powerful to face alone.

Although Keegan and Monju were skilled, I didn't like their odds one bit.

"Hey!" I yelled, holding out the Orb.

I couldn't be heard over the sounds of the fight. I banged the flat side of my knife against the well-worn bar counter. Nothing. Sheathing the knife in my belt, I focussed on the Orb. Tendrils of blue lightning cracked the air and snapped at my hands, the bar, and the floor, effectively capturing Keegan's and Monju's attention, as well as the Frostfires'.

The illuminated blue artefact fascinated the Frostfire men, and they were right to fear it. Still, their fear did not belay their curiosity, and they inched forward on the sloped wood. Their fallen comrades proved tricky obstacles for their unsteady feet. Leon, somehow still conscious, though badly bruised and bloodied from a wound on his upper left arm, tripped and fell face first onto the floor. That didn't stop him. He righted himself, grinning like a wolf that had just cornered its prey.

"Stay back!" I shouted, holding out the glowing artefact.

The men hesitated, looked from me to the Orb, and back to me again. The artefact was warm, but not as hot as I wanted.

I took a careful step towards the door, holding the Orb as a shield as I concentrated on activating its magic. "I *will* use it against you."

Another step. Monju and Keegan slipped behind the bar. This was the first time Monju had seen the Orb, I realized. Just a few more seconds, and they'd be at the door.

One of the soldiers drunkenly shouted, "She don't know how to work that thing!"

Uh-oh.

I threw open the inn door and bolted.

The night cut through the heavy monk robe and whipped the fabric as if it weighed nothing. Behind me, Keegan's and Monju's footsteps fell into line, and the shouts of the East echoed on their heels. My sack bounced on my hip as I ran; I gathered it under my arm and shoved the glowing Orb inside, praying it wouldn't destroy my journal. Besides my knife, they were the only two things I'd managed to recover from the inn. My father's expedition notes still lay at the bottom of the stairs.

Couldn't worry about that now. The dusty road was wide and the houses became few and far between as I neared the mountains. They towered, dark and unmoveable in the night, though a glimmer of light shone from within the Throat. A sign, perhaps, to run towards the place my people once called home. The pass appeared unguarded.

"Don't let them get through!" came the now-sobered shouts of the soldiers.

I'd been wrong. I slowed and kicked up a dust storm as two shapes slunk around the opening of the pass.

The roar of hooves pounding on the road came up fast behind me. Likely Leon was leading the charge. I wouldn't give him or Sylvia the satisfaction of taking any of us alive. I veered to the right, thinking of kicking down the door of one of the unlit residences, when Keegan shouted my name once more.

How had they—? Never mind. Keegan urged the horse to slow and held out his hand. I ran up alongside the trotting animal, reaching for my prince. He leaned further over the side of the unsaddled horse towards me.

There was a moment where moonlight and his golden irises melded and became one, and I saw the determination that lived there. He wasn't about to give up yet. Neither was I.

I leapt for the horse's wild mane and Keegan grabbed me. Both of us cried for purchase and the horse made a sound of displeasure, but Keegan somehow managed to lift me from the ground. I hung onto his torso, splayed a leg, and squeezed with my thighs, righting myself on the back of the beast.

Sweat poured down my forehead. "Thanks," I muttered.

"Are you all right?" he asked. His favourite thing to say to me.

"Fine."

More galloping, from behind. Monju? No, though I glimpsed him on horseback as well. He was gaining on the Frostfires behind us who had also found beasts to ride. Rats, they were never as dumb as I wanted them to be.

The mountain pass was barely large enough for two horses to squeeze through, and was not nearly as lit as I had first assumed. We were trading open, dark space for closed-off, complete blackness. As the East closed in behind us, Monju charged ahead, grinning as if we were in a race. The two guards at the pass drew their long swords and attacked.

The first guard slashed our horse's side.

The second attempted to stop Monju's horse by spooking it; the beast could not be deterred. The guard barely made it out of the way of the deadly hooves as Monju raced by and was engulfed by the pass.

I gasped as we slid between the tall mountain walls. Immediately we were met with a fierce, cold wind that ripped at our faces, urging us to turn around. My grip on Keegan tightened. The monk robes offered some protection, but not much. I could scarcely breathe as we caught up with Monju's pace. Here we could race side by side, but it would narrow soon enough. I was used to cramped, earthy spaces, but not whipping through them at top speeds against a torrent. I feared that any moment now, the horse would trip and fall and the forces-that-be would force the mountain walls to meet once more, squeezing the life out of us.

"How long is the Throat? Can we lose them in it?" Keegan asked breathlessly. I could barely hear him over the whistling wind. He threw a quick glance at me. "What do your notes say?"

"They're gone," I yelled. "But we still have this."

Clutching Keegan's waist for dear life, I dug into the sack and retrieved the Orb. Unlike before, it warmed immediately under my touch, perhaps in response to the biting wind. It was so smooth and we were riding so fast that I was afraid I'd lose it beneath the horse.

Monju gave me a curious look. "What is...?"

"Later," I said, as it became like fire in my hands. I twisted around as far as my back would allow. Five men on three horses were closing in fast behind us. Taking a deep breath, I closed my eyes.

The Violet Fox called lightning to evil's lie...

Rocks and dirt rumbled as nature bowed to magic's will. Something cracked behind us and fell; men screamed.

...and won the prince's heart on Mountain High.

"Wait, don't! Stop!"

Keegan's interruption jolted me from my connection with the Orb. The bottom of the mountain wall had splintered and flopped onto the pass. One of the enemy horses had tripped, sending its two riders flying. The two other horses attempted to make the jump but fell over themselves, blocking the pass. We took a sharp turn, and then they were out of sight entirely.

"We'll need the passage to find our way back," he said shortly.

I sighed. "And they'll be there waiting for us."

Grimly, he urged the horse on. "That's the way it is."

* * *

We could only move forward, against the wind. I had never been afraid of closed-in, rocky places, though if there were a place that would inspire that kind of fear, it would be the Throat. We travelled in single file through the mountain pass as it narrowed and wound left and right through the centre of the mountain. Our horse wheezed heavily; I doubted it would survive another day. Keegan and I took turns riding to ease the animal, and to stretch its usefulness until we'd have to do the inevitable.

There were places of absolute darkness that even my vision couldn't penetrate. For a while, I ran my hand along the rough mountain walls that rose several hundred thousand hands into the sky—roughly twelve thousand feet, by Marlenian measurements.

Some time later, when the dawn inked the sky with pink and

blue blotches, Monju touched my arm and pointed to a well-hidden path to our left. It sloped sharply upward, and seemed to disappear into the belly of the mountain itself.

"God Tears is in there," he shouted above the wind. "May be a safe place to rest, should the prince wish it."

Keegan squinted in the darkness, and stepped forward to feel for the path. I took his hand as I dismounted from our tired horse. Together we were stronger than the wind.

"I can lead you," he said.

"Will stay here," Monju said as he stepped into the path, away from the wind. He leaned against the centuries-old rock and held onto his horse's reins, attempting to calm the animal.

It was not far. The narrow cavernous path became more open as we climbed, sometimes hand over hand, up and into the belly of the mountain. Bits of grass sprouted from the rock as it softened beneath our touch. It reminded me of potter's clay. Even the smells were different here: sweet wet grass, with the undercurrent of rot. Not unpleasant, but not the first place I'd choose to be.

At least, I thought, until the path widened further into a large, open cavern.

It was as Keegan and the scholars had described. The basin surrounded us on all sides, and opened to the cloudy, near-dawn sky. Unlike in the Great Cavern, where magic had smoothed away all imperfections, the walls here were rough and untamed. Dark water trickled freely down grooves that looked hundreds of years old, and trailed into the giant purple pool that occupied much of the cavern. Tears of the man-god.

The cavern was supposedly carved by time and water—I had trouble seeing how that could be. Magic and man-gods were catch-all explanations I was used to: surely the hand of Dashiell played more of a part in the creation of the Tears, rather than time, and something as simple as water?

The air was hot, stuffy, and still, a respite from the Throat below. Rock groupings surrounded the pool. Thick with the royal colour, it looked deep enough to submerge me. I was certainly cold enough to be tempted to swim.

"Everything here is more beautiful than I could have imagined," Keegan said. His face was alight with faith.

"It doesn't seem real," I said, wishing I could feel the same reverence for the randomly placed water and earth.

"No, it doesn't."

He settled on the rock next to me. I found no need to fill the silence as the water trickled into the pool and warmed my weary toes. Warmer than the bath water at the castle, the supposedly holy liquid was a splash of luxury in the harsh backdrop of the world's end. Keegan removed his flats that carried bits of our journey through the forest on their soles, and tossed them aside as his feet joined mine in the pool.

"None of this seems real anymore," Keegan added above the sounds of the water.

"Everything will be fine once we have the Spear," I said, gritting my teeth, willing myself to believe it.

"They may kill us first," he said quietly.

"Maybe."

He bowed his head and leaned his shoulder into mine. "Sometimes I forget that the threat of death was part of your life."

It wasn't easy for me to speak about being the Violet Fox with Keegan. It was one thing to recount a valiant story about knicking food from an unsympathetic vendor. It was another to describe how it felt to be hungry all the time. How easy it was to give over everything I had stolen just to feed the family next door, and feel angry that I had borne the brunt of the risk only to receive the same ration as every other Fighter.

"I survived," I replied, chucking a small stone into the pool. "And some didn't."

"Kiera." He said my name with such softness as he took my hand. "You don't have to wall me away."

How could I tell him my fears? I had to be strong. I had carried my faith in the Spear with me, wrapped tightly about my being.

When shared, my belief in the mythical object had been lambasted. Keegan wasn't here for the Spear—he was here for me, but that wasn't enough.

For if we got to the cavern, and the only thing true about the Spear was the story...

At least I would have kept him out of Sylvia's hands. And I had gotten him this far. With Monju's help, I might be able to take him back to Baile Gareth, providing that was still a safe haven.

Providing no one else was dead.

All because of me.

My knuckles blazed white, I was gripping him so tightly. I wanted to hide my concern. To be a stone wall, like him. But I was just sand and dirt shaped like a girl. The longer I remained with Keegan, the harder it became to hide my fears from him. Was this ... love?

"It's all right," he said. "I'm afraid too."

I didn't want him to see me cry, but there was nowhere to hide in this holy place, not from him. I tilted my chin to catch the remaining moonlight and showed him the brewing tears.

"How many more of us must die before we can be together?"

Keegan gripped my hands firmly. "We are already together. Nothing is going to tear us apart."

"This war will tear everyone apart," I whispered, leaning into him more. "I can count the number of people I trust on one hand. Before, I could count on my people ... but if we don't get the Spear ... everyone is doomed. I can't fail, Keegan. If we stop moving, we'll lose what little we have left."

"Look at me," he said.

I lifted my gaze to his as the tears fell freely.

"You wanted to know why I changed my mind about coming with you," he said. "I couldn't leave you alone with Monju—that was the underlying reason. But you made me believe that we have a chance against the East. You make me want to be better. And because of that, I will never leave you. I will always be here for you, no matter what hare-brained scheme you hatch from that delightfully stubborn mind."

His words melted my heart and stilled my tears, but I wished I could believe him.

"You're not mad at me anymore, then? For what happened with the Roamers?"

"Of course not," he said. "I shouldn't have overreacted."

"I reacted in the same way." I pursed my lips, ashamed. "I should've known better."

He smiled. "There's still so much we don't know about each other."

"We have time. I don't suppose our wedding will be for a while."

Keegan looked thoughtful. "There is an old practice," he said slowly, gazing up at the fading moon. "Two lovers who wish to be wed, but who have no means, can say the holy words at a sacred place and be considered man and wife by law. So long as they visit a priest within the year to bless the union, the marriage is upheld in the eyes of the Church, and the community."

My heart leapt. "Are you saying...?"

He took my hands and gently turned my palms skyward. "Marry me, here. Now. With only the mountain and the earth as our witnesses."

"I...I'm surprised you would even want to...I mean..." I felt as flustered as a Marlenian lady-in-waiting on her first day at court. "Are you sure that's what you want?"

"Only if you don't mind not having a proper dress, proper shoes, proper headdress..."

A smile broke through my road-weary face.

"Yeah. I mean, *yes*. A Freetor wedding, then." Vows uttered between Freetors on their wedding day were said to be bound by magic, and breakable only by death. No Elders stood by to hear our promises, so the holy water and the mountains would have to do.

"I was planning to give you my mother's ring, or have a new one forged." He looked bitter. "I suppose the Frostfires will have plundered all that by now."

I didn't want to think about that, not now. "We don't usually exchange rings anyway." An idea struck me. My tattered cloak had not escaped my sack, as blood and sweat had glued it to the bottom. It had seen blood and magic, forests and mountains, and was nearly spent, but it could do one last thing. Carefully, I removed it from around the Orb and tore a long piece from its frayed end, and then tore that in two. "Hold out your hand."

He gave me his left, palm up. I folded one of the frayed pieces of violet fabric and twined it around his forefinger.

"I swear to protect you," I said. There were no formal words to Freetor wedding ceremonies. The bride and the groom spoke from the heart. "I will not stray from you. I will fight by your side until I am no longer able. I..." The words floated on my tongue, afraid of being made real. People I loved ended up dead, or morphing into strangers. I said the words to myself. If he truly felt for me as I did for him, he would understand. I gave him the string. "Now you."

I expected bewilderment. Not so. Keegan gingerly plucked the fabric from my fingers, and I held out my right hand. The hand the makeshift ring graced didn't matter. The significance behind the gesture, made truthfully in a special place—that was what bound us.

As he wrapped the worn fabric again and again around my forefinger, he said solemnly, "I have followed you to the end of the world. And I will follow you back again. I will fight by your side, until and beyond when I am able." He smiled good-naturedly, happy to flaunt his superior vow. "I will protect you, and I will not tie you to the throne." He knotted the fabric as best he could in the dim light, and tucked the ends. "I will never take anything from you, and I will give you whatever you ask of me, as long as I am able to provide it." He hesitated, and then released one of my hands to touch the scar I had given him on our first meeting. "I would not trade this for anything."

I cupped his cheek, and brought him closer, and kissed the scar, the man, the king. The fabric of the promise brushed his stubble. He smelled familiar, and for a fleeting moment, I understood the desires of women older than myself, and wanted to disregard responsibility for the mind-numbing passions of the present. He kissed my face, my nose, my eyelids, and my neck, sending previously unknown shivers through me, ones not explainable from the heat of the springs.

I pulled away, half terrified, half crazy. In the eyes of our peoples, we were married. And after a man and a woman exchanged words... Keegan made no further move to sate our desires, and I let out a slow breath of relief. Instead he took my hand, and traced the lines on my fingers aimlessly, stealing glances as if working up the courage to say something important.

"Usually the groom gives the bride a gift. A physical gift, I mean," he said quickly, blushing. "I don't have anything to give you, unless..."

Tell me you believe in me. A selfish wish for an unselfish night. The need for his blessing, his validation of my desires, trumped any kind of signal my body gave me.

"I don't need anything," I whispered. I had enough faith in the mission for the both of us.

He nodded, and squeezed my hand. "A promise, then, in addition to the vows," he said. "I won't ever leave your side again."

"And," I added, wiping away the tears, "you have to promise to say my name at least once a day. My real name."

He reflected my smile. "Kiera Driscoll, Kiera Driscoll, Kiera Driscoll, I will say your name gladly, and more than once."

My foot nudged his beneath the water, and I leaned against his chest, listening to the consistent rhythm of his strong heart as it observed the seconds of the night. I shivered as a sharp breeze whipped about the rock, and disappeared just as quickly as it had been summoned. He wrapped an arm around me. We had nothing but our battle-torn robes and our body heat to keep us warm.

"We should go soon," he said reluctantly.

He was right. Sleeping here and awaking to the monks and scholars who tended the holy ground would be awkward to explain away.

Keegan lifted his foot out of the water and allowed purple liquid to drip onto the ground before settling it into the earth. "It wouldn't feel right leaving without observing at least one of the customs of my ancestors."

"Customs?"

"Besides meditation—which I'm truthfully not in the mood for at present—it is customary to leave an offering to the pool before departing."

I stared at the murky depths, wondering what treasures previous kings had thrown to rest below. "What are you going to leave behind?"

"What haven't I left behind already?" he said glibly. But he looked thoughtful, and pulled his sword from its scabbard at his hip.

"Not your weapon!" I said, incredulous.

He smiled, and then shook his head. Swiftly, he slid his left palm across the sharp edge of the blade. The bright red wound dripped blood into the purple pool.

"My heritage is all I have left," he said, watching as the tiny droplets rippled the hot springs. "My value is in my blood. Material wealth seems so far away now."

Spoken like a monk. Or a Freetor, I thought wistfully.

Satisfied with the offering, he resheathed his sword, slipped back into his worn flats, and brushed his unsullied hand over my shoulder. "Take your time," he said.

He descended along the path, rustling the loose rocks as he went. When his footsteps were inaudible, I removed my journal from the pack. The leather scraped against the gritty rock. The journal did not glow; my father had not responded. Perhaps he was gone forever this time.

I'd poured my hopes and dreams and tales of success and failure onto its pages, hoping beyond hope that my father could read them. Rordan lived in them. So did Laoise, Bidelia, the Elders, and my naive, younger self.

The lie was burned on its pages now. I could not afford to have it used against me again.

I sat there for a while, with my hand splayed on the cover. Nothing was forever, not even magic. The best parts of Rordan lived within me. I could not continue forward while living with the temptation to go back.

With a deep, tight breath, I took the journal in trembling hands, held it over the dark water, and let go.

Sixteen

WHEN I WAS the Violet Fox, and worried only about the people of the underground, I gave little thought to which part of the surface I'd like to someday inhabit. *Freedom under the sun*, we'd shouted. Having our own piece of Marlenia, bathed in sunlight, that was always the goal. Obtaining it, standing on it as a free person, that was the difficult part.

The cold whistling wind whipping through the Throat died down as the sun rose, and I was thankful for the heat on my back as we wound through the narrow pass. Our horse succumbed to its wound several hours after we left the Tears, and we were forced to leave it—there were no other side paths on which to hide the body, or loose dirt to give it a proper burial to keep away beasts.

Monju sang our song and others to keep us entertained as we took turns riding and leading our remaining horse. Keegan, invigorated from the Tears, even joined in on a few. The singing helped us keep our focus, and made us forget the inevitable hunger, which settled in when the sun reached its peak. It was impossible to make a fire with the wind, and we had nothing to burn: bitter weeds grew here and there from the clay, and my stomach felt weak after munching on a few.

As the pass inclined steeply, Monju ceased the singing. I wondered how high we'd have to climb: over the clouds, to the stars? How had my ancestors lived, so isolated from the rest of the world? I entertained myself with the possibilities to keep my spirits high as sweat poured down my face and my back. Surely there was an end to the pass somewhere.

I missed my father's notes.

I missed my father.

Overhead, a screeching white crow announced that there was life nearby, soaring high into the clouds to the surrounding mountain tips. I hoped he was telling me that there was more to the edge of the world than the Shoulder Mountains and the void rocky pass. A distinctive, salty smell permeated the air. I curled my nose.

"Are close," Monju told us. "That is the scent of the sea. Reminds Monju of home."

Grass peeked through the rock, blade by blade, until the hard, mountainous trail underfoot became soft with untrodden wildflowers. Not many people came this far. As the Throat widened and expanded into a meadow, and the sun dropped lower in the sky, furry animals the size of cows with large, curled horns spotted us from a distance. They looked up from their grazing, observing us carefully as our shadows elongated behind us.

Just when I thought my body would give out to exhaustion, the meadow plateaued, and the mountain walls parted extravagantly to reveal the open blue mass that stretched as far as I could see.

The Forever Sea.

Driscoll's End.

Propelled by hope, I ran to the edge of the meadow, and tumbled down a rocky slope to a long cliff edge—truly, the end of the world. Keegan called my name and slid down after me. Wind tossed my hair and ran through my robe, but the sun toasted my face as it began its descent into the water before us. The cliff edge stretched for half a league in either direction along the mountain face, overlooking the sea. The mountains towered behind us now, though only twenty stone-throws separated the unmovable rock and stone from the edge of the cliff, and the sea below.

So this was where my ancestors had lived. Why had we left this place?

We stood together at the end of the world, Keegan and I, and surveyed the untouchable part of our realm. The sea stretched on and on, and seemed almost measureable from up on high, and became larger and more untenable the closer I came to the edge of the cliff. The cliff was rocky, barren, and void of life. The meadow mountainside we'd descended earlier had grown on rocks, and seemed unsuitable for farming. A dilapidated cabin stood a quarter of a league away, at the other end of the cliff. A lantern, rusty from hundreds of years of neglect, was bolted to the sole windowsill that faced the sea.

"You look disappointed," Keegan noted.

I bowed my head. My cheeks were already rosy from the chilly sea breeze. "I..." I smirked. "I guess I thought I'd feel...something. Rordan, maybe."

"Perhaps your ancestors warned passing ships of the rocks below," Keegan suggested.

Peering over the side made me nauseous. It was so far down—many, many leagues—to the sharp rocks below, and would be an unpleasant way to die. I took a step back from the edge. The undulating waves stretched far and wide to the horizon, and evoked a strong nausea that I fought to contain. Was this truly the end of the world? If I sailed a ship to the edge of the sky, would I ride up into the clouds? Did the ocean fall away to nothing? Or worse: what if the ocean continued infinitely?

"What's out there?" I asked.

"No one knows. Scholars say that if we journeyed far enough, we would wrap around back to the East. No one who has risked it ever survives," Keegan said.

My head swam at thought of sailing forever with no hope of seeing land again. It was not named the Forever Sea for nothing. The mountainous shores made mounting such a trip near-impossible anyway.

My ancestors may have stood in my very spot, and asked the same questions. I wondered if they ever found the answers. Because of the Marlenians' information purge, I would never know.

"A cave, that way," Monju said. His footsteps crunched on the dirt behind us. "That is what the lady said she wanted, yes? A cave?"

"Yeah," I said slowly. I retreated away further from the cliff. Turning my back on the ocean felt like a terrible idea. I wouldn't want to fall in.

"Long way down," Monju said absently. He smirked a little, backing even further away. "Monju is a good swimmer, though."

"Probably would die on impact on the sharp rocks below," Keegan replied bitterly. "Or be kept under by those big waves."

"Can hold breath for long time, Prince. Cave is this way."

Following Monju's frantic gesturing, I turned and spotted the cave to our right. Long blades of grass nearly obscured the entrance, but the frequent winds pushed them aside, revealing the large dark mouth leading into the mountain.

"Is the only cave in the area," Monju said.

I moved towards the entrance, intrigued. Keegan remained at the cliffside, lost in his musings about the large body of water announcing the end of our world. Monju followed beside me.

"Thanks," I said. I drew a deep breath, casting a brief glance at the expanse. "If you want to go...back, you can."

"Does the lady wish for Monju to leave?"

I hadn't really thought about Monju's involvement past his showing us the way. He still didn't know about the Spear, and I intended to keep it that way. "I don't want you travelling by yourself. Wait outside. If someone is coming, run into the cave, and try to find us." If he could. According to what I remembered of my father's notes, the cave was a labyrinth. We might be able to lose any attackers, but become lost in the process.

Monju's expression brightened. "Yes. Will keep watch. How long will the lady and her prince be?"

Would Keegan come into the cave with me? I supposed I hadn't thought about that much either. I had pictured doing this alone. "It might be a while. If I'm not back by sunrise, feel free to go back through the pass." I felt odd giving him the order. How many times had he saved my life? I was in his debt.

"Monju will stay for as long as the lady needs me," he said solemnly.

"I don't know what I did to deserve your loyalty."

A pained expression flirted with his face. His fingers danced and twitched over his curved sword sheathed at his side. "There is something to confess."

My eyebrows knitted as I whirled on him. Our unspoken agreement not to talk about what happened at the Roamer camp hung heavily in the air, pungent as the sea. "Whatever it is...it's all right. I...I mean..." My shoulders hunched awkwardly. Keegan faced the sea, and could not see us. Likely the sound of the waves drowned us out as well. "Keegan and I said the words at the God Tears. We're joined, at least in the eyes of the man-god."

Monju, normally bright and alert, looked suddenly wary. Surely it wasn't such a surprise to him? Keegan was my intended. Monju—I barely knew him. He had saved my life, serenaded me, made me into an immortal character that would no doubt be sung about long after we were all dirt and ash. But I was not that girl. The woman he idolized and romanced was not the flesh and blood before him.

Something else, so subtle I almost missed it, also clouded his round dark eyes: relief. I had given him a gift—he did not have to admit his ill-advised feelings, and I didn't have to hear them.

His words were soft and lost to the sea, but they were plain on his lips. "Congratulations to the lady and her prince."

"Thank you."

He fidgeted again, and stepped back to bow. "Will start a fire to keep warm. The damp will become cold soon enough."

A smile caught my lips and I dipped my head. "Stay safe, Monju Farin."

"And you, Lady Kiera." A troubled look crossed his face, broken by his smile, and he turned away to start his watch.

Right. This was what I'd travelled many leagues across the West for—to retrieve the artefact that could free my people from oppression. The cave entrance was before me, and all I had to do was enter. My sack felt heavier than it ever had, although I had lost so much, and with each noisy step on the large rocks, my heart weighed me down.

What if we've travelled all this way, and...and...?

"Kiera, wait."

Keegan's voice carried over the roar of the ocean, but I didn't stop. He caught up with me just as I neared the unforgiving entrance. I didn't want to linger long now, now that I was so close. Long reeds brushed against my legs, and I feared ensnarement.

"You don't have to come," I said. "If you don't want to."

He raised his eyebrows. "You think you're going in there alone?" Keegan asked, throwing a glance into the mouth of the dark, dank cave. "Because that's absurd. I'm coming with you."

"Don't risk your royal neck for me."

"I'll risk whatever body part I want for whomever I please, especially for my *wife*."

Despite myself, I smiled. He'd already risked so much. Too much. He was barely recovered. "Fine." I cast him a furtive glance as my hand hovered over my knife, secured at the belt of my robe.

Glancing over his shoulder and finding Monju at a satisfactory distance, Keegan leaned in and brushed his lips against my ears. "It's all right if the Spear isn't there, Kiera."

I savoured the words, wishing I could believe them and feel relieved. "It won't be all right if we find nothing," I replied, facing the open mouth of the cave that threatened to swallow us both. "We've suffered too much for *nothing*."

"Better to be here, than in the hands of the East, or the North. And I'd rather be by your side no matter where we may be."

I leaned into him, wishing only to be held, but I only allowed myself a moment of sentiment before urging my feet forward. Keegan, intuitively understanding my deep-seated desire, drew an arm around my waist to steady me.

I breathed in the salty sea air. "Let's go, then."

The cave sloped into the earth, gradual at first, and then alarmingly steep. We gripped the rough jagged walls, but the purchase was not enough. I slipped and slid downward on my back.

"Kiera!" Keegan's cry reverberated and I heard him crashing

down behind me. The loose rocks dug into my flesh and tore my robe, yet a slippery, soothing, *chilly* sensation replaced the pain and eased my wounds. I grabbed for my bag as my eyes adjusted to the darkness. It didn't feel as though it had come open. No—the Orb and my cloak were still inside.

"Here!" I shouted, when Keegan called for me again. I looked up. We'd come down a further distance than I'd realized: the entrance to the cave was barely the size of my fist. Though the daylight poured in, it was not enough for us to see properly.

I held up my hand, and felt him grab it. Warm, reassuring. He helped me to my feet—and I fell into him, and he slipped backwards into a smooth, hard wall.

"Ooph," Keegan said, trying to contain his pain. "Careful, the floor is... icy. The underground isn't always this cold, right?"

"Not like this."

"Wish we had a torch. Can you manage to stand?"

"I'll be all right. You?"

"Wish I hadn't just slammed into an ice wall. After falling down a rocky slope. May have just... yeah..."

I grimaced. "Keegan, I'm sorry... your back. Let me help you up to the entrance."

"I'm not leaving you. Not now," Keegan said firmly, in a tone that brooked no argument. "I'm fine."

Sighing, he didn't resist as I helped him find Monju's flint in his satchel. We ripped and balled the hems of our monk robes to create a temporary light source. Keegan fumbled in the darkness with the flint, the sword, and the balled fabric on the ground, but insisted on lighting the thing himself. I knew what it was like to distract myself from embarrassment and injury, so I didn't take the task away from him. Instead, I examined the walls, and the corridor that seemed to lead us deeper into the cavern. As my vision adjusted to the darkness, I realized that the walls up ahead glittered and glowed a faint light blue—the sign of Freetor magic.

"We're in the right place, at least," I said, venturing further.

Keegan drew the flint across the steel, creating sparks that momentarily lit up his determined face. "The cave must extend deep into the mountains," he mused. "I wonder how deep it goes."

My mental conjuring of the cave dissipated as something rustled further inside the dark, rocky expanse. That was when I remembered the most frightening part of the legend of the Silver Spear. My father hadn't mentioned it. Surely *that* part couldn't be real—could it?

"Hear something?" Keegan asked, feeling me tense.

"No, no, it can't be," I whispered.

"What? Here, I'm getting some light."

"Quiet. It will hear."

"What will—?"

Just as Keegan brought the flame to life, the creature padded into sight. Normally tigers would not exist this far west, as their natural habitat was in the northeast, where it was cooler and drier. But this wasn't any ordinary tiger. The sabre-toothed beast had sleek white and black fur that shimmered against the walls of ice. She had no trouble navigating the slippery floor, for this was her home.

According to the legend of the Silver Spear, sabre cats and other wild beasts guarded the cave. They evaluated each person who entered, only allowing those they thought worthy—no one, generally—to pass into the inner chambers. In some versions of the legend, when Alastar stumbled upon the cave, he was attacked by one of the sabre cats, and it took out his eye.

I gulped and took a wobbly step back. The grips on my soles wouldn't hold and I slipped. I would've fallen if it hadn't have been for Keegan behind me.

"What do we do?" he whispered in my ear.

"I...I'm not..."

"This is the—?"

"Yeah. Tiger from the legend."

"What does the legend say to do?"

Keegan didn't know about Alastar's misfortune, and now seemed like the most inopportune time to fill him in. The tiger stared up at us with gleaming eyes, considering her intruders. She didn't look starved. There had to be enough game for her in the mountains. But I was sure she wouldn't turn down two meals who had walked so conveniently into her lair.

"Run," I said to Keegan. I slowly drew my dagger.

"Are you insane? Where would we go? I'm not—"

The tiger's gaze slid from me to the knife, and a low warning growl rumbled in her throat. She crouched, preparing to pounce.

Then, the sound of falling rocks behind us, and the footsteps of steady boots. "Wait! Don't hurt the cat!"

Monju?

Baring her teeth, the tiger decided that Monju was a more challenging target, and leapt past Keegan and me. I shrieked and sliced her coat as she sailed by us. In one fluid moment, with the grace of a dancer, Monju brought up his curved sword just as the tiger threatened to close her jaw around his neck. The blade caught in the tiger's mouth, and the metal shattered into thousands of pieces as if it were made of glass.

"Go!" Monju yelled.

Even without his sword, Monju was a far better warrior than Keegan or I. I gripped Keegan's sleeve as he hastily grabbed the ball of flame from the ground and took off down the icy corridor. Together Keegan and I slipped and slid and almost fell but somehow we managed to keep ourselves mostly upright. We rounded a corner in the dark, narrow passageway. Keegan cursed as the fabric in his hands burned and licked his robe; it wouldn't last much longer. Sounds of Monju screaming and the tiger thrashing and growling bounced off the walls. I tried not to think about whether or not he would survive, and concentrated on putting one foot in front of the other.

"What if there are more tigers?" Keegan asked.

"I don't know."

"That's not a good enough answer."

"I don't have another answer, *Your Highness*."

"Now is not the time to be snarky, *Violet Fox*."

I guffawed but our banter was short-lived. Before us, the path forked three ways into equally frightening darkness. Keegan threw the last of the burning fabric down the centre passageway, but the fire extinguished with a hiss, and the darkness defied all natural light. I whipped my head around, expecting to see the white tiger bounding down the corridor after us with her sharper-than-steel teeth glinting in the ice-light.

"We need to choose," Keegan said, finding my hand and gripping it tightly. "Do you know which path is correct?"

"I don't even know if there *is* a correct path. The whole place is a maze."

"Your father's notes could've helped us here."

"I don't think so. The pages about the cave were torn out."

Keegan frowned and glanced behind us. The fighting had gone quiet. Too quiet. Any minute now, we could be tiger food. He advanced down the centre fork, turned, and silently sought my approval.

"Fire will be no good to us wherever we go. You don't happen to know a few magic spells to break through the darkness, do you?"

"No. But..." An idea struck me as I carefully swung the sack around. "The Orb. It generates light at my touch."

Keegan let go of my hand and slid behind me, keeping watch for threats, as I pulled the Orb of Dashiell from the sack. It was cool to the touch, but as I held it out into the darkness, it crackled and glowed with magic. The hair on my arms stood on end.

"Now are you glad I brought it?" I asked.

"Let's not get into that now," he replied. "Which way?"

I moved the Orb to the entrance of each passageway, and it could have been my imagination, but the cool, smooth texture seemed to warm at the centre path. "Here."

If we kept going straight, we'd be less likely to become lost—this was my logic for exploring underground caves. The tiger, if she was still living, would follow our scent regardless, but she hadn't caught us yet, which led me to believe that Monju had been victorious—hopefully not at the cost of his life. I etched a Freetor symbol into the wall before we continued, to mark our path. Even though Monju couldn't read Freetor code, he might recognize the freshness of the markings, and find us that way. The symbol glowed a bright white-blue within the ice, and the Orb's lightning tendrils reached and licked it as if recognizing the magic as its own.

Keegan and I trudged deeper into the ice cave. His face was cast in an eerie dark blue light and even darker shadows from the Orb's crackling lines of lightning.

"If the Advisor made this journey before, why would he give you the journal with the most crucial pages torn out?" he asked. He was trying to hide his chattering teeth.

The Orb lured us down a passageway to our left. The deeper we went into the cave, the colder our surroundings became. "He didn't want me to go. I thought that maybe giving me the notes was his way of discouraging me. Showing me the hard time he had. Ripping the pages out would prevent me from actually finding the Spear, but assure me that it does exist."

Keegan looked unconvinced. "I understand that, but your plan to retrieve the Spear—although far-fetched—had a better chance of working than his idea to infiltrate their forces. Why remove vital information that would ensure our success, especially when he gave you a map, travel information, and the courage to carry out the plan? I'm worried, Kiera."

I pursed my lips as the Orb grew hotter in my hands. "Do you think he's a traitor?"

"What? No. I don't think that. But don't you find it a tad strange?"

The thought gave me pause. "Yes, but... the expedition notes are legitimate, and they are written in his hand. I'm sure he had his reasons to exclude the information—believe me, I'm not happy about it. And we have the Orb to show us the way." I stopped at another junction as the Orb directed us down another left passageway, and I marked another Freetor symbol in the ice.

"But he didn't have the Orb the last time he came here," Keegan pointed out. His hand graced the small of my back, not to stop me, but to drive home his point. "We could be walking into a trap."

I stared at the icy floor. Keegan's words rang true. I had no idea how my father found the Spear before. Perhaps he made markings, as I was doing. If so, they had been worn by time, for there were no artificial scrapes on these pristine, smooth walls besides mine. "You think we should turn back, after we've come all this way?"

Keegan sighed. "No. Never. I just think we need to be prepared for trouble."

I smirked and stroked his cold cheek with my warm hand. "I usually am."

The colder the passageway, the warmer I felt, until sweat dripped down my forehead. Keegan unsuccessfully tried to hide his chill, and despite his wariness of the Orb, he held me by the shoulders with his stiff fingers. He refused offers to hold the Orb.

"Don't be stubborn," I said. "You'll freeze to death. We don't know how much further it is, and carrying you would be a nuisance." I meant to be flippant but the echoing nature of the caverns made my tone sound hostile. I sighed. "How is your back?"

"Numb-b-b-b, thank-k-k you."

That was a small blessing. My thoughts returned briefly to my father. Keegan did have a point. Why not warn us of the cold? How far had he made it in this labyrinth before feeling the magic's chill? Would he feel it at all, having access to magic himself?

"Look ahead," Keegan whispered hoarsely.

His now-blue fingers pointed at a glowing cavern off to the right. Holding him close against me, we pushed through the biting chill in the corridor and passed into the surprisingly cool—certainly warmer than the corridor—brightly lit chamber. The Orb crackled, shocking my palm, and my eyes ached as they adjusted to the change.

"That's it," I whispered. "The Silver Spear."

Encased in a block of ice as wide as my wingspan and hovering in mid-air, the Silver Spear was just barely visible through its thick, shiny prison. A sheen of blue light surrounded the ice, announcing the Freetor magic within. Keegan and I approached with reverence and caution. I clutched the Orb to my chest. It was almost unbearable to touch now, as if recognizing a fellow artefact in the room.

"It's frozen in a lot of ice," Keegan said. He tore another piece from his fraying robe, and patiently set to work with the flint and steel.

I worried my lip with my teeth. Tucking the Orb under my arm, I walked around the floating block, looking for structural weaknesses. The ice itself had so much texture, but it was thick for a spear this thin. Whoever froze it like this knew the power of the Spear and took precautions against those who would abuse it.

A small flame came to life, and Keegan quickly held up the fiery strip to the ice. It didn't even melt a lick. "More magic."

I leaned forward and breathed on the ice. My breath fogged but did nothing to weaken it.

"Weapon?" I asked.

Keegan, his face growing rosy as he warmed and recovered from the extreme cold, drew his sword. "It will take a while to chip away at this. We'll die of starvation first."

"We can't do nothing, either."

"I wasn't suggesting that." But he smiled a little, and eased the blade along the corner of the ice block. Keegan's attempt sounded like progress. I could hear the scraping of his blade. But no ice shavings fell to the floor, and the corner looked barely affected. We carefully examined the edge of Keegan's blade. If anything, the ice had *dulled* the steel.

I gritted my teeth and glared at the frozen block. "Why don't you just—?"

I raised my fist and pounded the block. Big mistake. I recoiled in pain. The Orb was comfortably hot, like a brick you'd wrap in cloth and put under your mattress for the night, but touching the ice was like dipping your hand into liquid metal. Boils popped up along the side of my pinky finger. The fabric ring around my forefinger suddenly felt too tight as my hand stiffened. I swore and slammed my fist into the regular icy floor, where I received some relief.

Keegan knelt before me, sheltering my form with his. Concern painted his features. "Are you all right?"

"Yeah, just... really hurts."

"I should have touched it first. To spare you the pain."

I looked up at him. "You can't protect me from everything."

He tucked a lock of stray hair behind my ear. "I can try."

I set the Orb gently on the ground as the icy floor consoled my wound. It rolled gently towards the floating block of ice, even though the floor was not sloped.

"Get that in case it touches the ice," I said.

"It's not going to touch the ice." But Keegan lunged for it despite his objection, probably because, like me, he couldn't stand to allow the ancient family artefact to roll out of reach.

"Keegan, watch out!"

He slid across the slippery floor after the rolling Orb. His hair just barely missed the burning ice block as he was propelled beneath it. I held my breath. If he lifted his head, he'd burn off all the hair on his head.

"It's all right," he reassured me as his fingertips grazed the Orb. It had stopped dead centre beneath the ice block. Keegan shimmied closer to the Orb, and took it triumphantly into his arms. It sparked and sizzled with energy. "Oh—ouch!"

"Keegan!"

I rushed to his side as he crawled out from beneath the block. He frowned and gritted his teeth as he rested the Orb between his legs and settled on the floor. "Didn't expect to be shocked by the bloody thing. I suppose no one's ever really touched it like this before."

"I never really noticed that it shocked. It's just... warm."

"Really." His eyebrows knitted. "Perhaps it has to do with Freetor magic."

"Maybe." Or maybe the artefacts liked Freetors better than Marlenians.

That was a big jump in logic, though. Making conclusions based on limited data. I had learned about that from the tutors at the castle. There was so much I knew now that I didn't before.

The smell of burning flesh permeated the air. My hand? No. I sniffed Keegan's hair. No. "You smell that?"

"Yes. Something is on fire."

"I don't see how. Everything here is made of ice."

Keeping the Orb encased in his grip, Keegan slid closer to the block and peeked beneath. I knelt beside him and peered at icy underbelly. Above where the Orb once rested, a black shadow sizzled and spread. The dark tendrils burned deep ridges in the ice and emitted hot steam.

"It must be the magic in the Orb," I said, staring at it in Keegan's arms.

Even as Keegan sat an arm's width from the ice, the block reacted, darkening like a shadow that did not fade, but burned. He held the Orb out as close as he dared, and the ice smouldered and blackened faster, like parchment near flame.

He grimaced and flinched. "Agh. It keeps shocking me."

"Here."

Relieved, Keegan handed me the Orb and set to chipping away at the blackened ice with his sword. The ice was more receptive this time, and fell in chunks to the slippery floor. At a safe distance, I circled the floating block and held the Orb as close to the magical ice as I dared. Soon the whole cavern stank of smoke, and tears lined my eyes at the memories it brought, but I pushed them away.

After ten rotations, I was feeling light-headed, though I pressed on. Keegan's blade had lost much of its sharpness, and I feared it would become useless altogether, but he refused to let that stop him. The magic weaved dark tendrils into the ice, spreading like a plague until the entire block was no longer reflective, glowing ice.

Keegan stood back. "Do you think...?"

I nodded, understanding his trail of thought. "Maybe."

"Careful."

Taking a deep breath, I shoved the Orb of Dashiell against the floating shell.

A hot shock attacked my core, and lightning coiled around my arms and legs. I held firm. A scream ripped from me and Keegan neared, though I warned him back. The dark tendrils deepened into ridges, which became cracks and fragments that soon broke into pieces. Large chunks fell to the floor, hissing and steaming. A piece the size of my torso dislodged before me: I backed against the icy wall as the floating protective structure collapsed. The black ice melted into the floor and lost its menacing colour. White-blue steam billowed, swelling wide and then deflating to reveal our prize.

The Spear remained afloat in all its glory. Near ten feet tall, the wooden shaft was carved with Freetor symbols that alternately glowed and shimmered. The silver head, perhaps made of steel or something stronger, shone and showed no signs of its previous battles. It was narrower than any spearhead I'd seen, and long too—perhaps precise enough to pierce an eye. I shuddered. The Spear shook.

Free of its prison, the Spear glowed a light blue, and then clattered to the icy ground.

I burst out laughing. We had come all this way, and I had hoped against hope that the Silver Spear existed, and so many had said it was a foolish dream, and yet, here I was, in the legendary cave of the Silver Spear, with the fabled weapon at my feet.

Keegan's features softened and he took my hand. "Well? Are you going to take it?"

"Me?"

"Why not you?" he asked. "The Holy One of the past spurned the gift. It is an artefact of the Freetor people. Pick it up, and tell me how it feels to hold history in your hands...my queen."

Grinning, I wrapped the Orb in my cloak and set it on the icy floor. It wobbled gently.

I picked up the Spear. It was warm to the touch, like the Orb, but a zing of power flew up my right arm and made every nerve in my hand tingle. Given its size, it should have been heavy and unbalanced in my grip. Instead, it wobbled, and the weight of it shifted until it felt comfortable to hold.

There was power in this weapon. And now, I wielded it. There was something unsettling about that. With the Spear, I could rally my people against the North and the East. No longer was I an underground rat.

I was a symbol of revolution and change.

"Kiera."

The way he said my name gave me pause. He drew his eyebrows together and looked at me as if seeing me for the first time.

"I'm sorry I doubted you. It's the worst thing I could do."

I shook my head. "It's all right."

"No, it's not. You never gave up hope, and I..."

"It's all right," I said again. "I carried enough hope for the both of us."

"I won't ever doubt you again," he said solemnly. He rested his hand over mine, which gripped the shaft tightly. "I love you, you know."

My heart lightened at his words. As he turned away, I pulled him back to me, and drew him down to my lips. How long had I waited for this moment, to show the world that my faith had not been in vain? To hear him say the words of our hearts? His hands travelled up my back and he held me close as he returned the kiss passionately. With the Spear in one hand, and Keegan in the other, I felt as if I were dreaming.

"We shouldn't camp in the meadow," he said, drawing away breathlessly. "We'll ride until we're near exhausted. The wind will be at our backs in the Throat, and maybe the Spear will help us against the Frostfires in—"

The crunch of unsteady footsteps outside the cavern put us on the alert. I tensed and Keegan drew his sword. I shook my head—it couldn't be the tiger; she was far lighter on her paws. "Monju?"

Fierce eyes peeked around the corner and into the cavern, but they did not belong to our Southern bard. Ash-black hair and high cheekbones sunken by hunger belonged to a face so out of place in the cavern, in this part of the world, that I blinked, expecting the image to disappear.

It didn't, and Apprentice Lorcán stepped into the cavern, carefully putting one bare foot in front of the other. Behind him, Apprentice Sinéad followed, and Apprentice Orrin clutched her arm as he nearly fell onto the floor.

"Apprentices," I said, in a tone that carried my shock and respect, just as Keegan asked, "How did you get here?"

Controlled by one will, they turned their heads precisely in unison to Keegan, and lay suspicious looks on the Prince of Marlenia. "We have been tracking your progress," said Apprentice Lorcán, though the other two apprentices mimed his words in tandem.

Keegan shot me a worried look. "*Tracking?*"

"Yes, Prince. We ensured your safe and successful arrival," Apprentice Sinéad replied. The other two mimed her words without speaking. "Or did you not find it strange that you were not eaten by wild animals, or not killed by the assassins that have sacked your city?"

Our city, they meant. I stepped forward, brandishing the Spear tightly. "You were the ones following us? But the assassins..."

"The East and the North tried, for a time," said Apprentice Lorcán.

"No match for us," added Apprentice Orrin.

Three nods, all quick and concise and uniform.

My heart pounded hard against my chest. Those assassins had been fast. Deadly. Trained to kill. And yet these apprentices had taken them out. The memory of the men transforming into ash before me invaded my senses. "When Lady Sylvia showed up with Bidelia and Laoise as prisoners...that was you, frying those men?"

Another perfectly timed nod from all three.

My gaze went immediately to the exit. They blocked our only escape. "Why not make yourself known to us?"

"The Violet Fox is capable of handling minor distractions," said Apprentice Lorcán.

"Several *minor distractions* almost got us killed," Keegan said flatly.

The three apprentices glared at him. "The Violet Fox is capable. The prince is less capable. Regardless, we lent our support from the shadows."

"But... you're only apprentices..." I murmured.

"Working together," said the three of them, their voices harmonizing in perfect pitch. Their tune echoed in the icy cave and chilled me more than the air.

"And the Roamer in the tent? That was your work too?" Keegan asked. His voice wavered slightly, betraying his fear. The idea that he had taken punishment for these shadowy apprentices didn't sit well with him—or with me.

The apprentices returned my stare, and said nothing.

Keegan narrowed his gaze. "I think the three of you had better explain yourselves quickly. Not coming to the aid of a prince and his companions when you are clearly capable only hinders the relations between our two peoples." His voice dripped with authority. It was the Prince of Marlenia speaking now, not just an eighteen-year-old man with a sword.

Wary of Keegan and his underlying threat, the apprentices directed their choppy dialogue towards me. "According to lore, the only thing to break the Spear's confinement is another artefact of Dashiell," said Apprentice Sinéad.

"You convinced me to come all this way because I held the Orb? You didn't mention that before. What if I hadn't brought it with me?" My eyes narrowed. "If you're so powerful, why didn't you use your magic and steal the Orb from me back at the castle?"

"Perhaps the Elders who are now gone may have been able to do that. Not us," said Apprentice Sinéad.

"Would not have left the castle without Orb! Far too precious, too powerful to resist," Orrin said in an annoying sing-song voice.

"And what a story this makes," continued Lorcán. "Kiera Driscoll, the Violet Fox, the Lady Who Climbed the Mountain High and fell in love with the prince, retrieves Dashiell's Spear, once spurned by a Holy One of old, and returns it to its rightful owners. The struggling, starving people of the underground."

"You forgot the part where the meddling apprentices come and try to steal it from us," Keegan said.

"We do not meddle. There is no stealing. We oversee, as the Elders have taught us to do," said Apprentice Sinéad. "The Spear belongs with the apprentices, the Freetor people. It represents the freedom we have worked hard to achieve."

"It is freedom," Orrin added.

"Give us the Spear, Violet Fox," said Apprentice Lorcán. He held out his frail hands, palms up. "You know its rightful place is with us."

I almost listened. Letting them hold the Spear would do no harm. Instead, my grip tightened.

"What about our deal?" I asked slowly. "Retrieving the Spear, and inspiring the respect of a Freetor army, in exchange for your help against the East and the North."

"Freedom first," Lorcán said. His gesturing was more frantic this time—Sinéad and Orrin also flicked their right hands, almost uncontrollably, as if pulled by puppet strings.

"You are free," I said. "Free enough to follow me, and abandon the underground. You didn't need the Spear for that. Who is protecting the entrances to the Freetor underground now?"

They exchanged glances. "Other apprentices."

"And if you were so keen to protect me on my *journey*"—I couldn't say the word without disdain—"why could you not protect the innocents who swore their loyalty to the Crown? Those who were murdered in the Grand Square just because they called Eamon Tramore and Keegan their rightful rulers?"

Lorcán's stare was void of compassion. "They are not our people."

His words were colder than the icy cavern we shared. "We are all Marlenians now," I said, shaking the Spear to hide my fear. "You'd let innocent people die just because they don't share your ancestor?"

"They are not innocent!" Orrin said suddenly, his eyes wide with rage. "The blood of our people is on all their hands! Let them kill each other so that we may have their lands!"

The old argument struck a familiar chord, one so easy to strum. I gritted my teeth. "We have to forgive them if we are going to move—"

The Silver Spear

"Let them kill each other," Sinéad interrupted, echoing Orrin's words in harmony.

"We will take back our old homes," Lorcán chimed in above Sinéad and Orrin's chorus. "And use the Spear to do it."

So that was the heart of it. They never intended to help us. The hate in the apprentices' eyes was the most truthful thing they had imparted to me thus far. They would use magic to destroy the Marlenians, no matter what colours they wore, just so they could take their land and farm it as their own.

My grip on the Spear loosened. I had been played for a fool, once again. Foolish and young, I had been swept along by childish dreams of adventure and romance, led and encouraged by monsters who shared my flesh and blood.

No more.

"I'm so sorry," I said, and pointed the Spear at them. "I don't want to hurt you. No one has to die to get land on the surface. We will find a way. Once we have settled things with the East and the North, we'll find homes for everyone. We just have to wait a bit longer—"

Their haunting chorus ceased at once. "You speak like one of *them*," Apprentice Lorcán hissed, pointing at Keegan. "You have put the needs of your people second to the needs of the Tramores. You have strayed from your true purpose." The apprentices shook their heads slowly to the left, and then to the right, and then they fixated on me once more, speaking as one: "The matter must be taken into our hands."

Rolling their wrists, the apprentices' hands glowed a bright blue.

"Duck!" Keegan yelled as I dropped to the cold, icy floor beside him. He threw an arm around me, pulling me close to his chest as a bolt of magic whizzed above our heads. The smell of smoke invaded my nostrils as the bolt hit the back wall with a loud sizzling explosion.

"Give us the Spear," they said. "Give us our freedom."

Swearing, I rolled and narrowly evaded another blast of magic. The Orb lay where I'd left it. If it could stop the most powerful Elder, it could maim the apprentices long enough to get them to see reason, to give them a fair trial. Killing them would only ruin our chance for a proper alliance between the Freetors and the Western Marlenians—if there were any Freetors left in the underground.

Keegan seemed to have the same idea. As we scrambled for the Orb, I glanced over my shoulder to gauge the distance between us and the apprentices. The icy floor was unforgiving to my desperate stride. I lunged, checking my reach too late. I tripped and fell, the weight of the Spear bringing me down fast beside the Orb. The sharp tip barely grazed the smooth surface of the Orb of Dashiell, yet that was all it took to shatter the artefact.

"No," I said under my breath, touching the shards gingerly.

Keegan rolled out of the way as another blast of magic hurled towards him, while a blur at the entrance of the cavern drew my eye.

The crunch of his boots on the ice outside should've given him away, even in the commotion. But I hadn't been expecting him to return. Monju's dark skin contrasted with the sparkling crystal ice, so much so that I barely noticed the blade he held in his fist as he raised it high into the air, aiming for Apprentice Lorcán.

"No!"

The warning came too late. My cry bounced off the crystalline walls as Monju's knife sank into Apprentice Lorcán's neck.

Seventeen

As the blood dripped down Lorcán's neck, we all froze, transfixed by the slow-moving red liquid. As if pulled by invisible strings, he collapsed suddenly to the icy floor. Sinéad and Orrin tilted their heads, exposing their necks for Monju, unable to adjust their behaviour and cope with a third of their unit missing. Drawing back, Monju prepared his next attack.

If Monju killed them, any hope for an alliance with the Freetor apprentices would be lost.

"No!" I cried. I swung the Spear around and aimed the end at Monju, hoping that it possessed the same lightning ability as the Orb of Dashiell. The weight of the weapon carried me across the slippery floor. "Monju, don't—"

Monju swirled around, ignoring my cries. He'd never acted like this. If Monju was abandoning his ethics, something was seriously wrong.

"We can't let them die!" I said to Keegan. He watched Monju's deadly skill with a touch of envy, and plenty more apprehension.

Sinéad and Orrin slid backwards on the ice as their fingers danced, preparing spells.

"Shadow murderer," Sinéad said, her voice heavy with rage as she pointed at Monju.

Orrin yelled something unintelligible, and twirled his fingers to create the beginnings of another lightning strike. Torn between the two opposing forces, I threw shards of the Orb at both apprentices, distracting them. Keegan carefully dashed towards them to draw their fire. Eager to face their sworn foe, Sinéad and Orrin fashioned bolts of lightning and white-hot fire and flung them at Keegan's feet, and just over his shoulders. They were taunting him. Keegan manoeuvred as best he could, but whenever a magic projectile caught him, it left a nasty black burn in the fabric of his clothes, or a striking red gash on his skin.

I grabbed Monju, pushed him against the slippery wall, and held the long Spear an inch away from his throat. "What are you doing?"

He looked apprehensive. "The lady was in danger."

"Are you mad? We could have settled this!"

Keegan could only entertain the apprentices for so long. A blinding flash of light shot by us and left a smoking hole right of Monju's ear. We dove in separate directions when Sinéad hurled a massive swirling ball of lightning towards us. It landed where we once stood. With a delayed, deafening crack, the tendrils of lightning spread across the floor and created deep black ridges in the floor. Her dark blue eyes, raging with a familiar anger, darted between Monju and me and then settled on her brother's killer as the most appropriate target.

"Apprentice Sinéad!"

My plea rang through the chamber, and to my surprise, she turned towards me. Lightning crackled between her fingers. I crawled quickly to my feet.

Unfortunately one moment of pause in the heat of battle meant your death.

"Duck!" I screamed at her.

Keegan dove towards her, but Monju was far more agile. Sinéad's hair whipped as she spun to face him, and unleashed her lightning. The Southern bard grimaced as the blue-and-white energy swarmed him, and acted on impulse. His blade hooked on her robe, and as Monju pulled, it lodged itself deep into her side. From the other side of the room, Orrin collapsed to the floor, hands clasping his head, screaming.

"Enough!" Keegan shouted, and swung his dulled sword at Monju.

Monju ripped the knife from Sinéad's side and blocked Keegan's attack. "Fight is not with the prince! Protect the lady."

"You don't have to kill them!" My voice was hoarse from yelling as I aimed the Spear at him.

"They'll kill if the lady doesn't!" Monju retorted, and as their blades crossed, he threw Keegan back and out of his way. "Not part of plan..."

Sinéad lay in a puddle of blood. She attempted to crawl towards her brother. Lightning sputtered and fizzled out in her palms. I knelt beside her.

"I'm sorry. I didn't want this to happen. You didn't have to attack us," I murmured.

Don't let their deaths be on my hands, I prayed to whoever was listening.

She threw a tearful glance at the Spear. "No...hope..." she croaked. She uttered something else, perhaps a spell, but blood prevented her words from taking full form, and life left her.

"AGHHHHHHH!" The youngest apprentice, now without two minds to consult, flew into an animalistic rage. He dodged Monju's swing just as the bard evaded my blow.

"Stay back, Lady Kiera!" Monju warned.

"Kill YOU BOTH!" Orrin screeched.

Sparks flew from the apprentice's fingers as he leapt to avoid Monju again. He stumbled over Lorcán's body, which only angered him further. I lunged for Orrin to pin him to the ground, to shield his body with mine to prevent Monju from harming him, but the slippery apprentice evaded me. Wild with rage, Orrin fled the cave with unsteady feet.

Monju tore after him. He seemed more confident on the ice than any of us. I cursed his steady feet.

"He's out of control," Keegan muttered.

We had no choice but to chase Monju back through the bitter cold corridors. Without the Orb, my fingers and toes were numb within minutes. The Spear unfortunately didn't have the same warming effect as the Orb. I fought to focus on finding the Freetor symbols I'd left. At one point, Keegan's hand found mine, but my fingers were so numb I barely felt his touch.

Eventually we reached the slippery, rocky entrance where we'd landed. Rocks tumbled down before us as Monju climbed nimbly from the darkness into the light. Shouting from various voices outside confused me. A white blur crossed the entrance like a colour-inverted shadow, and tortured screams rang in my ears—followed by the sounds of bones crunching and snapping, and rocks trickling down the bank leading up to the meadow.

Keegan and I held each other tightly as we struggled to climb the perilous slope up to the red-yellow light of the outside. Sunset was well underway. Unsteady rocks fell away beneath our boots and hindered our progress. My heart was heavy with the knowledge that we were likely too late to save the young apprentice.

We emerged from the cave, blinded by the setting sun over the vast expanse of water and deafened by the waves crashing on the shores below. The light shimmered on the spearhead, and I was absently aware that this was probably the first time in more than a hundred years that the weapon had felt sunlight. Orrin lay half out of sight within the reeds that surrounded the entrance of the cave, twitching as life left him. Monju backed away from the mess, and swung around to face us. Keegan pointed his sword at Monju, and the bard held up his blood-soaked knife defensively.

It was the look on his face that made me angry. He looked *afraid*. He'd just killed three powerful magic users, barely injuring himself in the process. There was seemingly no premeditation to the act. He had slaughtered them.

Keegan had been right about him all along.

"You said that you weren't a killer," I shouted, advancing on him with my Spear. "Why kill them, Monju? Why *them*?"

He backed away, holding his hands at eye level—but he did not sheathe his knife, which dripped with the apprentices' blood. "Necessary deaths, to prevent other deaths."

"They were just trying to defend themselves. Bettering their situation. Now the other apprentices will retaliate! Do you know how powerful and dangerous magic can be? They will want revenge for their fallen!"

"It does not matter. Monju could not bear to see—"

"That's not your decision to make," Keegan said. "You made a promise to me. To Kiera. Justice is not yours to dole out whenever you please."

Monju looked apologetic. He shook his head. "The lady is not—"

A ravenous growl interrupted Monju's pleas.

From the meadow above us, the white tiger emerged, not so white anymore. Fresh blood dripped from her muzzle and stained her two large sabre teeth. The long gash on her side from earlier didn't slow her down as she padded down the slope behind Monju. A low growl rumbled in her throat as she stalked us.

"Monju," I said cautiously, not taking my gaze off the tiger. "How is it that both you and the tiger are still alive?"

"I..." He glanced between Keegan and me, and finally averted his hurt gaze to the ground. "Forgiveness. Did not mean for the lady to be..."

Soft footfalls from the meadow above drew Keegan's sword, while I kept my weapon on Monju. "Who's there?"

And then, a voice I'd know anywhere, rich with the familiar accent, cried, "Heel!"

The tiger turned an ear to the noise, and arrested her advance.

The woman who had promised revenge slid down the slope, stepped over Orrin's half-visible body in the reeds, and strode towards the white tiger. The dark cloud of tangled hair, so much like my own, whipped around her gaunt, unfeeling face. Icy eyes like tiny pinpoints stared down at me, although she was just a finger taller. The ground crunched beneath her black boots as she approached; her short dress undulated around her wool-ensconced legs.

Lady Dominique Castillo, daughter of Northern Marlenia, cast a disparaging look at the sea and found it worthy of her scorn.

"Driscoll's End," Dominique said slowly, pronouncing each syllable carefully with her vile tongue. She stroked the tiger's bloodied fur absently, with affection. "A fittin' place pour dis pretender to die."

"Don't tell me you came all this way just to see me dead," I spat.

My threat was undercut by the tiger as she flicked her tail wildly back and forth, eying me suspiciously. She growled, rivalling the sounds of the ocean below, baring more of her sharp teeth and drawing back her ears. Licking her chops, she prepared to pounce.

Dominique flicked her commanding gaze to the tiger. "Down, Salavajee," she ordered.

The striped beast immediately stopped growling, and crouched low. Her tail twitched in warning, and her large eyes gleamed, but she lay on Dominique's feet, eagerly waiting for the next command. Ready to strike at the first sign of hostility.

So the tiger didn't belong to the cave. It belonged to my enemy.

"Y'it was not easy," Dominique admitted. "But in de y'end...j'ou are y'exactly where we want j'ou to be."

I swallowed warily. "We?"

She snorted. "Y'of course, *we*. Did j'ou tink I would send j'ou away wit'out eyes to watch j'ou?" She splayed her fingers and gestured to Monju. "All de Freetor magic-wielders are dead, j'es?"

Monju nodded, staring at the ground. "Yes."

The truth settled upon me like an unwanted garment that weighed down my movement. "All this time...you've been spying...for her?"

I should've seen it. His convenient rescues. His appearance just as Keegan and I escaped the castle. His unwavering loyalty. His confession of admiration. The song...had that been a convenient ploy to attract my notice? To gain my favour?

Before I went into the cave. He'd tried to confess.

I forced myself to stare at Orrin's body. He was perhaps a year older than me. Too short a life, filled with the obsession of obtaining something that, if only he had waited...

Keegan shook his head. His knuckles were white around the hilt of his sword. "I knew we should never have trusted you."

Monju refused to meet our gaze. "No."

My throat tightened as I swallowed my sorrow to fuel my anger. "You could've been knighted. Given proper land. You and your family could've had everything. You would've been a hero to your people. Why would you give it away for this...this woman?"

And then it hit me. Why Monju had travelled so far from home while his father suffered; why he'd sought to sell his services to moneyed nobles and eager patrons of the arts. He'd sold himself to the first person who promised him his heart's desire.

"It's not for Dominique, is it Monju?" I said, stepping forward. "Keegan could've given you anything, but we don't know if there's really a cure for what the Race drug does to your body. You said that the North's poisons and antidotes were the best in the world. You promised him a cure, didn't you, Dominique?"

"More dan a promise," she said. She withdrew a cone-shaped pendant from her bosom, and popped the top open. "See, Monju? J'our fat'er will know life y'again."

He peered inside. The cone-shaped pendant was the size of a thimble. Liquid or powder, I didn't know, but Monju drew back suddenly, disgusted by the smell. Dominique snapped the pendant top shut once more.

"Lady Dominique is certain this will cure Peta's illness?" Monju asked.

"If j'our fat'er is not dead yet," she replied, as if she were talking about something inane like the weather.

Monju looked uncertain, but he held out his hand. She deposited the pendant. His palm bobbed down and then up again at the weight of everything he'd fought for.

"You may have just saved your father," Keegan said, failing to keep the emotion from his voice, "but what of mine? And the countless other fathers you've sentenced to death by raiding the castle with the East, and capturing my city?"

Curling his hand around the pendant and turning to leave, the bard said, "Is a long way back to the South."

"You helped them, in the castle—didn't you." Keegan trailed after Monju. "The East infiltrated our ranks. But for the shadow men, the Northern killers, you were their plant. You said yourself that you had been trained by such masters. And you slayed them, to woo us into trusting you."

Monju's silence was confirmation enough.

"D'East can have dere stone walls and mountains," Dominique said. "Monju did much more dan dat. Tell dem how j'ou brought dem here, to dis spot, and den we finish."

She looked more than pleased with herself, a cat with its cream. Monju was the solemn mouse, forced to lament the tale at his master's bidding.

"The Freetor apprentices had been trying to meet with Lady Kiera, to tell her of the Spear," Monju began. He cast a sorrowful look at the mountains above us, and then took the tiger's impatient, hungry stare into account before continuing. "This the Northern eyes and ears knew. An alluring treasure for the lady and her prince to chase—"

"De prince was not esupposed to chase y'anythin'," Dominique said demurely, crossing her arms. "Hurry on wit' d'story, Bard, and den I release j'ou."

"Yes, Lady Dominique is right," Monju said slowly, his eyebrows furrowing slightly. He composed himself, drawing his shoulders back as he started to get a feel for the rhythm of the tale. "For the rumours were true. The North and the East had allied, with a shared goal: to *liberate* the throne from the Tramore family." He cast an apologetic glance at Keegan. "So the spies, the guards, every man was planted to ensure success. But removing the royals would take a more... delicate plan."

"Do not prolong dis, Bard. Dis is not a show," Dominique warned him. Her hand played with the hilt of a blade tucked at her belt.

"Of course." But he flicked a quick, chancy gaze at me that belied his words. He was stalling. For what, and why? "Certain incentives had to be placed to rid the castle of the Lady Kiera."

"Incentives? But..." And then it hit me. "My father's expedition notes. That was you? You put that at my door?" I frowned. "You said you couldn't read Freetor code."

"Can't," Monju admitted. "Had to steal many tomes, or tear out single pages, find willing Freetors to translate bits and pieces, until found Spear information to persuade the lady."

I felt so stupid. My father had mentioned that his books were disappearing. Why had I not paid attention? Dumb misfortune was responsible, not my father, for the missing pages in the tome. I had been so mad at him, too focussed and determined to find the Spear that I couldn't see the bigger picture.

"I suspect you were also the one who forged my handwriting, and created a letter addressed to Sylvia?" Keegan asked.

Dominique scowled. Her fingers danced over the hilt, as if she itched to use it. "Dat spoiled Eastern daughter convinced Monju to do dat."

"Driving a wedge between the lady and the prince was key to the plan," Monju said flatly. He twisted the pendant in his hands, allowing the chain to coil along his long fingers. "So Monju, good with words, with copying writing, did such, in exchange for coin."

I felt sick. That letter had caused us so much grief, and to hear him speak of it in his detached, pensive voice fuelled my anger. My pinky finger ached as I balled my hands into fists. Keegan seethed with rage.

"Whether or not the Spear was found, it did not matter. The promise of adventure drew the lady away from the castle, where... where she would be delivered to the Roamers, and be... put to rest... without reliable witnesses."

Put to rest? Dominique rolled her eyes at Monju's hesitant delivery. Keegan wrapped his arm around me and drew me close to his chest. "You *knew* someone would make an attempt to murder her."

Monju hadn't just seen suspicious characters in the crowd. He had helped arrange it.

And yet, he'd saved me.

"D'Eastern men got de wrong girl," Dominique muttered sourly. She narrowed her gaze at me, and then at Monju. "Too caught up in j'our stories and songs to keep an eye on de prize."

My heart pounded. Dominique didn't know that Monju tried to save me. I squeezed Keegan's arm, praying he would not say a word.

"I was not deterred, anyway. Dat plan was not mine," Dominique continued, scowling. "Lady Sylvia's dainty hand waved dat into y'existance. Y'Eastern men are not as good as Nort'ern men. Sloppy. Figured I would give her a chance, y'and take what I wanted if she succeeded. De real plan, if j'ou survived, would see j'ou to de y'edge of de world."

"Why not just kill me the first night, when we were in the woods? Why go to all the effort to make us trust him, and bring us so close to the Spear?" I asked.

Dominique's lips curled up in a cruel smile. "Had to be convincin'," she replied. "To put j'our trust in someone. To make j'ou feel safe. So j'ou would suffer by comin' so close to j'our goal, and den have dat yanked from j'ou." She glanced at the vast expanse of mountains ascending into the clouds. "I y'also tought, maybe de wilderness kill j'ou on de way. Couldn't have dat. I wanted j'our tongue as a trophy. So Monju guided j'ou to me."

The North—or Lady Dominique at least—had a fondness for cutting out Freetor tongues. As a prisoner, she'd threatened to torture me once she was freed: *Not only will j'our tongue be ripped out, but I'll see dat j'ou are drawn, quartered, and hung. De crows will eat out j'our eyes and j'our insides and den I'll feed de rest of j'ou to my dogs.*

I'd not given her threat much thought. Now, with a sickly deep dread swirling in my stomach, I regretted underestimating her. Especially with Salavajee reevaluating me with interest.

My knees bent as I immediately adopted a defensive position. She wanted my tongue, she'd have to fight for it. "Do your worst."

She sneered at the weapon clutched tightly in my hand. "J'our undoing. J'ou have risked j'our life pour an idea."

I was ready to tear her to pieces if needs be. "You don't think this can do any damage? Maybe I should stick it in you to make sure."

The tiger perked up and emitted a low warning growl. Dominique laughed. "Salavajee would attack de moment she knows I y'am in danger. And"—she smoothly adopted a defensive pose—"my shadows are not de y'only ones trained in de deadly arts."

A tinge of fear flew down my spine. My fingers tightened around the Spear as I pointed it upward, at Dominique.

"Thought you said you were afraid of blood," I said, hoping to stall.

"Fears can be y'overcome," she said with a sneer. "Had no choice, after j'ou ruined my life. Salavajee," Dominique said suddenly to the tiger. "*Ignata de pri!*"

The white tiger leapt towards Keegan, growling and hissing with the promise of another meal. Keegan swung at the air in front of the tiger as she advanced. The tiger had been wounded in her fight with Monju, and Keegan's cheeks were only now recovering their rosy complexion from the setting sun. Both could be easily felled, though the angry tiger was unpredictable. I feared the worst.

Monju tucked his pendant into his belt satchel and remained on the sidelines with his raised knife. His dark eyes roamed the scene, but he seemed torn on his place in it.

Dwelling on Keegan and Monju and the tiger would be my death, for Dominique was focussed on bringing me down—and I could not be distracted. She lunged, but, threatened by the sharp point of the mysterious Spear, recoiled just as immediately. And so our dance began.

In general, spears tended to have an advantage over swords and shorter weapons. Its long reach allowed distance between us as she flitted from left to right, searching for an opening. When she advanced, so did I, rushing the Spear's dangerous tip towards her unarmoured but well-covered body. But getting too close allowed her the advantage:

she reached for the shaft more than once in an attempt to draw me closer. I swiped away quickly.

Each movement was a fight for my survival. One wrong move and I could find myself with a blade in my chest, dying on the edge of the world. Though the Spear felt the same kind of *right* as the Orb had in my grip, I was not trained in pole weapons. The shaft was longer than me, and thinner than a sword hilt, and heavier than the knives I was used to. The knife was a weapon of intimacy. The spear embodied a warrior's fear of getting too close to the enemy. It was fitting that the Elders had adopted the Spear as their sigil, while we Fighters had engaged our enemies in close quarters.

Dominique suddenly barked a command in her native tongue, and feigned left. I struck, leaning forward with the movement of the Spear, when Salavajee sprung towards me from my left. Her curved sabre teeth and raged-filled eyes and the idea of being devoured alive frightened me more than Dominique cutting out my tongue. My first instinct: run.

I dove for the rocky slope, away from the cliffside, hugging the Spear as I landed. I rolled, startled by Dominique and how quickly she had leapt to my side, already bringing her knife down. I tried to keep hold on the Spear but it was of no use: rolling and dodging required flexibility, and the Spear was too long to move with me. I left it on the rocks, panicking, hating to leave it, and pulled out my knife.

With both the tiger and Dominique on me, I scrambled to my feet. Keegan came to my rescue and flanked them, poking the tiger's side to draw it away. She couldn't hear Dominique's command for it to focus on me, and swatted a large paw at Keegan's leg.

Frustrated, Dominique lunged, propelled by anger. Good—anger led to sloppiness. I ducked and made my way back towards the Spear as Keegan led the large cat towards the other side of the cliff.

"Stay...*still*!" Dominique cried, and thrust her knife downward at me.

As I dove to retrieve the Spear, Dominque yanked my robe, throwing me off balance. Monju swooped in and grabbed me from behind as I fell, robbing me of my opportunity to retrieve the Spear.

"Stop it! Let me go!"

Monju pulled me tight against him, my back against his front, close enough to smell the fear in his sweat. Keegan raised his sword but Monju's grip on me tightened as he recoiled like a startled viper. With one hand, he squeezed my wounded right wrist, making me drop my weapon. "Stay back, Prince," Monju warned. Then, to Dominique: "To the carriage?"

Dominique's knife glinted in the setting sun and I squirmed. Monju prevented my escape—he was stronger than he looked.

"No," she said softly. She advanced. "I y'am makin' good on my promise. J'ou know what we do to Freetor eslaves?"

"You will not harm her!" Keegan shouted.

Lady Dominique laughed. "J'ou do not scare me, Prince."

"Maybe you should rethink that sentiment."

I squirmed. Keegan stalked around us, but before he could strike, Dominique caught my chin and plugged my nose. "Monju, hold her."

"Monju is holding, but—"

I was not going to make this easy, but already my lungs were burning. Monju had been watching Keegan's every move, but now that he was distracted, Keegan had the opportunity to strike. Hurry, Keegan, hurry!

In my flailing, I kicked Dominique in the shins. Startled, she stumbled back, managing to draw her knife across my cheek. I grimaced as the wound burned and I gulped in fresh air greedily. As Keegan lunged for Dominique, Salavajee, seeing her mistress was in danger, growled and pounced for my prince.

"Keegan, watch out!"

Man and tiger met in mid-air. Salavajee was far heavier and pushed Keegan to the rocky ground. She landed on Keegan's sword arm. He cried out and released the weapon, and attempted to roll over to shield his face from Salavajee's vicious long teeth, massive paws, and even deadlier claws.

Laughing, Dominique kicked away Keegan's sword as he reached for it. The tiger had Keegan pinned—but she looked to Dominique for approval.

A cruel smile crossed her face. "Hold, Salavajee." She sauntered towards me and held up her knife once more. "One ting at a time."

"Let him—"

I sucked in a deep breath as she came at me from the side, grabbing my nose and mouth with one hand. I twisted and tried to catch her in the shins but she would not be fooled twice. Her hands smelled musty and were laden with dirt. I pressed my lips firmly together as she squeezed my cheeks, hoping to force my tongue into the open to meet her sharp, looming knife. My left cheek stung where she'd cut me, and sent tendrils of pain up and down the left side of my face.

I shook my head violently while my lungs burned. I would not let her take my tongue. I would not let her win.

But while Dominique was busy exacting her revenge, Keegan busied himself with his own rescue. For what Keegan saw and Dominique didn't was the Silver Spear lying just out of his reach.

My teeth clung ferociously to my lips like a portcullis sunk deep into the ground, but my resolve was weakening. My head was light and airy. Resistance only hastened my end.

Almost...there...

With a grunt, Keegan wrapped his fingers around the shaft of the Silver Spear. The tiger's warning growl was interrupted by the sudden dull piercing sound of steel through flesh, and then she whined for her mother.

Dominque whipped around, forgetting me entirely. "Salavajee...?"

The tiger stumbled off of Keegan as the prince grunted and withdrew the Spear from her neck. She wobbled absently with unfocussed vision, mewling in pain and dripping a trail of blood. Before Dominique could stop her, Salavajee collapsed on the edge of the cliff, and, pulled by her own weight, tumbled off the side to the dangerous depths below.

"NO!" Dominique shrieked. She advanced as close as she dared to the edge, frozen in horror. There was no sound of the tiger hitting the water or the rocks, for the roar of the waves had taken that from her. A blip of white against the sea and the sharp grey rocks, and then forever blue once more.

Dominique wheeled on Keegan, her mad eyes wide with rage and tears. "How *dare* j'ou...!"

As Keegan climbed to his full height and raised the Spear to defend himself, his body stiffened. He sniffed, paled, and jutted his head to the side, as if suddenly struck by an idea.

"Keegan?" His name left my lips as a worried inquiry but was repeated in a desperate flurry. "Keegan!"

Dominique drew back her knife and charged.

Monju's grip on me loosened.

Springing from his sympathetic grip, I dove for Dominique and tackled her to the ground. She kicked and stabbed, tearing my robe and nicking me in the side with her sharp blade. Dizzy, I put all my weight on her right side and immobilized her knife-wielding arm.

"Let go," I muttered through gritted teeth.

"Never!" she shouted.

Monju appeared suddenly and took the knife from Dominique's hand, examined its edge, paled, and then tossed it out of reach. "Enough, North Daughter. The damage is done."

"J'ou weasel, double-crossin' *me*..."

She tore into him, but now that she was less of a threat, all of my worry went to Keegan. The left side of my face was numb from the wound, and I struggled to breathe normally as I found my feet and half crawled, half stumbled to where Keegan stood, still as a statue.

While Dominique and Monju argued behind me, and he prevented her from retrieving her knife to harm us further, I pressed my face as close as I dared to my husband. "Keegan? Are you all right?"

He stared into the distance, unblinking. A white sheeny frost was crawling from beneath his shirt. It covered his cheeks, his nose, his lips in a swift, light *clinking* sound. It rode along the strands of his hair and coated his eyebrows in silver-white. The frost claimed his eyeballs last, swiping over his irises in one swift movement.

My fingertips hovered over his left cheek. The magical chill that had surrounded us in the cave exuded from his skin. No heat, no life. Only ice.

"No," I whispered. "Please, Keegan...don't be dead..."

Hearing my plea, Dominique's attention refocussed. "What is wrong wit' him?" she demanded impatiently.

I felt his neck for a pulse and counted. An eternity passed. The chill bit my fingers, but I dared not move away. Finally, a beat. One measly beat, weak against my desperate fingers. Almost a minute passed before another beat surfaced.

Alive. But barely.

"I said," Dominique repeated, "what y'is wrong wit' him?"

One by one, his fingers peeled off the shaft of the Spear. The weapon clattered onto the rocks once more. The frost immediately spread at least a stone-throw from where the Spear landed, coating my boots and sending a biting chill up my legs.

At the Spear's display of power, Dominique drew back, so shocked that she didn't realize her knife now lay within grasp. Monju appeared to be just as surprised as I was. "Lady Kiera...is he...?"

Dominique struck Monju hard in the chest. He fell backwards onto the ground. I had never seen her so frightened, not since we had held her captive underground. The act reeked of desperation and not of malice; with her tiger gone, her loyal muscle existed only within her own body. Why had she not brought a dozen men, like Sylvia had days ago, when she was otherwise prepared to fight?

Unless the apprentices had done away with them all.

"Is he alive?" Monju sounded winded from his blow, and avoided Lady Dominique's gaze. His eyes were wide with fear and hope.

I nodded, numb with fear and shock, dumbfounded that I was telling Monju, who was supposed to be my enemy, the state of Keegan's body.

The air seemed thick as I tried to sort things out. I touched the Spear, and I was fine. This was the first time Keegan had touched it since we freed it a short time ago. Had I been the only one to hold it? *Yes*, I realized with a pang of dread. Not even the apprentices had lived long enough to retrieve it for themselves, and even in our brief sparring, it hadn't touched skin.

But Keegan was a Marlenian. Not a direct descendant of the man who originally spurned Alastar's gift, but he was a reigning prince. Perhaps the magic in the Spear had sensed this and was ensuring that Keegan would never rise again.

Had Alastar the Hero laid a curse on the Marlenian people?

Keegan, a standing statue, leaned leftward. I leapt to catch him as he fell. The cold shocked my senses, attacking my arms as I was forced to the ground. I was painfully aware of the cliffside as I swayed with the weight of my prince and the disorientation from my wounds. One push. That was all it would take. Then we'd both be gone.

Although the sea lashed below us, it did not disguise the approaching footsteps from the above meadow. I readied the abandoned Spear, yet Dominique and Monju seemed unconcerned and unsurprised that we were not the only visitors to the world's end. Finally, I thought in my mind fog. More men to fight.

Yet it was none other than Lady Sylvia Frostfire, her full dress putting her portly figure off balance. Her noisy shuffling alerted the three of us at once, and I pulled Keegan's stiff, freezing form onto my lap, hoping against hope that my body heat would break the icy spell and wake him.

"I told j'ou to stay in de carriage!" Dominique shouted.

Sylvia gave her cohort an indignant look and fanned herself. "In that stuffed-up closet? No, better that I also oversee the proceedings. Leaving your dirty work to the animals"—she glanced at Monju—"is most uncivilized." Blinking several times, she seemed to notice that the tiger was no longer in sight—and that Keegan lay motionless in my clutches.

"My prince...?" she whispered, in a high, shrill shriek.

She tottled down the slope towards Keegan's cold body. Tears ran down her face as she cried Keegan's name repeatedly. The cold seemed to guard Keegan from her touch. Her ugly cries became heated, angry screams as she threw a nasty gaze at me, eager to cast blame.

"What have you *done*!" she screamed, clutching her long skirts. "Killing my prince, to take the throne for yourself?"

I slapped her across the face. Shocked, she yelped, but I did not dare leave Keegan's side. I offered her the Spear.

"Don't!" Dominique yelled, as Sylvia held out a curious hand. "Cursed!"

Sylvia stepped back, looking disgusted. "I *knew* you had him under some sort of spell. Filthy Freetor magic."

"Why are you so concerned?" I demanded. "Your family has been executing people in the streets for their loyalty to the Tramore line. With that sort of talk, I'm surprised you're not among them."

She blinked, surprised that I knew. "They were saying terrible things about me and my father and my family. We couldn't have that. Just like we can't have commoners sympathizing with the Freetor plague."

I glanced between Sylvia and Dominique. "Your families don't know you're here, do they. You're acting on your own accord. Your father, Sylvia, would never approve of your marrying Keegan. Not now, since he has established himself as the new...what did you call it, emperor?"

"Dat is none of j'our concern, rat," Dominique replied haughtily.

There was some comfort in the knowledge that the North-East alliance had cracks, but the knowledge would mean nothing if we didn't survive to use it. I hugged Keegan ever closer. My legs were numb, and so was the entire left half of my body, but there was no way I was abandoning him. I breathed on his forehead, hoping to clear the icy sheen, to no avail.

"Cure him, then!" Sylvia commanded. Her angry gaze melted into a desperate plea. "Why won't you *help* him?"

"I...I don't think..."

My hesitation was too much for her. "He's mine. I'll have him, alive or...sleeping." She bent and took him by the underarms.

Shrieking, she immediately released him and blew on her fingers. "He's so cold!"

Dominique seemed to have lost interest in the frozen prince and my vulnerable state. She stared out into the sea, wearing a mournful expression as she searched for her now-dead tiger among the restless waters.

I needed to focus. So far Dominique's actions had been carefully calculated—if our situations were reversed, she would not hesitate to seize the opportunity and run me through. My head spun and I fought to maintain my nerve. "Not having your family's support in your little revenge plot isn't doing you any favours. Is this all you have to fight me with?"

"I could say de same ting about j'ou."

Reluctantly, I slid Keegan from my lap. Frosty residue remained on my robe, and the biting cold made it hard to stand. I wobbled. The Spear was still on the ground. Had I set it down? So hard to remember. So far down. My knife was close to the rocky slope, where Monju had made me drop it.

My unsteady movements were not lost on Dominique. Her cruel smile returned as she addressed Monju. "J'ou will not put de Freetor rat out of her misery?"

"That was not the agreement."

"Hmm." She crossed her arms, and shifted her weight from one foot to the other.

"What are you going to do?" I spread my arms in challenge—left arm up first, then the right, yes, very good. "There's nowhere else to go. Keegan, unconscious. Monju..." I cast him a hopeful glance, but he looked away. Fine. "It's just you and me, Dominique. Fight me. Show me just how good you are."

Dominique's sour lips curled. "I y'already fought j'ou and won, rat. Five minutes ago, y'in fact. Our poisons are subtle, but effective."

My face tingled where she had wounded me. Black, powdery residue rested on my fingers after I touched my numb cheek.

"No," I whispered. "How long?"

"Anot'er five. Perhaps ten minutes. Some poisons are faster, but less painful. Dis one y'is slow."

This was it, then. Before I became the Queen of Marlenia, I had suspected I would die in battle, fighting the Marlenian city guards. But to be killed by poison—that was an insult. I would not let her cleverness get the better of me. A warrior's death I would get.

My right hand was sore from the ice-block burn, and looking at my forefinger reminded me of Keegan's promise. There was no way but forward. Needed a weapon. I knelt, intending to pick up the Spear, but I stumbled and fell on the rocks. Spear: too far away now. I released my knife was within reach, and clasped it clumsily.

Dominique was equally amused and cautious. "J'ou would fight me, in j'our condition?"

"If you have to ask that," I muttered, "then you've truly underestimated me."

I attacked. She was ready for me. My movements weren't what I wanted them to be; my weakened state lent her the advantage, making her a prophet in the battlefield as she predicted my advances. I thrust the knife down, aiming for her belly, but she sidestepped me easily. She had a knife of her own now. Where it had come from, my increasingly fuzzy mind had no time to contemplate.

Monju gave us a wide berth, torn between helping the woman who had promised his father's life for his loyalty, and saving the street rat turned royalty who had enraptured his muse.

"Don't count on him," Dominique said through gritted teeth as she evaded me for the tenth time. Seizing the opportunity at my distraction, she pushed me to the ground. I fell on the rocky grass as if my spine had turned to jelly, and she climbed on top of me. "He won't help either of us now."

She pressed a heavy hand on my forehead. My strength melted into the ground with each passing second. As she tried one last time to force my tongue from my ever-relaxing mouth, I realized in a haze of confusion that my knife was still in my hand.

Growling like a feral animal, I put all of my strength into my arm and thrust the knife upward. The blade sank into her dress, to the left of her heart, and met with solid corset, and then flesh.

Did I get her? I wondered, though one part of me felt apathetic about matters of the body. She rolled off me, and disappeared somewhere off to my left, muttering in her native tongue.

Keegan. Where are you?

In my periphery, Sylvia had overcome her aversion to Keegan's cold body. She was dragging him up the slope using two long pieces of cloth tied around his underarms. Her torn skirts fluttered around her.

"Come...back..." My words came out slow and slurred. My mouth felt as if it were full of liquid. Was I drowning? I couldn't feel my arms, or legs. My head was on fire. Eyelids heavy. Lips and tongue, large and unmovable. Ground—comfortable. A good place to rest.

Then, someone above me. My head lifted onto another's lap.

"Monju..." Dominique wailed, somewhere to my left. I must have gotten her. She sounded desperate.

Liquid running over my lips, running down my chin. I wasn't even sure I had a face anymore, it was so numb. I struggled to lap up the liquid. It tasted spicy and cold; a sensation that quickly evolved into sweet and warm. It ran down my throat with little resistance. The ambrosia trailed through my body like hot liquid on ice, breaking the rigidity of my thoughts and movements.

"Kee...gan..."

No. Monju. He stroked my hair and urged his tiny vial—the cure for the effects of his father's illness—into my mouth. I struggled. I couldn't accept it, even though he had betrayed me for it—for what else in this life did he have that was good? But it was too late. All the liquid had been drained, and my dry tongue searched my chin for something to sate the desert it had become.

"Why?" I managed to ask.

"The lady must not die," he said. His voice was wobbly, and distant. Perhaps he was crying. "That was not part of the song."

"New...songs," I said. My tongue was less heavy now.

"Not anymore."

He laid me back down on the ground and kissed me on the forehead. My vision cleared just as he stood, and Dominique charged forward, clutching her side, knife in hand. Monju did not fight her. His eyes were closed, and he was humming the tune that men and women everywhere sang.

Dominique lunged, and her blade slid between the Southern bard's shoulders. She screamed something akin to a war cry and an apology that wasn't sincere. Monju, with his vibrating tenor, hit a pure high note that harmonized with Dominique's bawl, holding it even as she withdrew the knife. He slumped backwards to the earth, beside me.

His gaze found mine. He sucked in a breath to sing another note.

And then let it out. He did not inhale again.

The air in that agonizing moment was still. Monju sang for the world. But no one sang for Monju.

Dominique panted heavily. She had been good on her word—whatever had been in Monju's vial, promised to his father, had been fast acting. The numbness receded, though my left cheek still burned, and the wound from the ice block on my right hand still plagued me. I was a far cry from dead, at least at the moment.

Blood seeped from Dominique's wound as she fell to her knees beside me. "J'our turn, rat."

I rolled over just before her clumsy attempt to give me a matching wound could succeed. This further infuriated her.

"All I wanted," she said, "was to see everytin' takin' away from j'ou. Like j'ou took everytin' from me."

I climbed to my feet. My hand was empty. My knife must have fallen in my daze. Dominique swung lazily, and I recoiled. All of my faculties had not yet recovered, and I had no way of knowing if Monju's Race cure was a stop-gap measure, or a miracle cure to the poison coursing through my veins.

"At least we succeeded in takin' j'our prince away," she mused lightly.

Her words jerked me to full attention. Hand over hand, I crawled up the slope to the meadow. In the distance, Sylvia was but a speck as she hoisted Keegan's frozen body inside a small carriage.

I started towards them. Dominique crawled up the slope behind me and grabbed my arm. I tried to wrench myself away, but she swung at me with a rock-fisted hand and struck me in the left temple. Though it felt like a dull thud through the still-lingering numbness, it stunned me, and I fell to my knees, dazed.

Swiftly tearing fabric from her already-tattered dress, Dominique hobbled back down the slope for the Spear, abandoned on the cliffside. She gloved her hand in the torn fabric, taking the time to ensure every bit of skin was covered. I groaned. Strength seemed to have left me again, and my head weighed heavily with sleep and the promise of nothingness.

Lady Dominique lifted the Spear with her protected hand and whirled around, breathing heavily as she made for me again. I had to get up. My boots caught in the dry grass, kicking the useless green blades into the air as I struggled for purchase. Grinning, Lady Dominique brandished the Spear and advanced patiently on me. Blood dripped from the wound in her side and she paid it no mind.

She could have said so many things in that moment. *I have waited so long to kill you. This is payback for what you did to me. Die, filthy Freetor.* Her silence was terrifying. The knowing grin said everything. I was going to die. She was going to kill me with the artefact I had travelled so far to find.

There came a point where I stopped struggling. Perhaps it was the lingering poison that held me still as Lady Dominique raised the Spear and slammed it into my body.

That's not where my heart is, I thought, as well as, At least it's not in my gut. Being stabbed in the intestines was a slow, painful death.

I cried out as a cold burn rippled through me, beginning near my stomach. I doubted this kind of death would be any faster. My brain tried to calm my panicking body: *It's all right, the Spear is part of us now, just relax, everything will be okay.*

I had wanted the Spear, I told myself deliriously. Now I had it. Forever.

Dominique's form blurred as she loomed above me.

"Sure you...you don't want this?" I wheezed, fingering the long carved shaft lodged in my chest. Even touching it sent a shock through my system.

She clutched her side again; her face was noticeably pale as she knelt, her blade ready to take its prize. "J'ou can have j'our stick," she said spitefully, as she tipped my chin back. "Dat is all it is."

During the past several days, what I'd wanted had become so foggy, so unclear. And yet, as the carriage that held my future husband captive rolled further away from me to the mountains filled with usurpers and holy promises, everything sharpened and became clear.

No one, not even the most powerful, dangerous assassins could stop me from getting him back. Not because I had fought so hard to be with him. Not because he had been torn so suddenly from my side. But because of a clear fact I had dismissed so often since I went to live at the castle: I loved Keegan. I had always loved him. I would not stop loving him. I loved him not because he completed me, but because together we completed something greater, something I didn't have words to describe.

It didn't matter why I loved him. I simply did.

I would get him back, with or without my tongue.

Dominique parted my lips, and I felt the fabric wrapped around my forefinger.

My vision blurred once more as the sharp knife pressed on my now-exposed tongue. The sweet smell of grass surrounded me, invoking a memory of the earthy home I once knew. The heavy hand of death touched my shoulder, also familiar and comforting, and speaking in soothing tones as I fell away from myself into unthinking nonexistence.

Eighteen

THE POTENT SMELL of salt invaded my nostrils.

Keegan. Lady Sylvia had Keegan.

Keegan was under an ice spell.

I sat up, realizing three things in the space of one moment. First: the room was small, warm, and made of stone, and allowed the morning light to seep in through a lancet. Second: the Spear was no longer lodged in my chest. My hand brushed the wound, neatly bandaged beneath a fresh grey wool dress.

Third, I was not alone.

I wet my cracked lips. Fourth: I still had my tongue. "Where—?"

"Lie back, Kiera, or you'll reopen the wound."

My father hovered over the cot where I lay. His moustache, once long, pointed, and groomed immaculately with waxed tips, now blended with his greying beard. The flashy, bright robes of his office had been replaced with a dark tunic, a grey vest, and simple black trousers. These were not the clothes of an advisor to the Holy One.

"We're in Baile Gareth," he said. "In Feenagh Forest."

Though I knew the answer, I had to ask. "And Keegan?"

He looked troubled. "The East has him."

He was alive, at least. Or so far as we knew. I shivered at the memory of the ice spell that had cursed him.

"Dominique almost killed me."

"She was almost dead herself, and rightfully frightened by my hand fire, especially when it singed her clothing. She ran after her carriage, and made it, even though Lady Sylvia was determined not to stop for her."

Rats. "And the—?"

He gestured to the surface behind him. His back dug into the desk, and his knees into the cot, as the room was cramped and narrow. On the desk, wrapped in white linen, was the Spear.

"You didn't let anyone touch it, did you?" I asked.

Frowning, he shook his head. I let out a breath of relief, and grimaced. The fewer people who knew about the Spear's abilities, the better. Dull pain radiated from the wound in my chest.

"It's cursed," I explained, relaxing into the rough pillow behind me. "I should have known. If I'd had more time to research it—"

"I've been studying the Spear for the better part of fifteen years, and I didn't know. The Freetors were never very good at recording the history of magic. I still can't believe you managed to find it, let alone free it."

"I'll tell you all about it sometime," I said with a tired sigh.

A silence hung between us. Outside, birds chirped their morning songs, and the wind swirled through the tall evergreens.

"How long have I been here?"

"Three days. I stitched you up and used what herbs I had to keep you alive as we travelled back on the road." A pained expression haunted his face. "There were times when...I wasn't sure if..." He cleared his throat, unwilling to say the words.

It was hard to fathom that so much time had passed and I remembered nothing of it. Moments ago, I had been fighting for my life against Lady Dominique. Vaguely I recalled his mentioning that he could move quickly and unseen at great speeds. "I thought I was going to die."

My father stared grimly at my chest. "If I would've been faster, I could have saved both you and Keegan. But Keegan was already in the carriage, barrelling past me, and when I saw you on the ground...well..."

He trailed off. I swallowed over the lump in my throat. "I'm your daughter."

A bright smile spread across his weary face. "Yes."

He inched his hand forward and rested it cautiously near mine. It was a question. A test. Slowly, I turned my palm upward, and looked up at him.

"Thank you," I whispered.

Grasping my hand, he leaned forward and closed his eyes. "I wanted to make sure you succeeded."

"So all this time, you were following me."

"Of course I was. I thought I'd made that clear."

I snorted. "No, not really."

"Hmm. I suppose subtlety is hard to convey in writing. You didn't get my last messages...?"

"I left the journal at the God Tears. As an offering." I squeezed his hand. "I don't think I need it anymore. Not...if you're here."

He dipped his head, smiled a little, and then cast a sideways glance at the Spear. "The apprentices are dead. I suppose you knew that, at least."

"Monju Farin killed them."

He appeared unsurprised. "They would have killed you, if you weren't compliant."

"You sound like him. I could have gotten them to listen...if I'd just had more time..." I clenched my hands. The ice wound on my right hand had made my pinky finger stiff; it would not fully fit in a fist. "The Orb is destroyed."

A faint clinking sound, and then my father set my bag on the edge of the cot. He opened the flap, revealing its shimmering contents. "It may have been shattered, but that doesn't mean it's destroyed."

My eyes widened. "You went into the cave and recovered the pieces? How did you manage to rescue me *and* do that?"

"Not easily," he admitted. "I had some help, though."

"Who? How? Did you use magic? Did Bidelia and Laoise make it here safe?"

He waved his hand dismissively. "You should rest, Kiera. You'll heal faster and not have such a nasty scar. Then we can talk."

"I don't care about scars. I've done enough resting. I have to know now." I wasn't about to spend days dreaming up the worst scenarios in this closet of a room in an unfamiliar fortress.

He sighed. "It's not that important. What's important is dealing with Keegan's capture, and using the precious few days we have left in Baile Gareth wisely. We cannot stay here for much longer. Over half of the bailes west of Marlenia City have sworn to the Frostfires, fearing death or invasion. More are following their lead. Lord Ansel Gareth is feeling the pressure, as he will be executed if the Frostfires find evidence that he is harbouring people loyal to the Tramore family."

"We can return underground," I said. "With the Spear, we can rally the remaining apprentices to our side."

"Returning underground is a possibility, though it is no longer as safe as it once was. The three most powerful magic-wielders—Lorcán, Sinéad, and Orrin—are dead at Driscoll's End. The remaining apprentices are barely better at magic than I am, and may blame you for the death of their brethren," he replied.

"Some magic-wielders are better than none, if they can see past the apprentices' deaths."

"If you appeared before them with the Spear, and steered their vengeful anger towards the North and the East, then yes, they may follow you. Perhaps. But they need direction and protection, and their loyalty is only the first step to winning a war against the East. Right now they are cowering in the underground, using what little knowledge they have of their craft to keep the Freetor people safe. They cannot fight the East and defend our people at the same time."

I closed my eyes, remembering when I only had to worry about stealing enough food to feed my neighbours, and occasionally freeing slaves from unattended caravans. "But I am the regent in Keegan's absence," I said. I thumbed the fabric around my forefinger, thankful it was still there. "Surely that carries some weight in attracting allies?"

"You're a Freetor with no lands and a bad name," my father said, not unkindly. "He never married you, and engagements are far easier to annul than marriages."

"But we said the words at the God Tears. Keegan said that that was enough, as long as we sought a priest within the year." I held up my right hand to show him the makeshift ring.

"Were there any witnesses?"

My silence was answer enough. He exhaled slowly.

"Lord Ansel has been kind enough to shelter me and those loyal to me because of my reputation, though that reputation means less and less with each passing hour. Being loyal to the Tramore family is now a dangerous crime."

"Will the East attack Baile Gareth?"

He studied the tough, worn stone comprising the walls. Judging by the size of the room, it probably belonged to a servant. My father did not look impressed. "From what I have gathered, they're just barely holding Marlenia City. To attack Baile Gareth, so fortified and deep in Feenagh Forest as it is, would be foolhardy. Though, High King Lezsek is an ambitious man, and they have ventured this far already. To take Baile Gareth would show the other lesser lords that they should not dare oppose him.

"We have two advantages, perhaps. One, many believe you are dead, although Lady Dominique lingered long enough to see me rescue you. A chest wound is not easy to recover from. Not sure if she recognized my face, alas, that is a different problem.

"Second advantage, they fear the Spear. They are taking great pains to avoid contact with the sleeping prince, in case the spell is contagious."

"If we were to find a way to wake him up...?"

"Then it may strengthen our cause. There are many still loyal to Keegan's family and their reign, and many more still loyal to the idea of you at his side. To reclaim Marlenia City and reunite the West, we will need to rescue Keegan."

"Lady Sylvia seemed intent on keeping Keegan alive," I said slowly, tracing the outline of the bandage beneath my shift. My stomach coiled as I pictured Keegan, frozen in his pensive gaze, melting into water at the cathedral altar as Sylvia recited wedding vows. "Yet her father is killing everyone loyal to Keegan. Why? How long will his sleeping body be safe with them?"

"If he is still with them. My contacts have gone into hiding, and all of them say something different: Keegan is in the East. Keegan is in the North. Some say he's made it as far as Xii, the Southern capital." He sighed. "It was General Killan Tramore who put the Freetors in their place two hundred years ago, declaring himself the new Holy One after the members of the old line died by Alastar's hand in battle. The Tramores set an example that the rest of the world followed. Now the East, made wealthy through Freetor slavery and trade, sees the once-powerful Tramores softening their hearts to the people they once swore to eradicate—it is not just an affront to their way of life. It is an opportunity. Control the West, and you control the world.

"All we know for sure is that he hasn't woken, and Leszek is content to keep him asleep. He was ready to announce Keegan's death, and then Lady Sylvia paraded into town with his sleeping body, spreading the rumour that you put a curse on him. That put a hiccup in the Frostfire plans, certainly. Now there are rumours that Keegan submitted to a marriage with Sylvia before his magical slumber, and that the invasion truly happened to stop *you* from committing regicide. I heard one Frostfire bannerman preaching in the neighbouring baile that the public executions were not of Tramore loyalists but of Freetor sympathetics, loyal to the notion of your romantic relationship with Keegan. They're using your infiltration of the castle and the theft of Lady Dominique's identity as proof that you were up to no good from the very beginning of your involvement."

"And people believe that?"

He half shrugged. "If the story is convincing, and simple enough to digest, people can be made to believe anything."

"What happened to people not being sheep?"

"This isn't about Marlenians being stupid. I don't think for a second that the Frostfires assume that the average Marlenian is stupid. This is about the Frostfires recolouring history in their image. This is about playing into the desires of the people, and the Frostfires doing whatever they can to fix the mistakes they've made, so that the people of Marlenia can return to the *normal* lives they desperately crave."

He climbed to his feet, unable to hide the cracking of his knees and the groan when he put weight on his left leg.

I gazed at the stone wall. "I don't want anyone else to die for me, or because of me."

"Then we had best formulate a plan as soon as you're feeling better." His voice carried a sophisticated mix of aristocracy and adventure as he neared the door, barely two stone-throws from my bed. "In the meantime, there are some people who have been anxiously waiting for you to wake up. Should I let them in?"

I drew a deep breath, composing myself, as I sat up. I grimaced, and nodded.

The door screeched open. Laoise burst in, wearing a clean long blue-and-white wool dress. Her mother trailed in quickly behind, shutting the door promptly. I noted the high collar of her dress, and the long sleeves, and the loose bun that kept her hair at bay. Hiding her scars beneath warm clothes had frizzed her greying hair.

"Have they still got you working, Bidelia?" I asked good-naturedly.

"I wasn't about to let my mind go to waste," Bidelia replied, raising an eyebrow at my father in disapproval. "Protection does not come free."

"I'm just glad you're finally awake," Laoise said, kneeling at my side and taking my hands.

"Yes, not all of us have the luxury of sleeping so soundly in a private room," Bidelia said demurely, but she was smiling too.

"I was going to sleep in here with you, but there were so many healers coming in and out, attending you, that it got too chaotic," Laoise explained. "Our room is perfectly fine, especially after days of not sleeping, or sleeping in bug-ridden moss."

I squeezed Laoise's hands. "Lord Ansel knows who you are, then?"

"He does," Bidelia said. "We are lying low to ease suspicion amongst his household. Though we have the larger issue of—"

My father quickly interrupted her. "Let's not trouble her with that now. Later."

Steeling herself, Bidelia clasped her hands. She did not like being interrupted. "Very well, Conal. But dispense with the theatrics and show him in. Laoise and I must return to the kitchens, and you, I imagine, have noble minds to befuddle."

Laoise gave me an exasperated look.

"What are you hiding now?" I asked my father.

Somewhat annoyed, my father brushed past Bidelia and laid a hand on the doorknob. "I was getting to that, thank you, Bidelia." He gave her a chilly glance. Their years of playing prescribed parts began to show—likely the "Advisor" wasn't used to "Mother Margaret" being so bold with her address. "You wanted to know how you survived the journey here. You have another person to thank."

For the third time, surprise welled in my chest at the sight of Monju Farin, alive, as he sauntered into the cramped room. I recoiled against the wall, and then groaned as my wound protested. My father offered me a foul-smelling concoction in a clay cup from the desk, and I waved it away.

"Happy to see the lady awake," he said, bowing.

Shock sedated my tongue.

My father answered my unasked questions. "He was wounded, but not fatally. Without his help, it would've been impossible to remove the Spear and stitch you up enough to get you to a healer in Iar Bunsula. He also distracted the Eastern forces patrolling the roads, which allowed us safe passage into Feenagh Forest."

The four of them stared at me as if they were expecting me to applaud Monju for his bravery, quick thinking, and secret loyalty. "You died before my eyes." It had been intimate and familial, and to see him alive and well seemed to be a betrayal of the moment we had shared.

"The contract with Lady Dominique was to be honoured until the safe delivery of the Race cure to Peta, or until Monju's death. And Monju told the lady before," he said, with a small, amused smile, "Monju can hold his breath for some time."

My father read the room and addressed each of us. "I know that trusting a man who sells his word and his sword might be counter-intuitive, but we need all the allies we can get."

I never enjoyed admitting it when my father was right. Monju knelt by the bedside.

"I am sorry that I lied," Monju said. His eyes were pools of sincerity as he lost the formal speech patterns of his people. "If the lady wishes for me to leave...I will."

I drew in a deep, painful breath. Trust was not an easy thing. I had been burned too many times by people ensuring that their interests aligned with mine.

"What about your father?" I asked him slowly.

His lips twitched. "The South is far, and the Race is quick. It has been a year since Monju left, promising to return only when he had a cure. The cure from Lady Dominique was not guaranteed. Had been hoping...but...there is a time when hope must harden, or be transferred."

"I'm sorry," I said quietly.

"I'm not," my father said. "Monju saved your life."

Yes, but at what cost? What if Monju had used his vial on Keegan instead? I would not be here, and retaking Marlenia City would be a far easier task.

"Will work hard to regain the lady's trust," Monju said, patting the soft mattress.

I only nodded, thinking of the tenderness of his kiss when I had been in danger, and the violent and merciless way he had slain the apprentices.

Ever the diplomat, my father gestured to the door. "Kiera should rest some more. Perhaps she'll be up for joining us for some dinner later?"

"In the kitchen, out of sight from the nosy Gareth servants," Laoise added.

"Sure," I said, forcing a smile.

Bidelia opened the door, and let Laoise and Monju out. An encouraging smile lit her face briefly before she composed herself for the outside world. Even as a free woman, she still wore a mask.

Once more, it was just my father and me.

Feeling rejuvenated at the reassurance that Laoise and Bidelia were safe, I found the strength to place my bare feet on the cold stone floor. My father didn't reprimand me for wanting to stand. He offered his hand, and gratefully I took it. My head swam as swirling dots overcame my vision, but I persisted, fighting the urge to surrender to weightlessness.

"Easy," he said gently. He wrapped his arms around me. "It's all right. You're not alone. Not anymore."

Despite the pain in my chest and the distance the rift between us had brought, I returned his embrace, digging my fingernails into his shoulder, fearing he would leave me again. He stroked my hair, holding me for as long as I wanted, not resisting when I finally pulled away. It was a start, a sign that he would allow me to set the boundaries, that he was willing to be more than just his mask.

"I'll leave you be now. We have a long few days ahead of us."

Without so much as a backwards glance, he opened and then shut the door aggressively, as if jumping back into the fray of a raging battle. He had come into that room as my father, but had left as Advisor Ferguson.

Another round of throbbing pain radiated from my wound as I wondered what mask I would don when I stepped across the threshold.

Hooded, hiding in plain sight—exactly what the two of us were good at doing. While the men loyal to the East patrolled the busy streets of what used to be my home, tallying cooperating souls, I was ensconced in a fortress just out of reach. Staying here was not an option, for the Violet Fox never stayed put for long, and neither did Kiera Driscoll.

I laid a hand on the weapon I'd sacrificed everything to find, and looked out the lancet into the thick forest. Somewhere out there, Keegan lay in the clutches of our enemies, unfeeling and alone. Beneath the earth, my people fought for their lives just because of where they were born. The violet strip of cloth around my forefinger reminded me of my commitment to Keegan, yet both of us had strived to put our people's needs first, to make peace between us all.

I would remain true to the vows I made as a Freetor, and as a queen.

To ensure my people's future, I would fight those who had wronged us all.

I would find my love, and I would free him.

Stay tuned as Kiera Driscoll's adventures continue in...

The

EMERALD CLOTH

THE VIOLET FOX SERIES #3

Resist.
That's what my friends tell me.
But to free my prince
And save my people from disease,
I must cooperate with my greatest rival.

COMING SOON

Acknowledgements

In September 2014, I launched a crowdfunding campaign for *The Silver Spear*. Everyone in this list contributed, and because of you, the project was fully funded! You are awesome, and thank you very much for supporting independently created books.

Wendy Breen
Rhonda Burke
Peter Chiykowski
Evan Cormier
Clare Davidson
John Eddy
Patricia Eddy
Elizabeth Ewert
Holly Geely
Chadwick Ginther
Brittney Hartling
Jenna Harvie
Patricia Lynne
Jay Marshall
Jessie Marshall
Jennifer Messerschmidt
Jessie Miller
Robert Rudolph
Liz Schwinghamer
Adam Sigrist
Kayla West
Myra White

Also special thanks to: Mum, Dad, Jessie, Aunt Kerry & family; Marie & Joe—my other family. Sam and Chadwick, for being great friends. My social media followers & fans for following my journey, and all the people who have ever told me they love my work.

And Dave. It's tough being a kitty.

- THE AUTHOR -

CLARE C. MARSHALL grew up in rural Nova Scotia with very little television and dial-up internet, and yet she turned out okay. Her YA sci-fi novel *Dreams In Her Head* was nominated for the 2014 Creation of Stories award. She is a full-time freelance editor, book designer, ghostwriter, and web manager. If there's time left in the day, she devotes it to Faery Ink Press, her publishing imprint. When she's not writing or fiddling up a storm, she enjoys computer games and making silly noises at cats.

Photo Credit: Terence Yung

Website: FaeryInkPress.com
Facebook: Facebook.com/faeryinkpress
Twitter: @ClareMarshall13

If you enjoyed this book, please consider writing a review on Amazon or on Goodreads. Thank you!

STARS IN HER EYES
Sparkstone Saga #1
by Clare C. Marshall
$13.95
165 pages

YA Science Fiction
Ages 12+
ISBN: 9780987779489

Burn hot and cold. Read minds. Disappear at will. Dream your own death. Welcome to Sparkstone University, where some students are more gifted than others.

When Ingrid learns she's been accepted at the hyper-secretive Sparkstone University, she is sceptical. It's an honour to attend, apparently, and yet barely anyone has ever heard of the place.

And everyone seems a little too happy that she's there: especially when she meets Sunni and her group of friends. They seem to already know Ingrid. As if she was expected. Expected to save Earth from an imminent alien invasion. Like she has superpowers or something.

As if magic and mutations exist. As if aliens are really planning to attack.

That just sounds ridiculous. There's no such thing.

…right?

Wrong.

DREAMS IN HER HEAD
Sparkstone Saga #2
by Clare C. Marshall
$15.95
249 pages

YA Science Fiction
Ages 12+
ISBN: 9780991961023

Open the door.
Step quickly, step through.
Breathe in the darkness,
Until you are its master.

Ingrid Stanley is in more trouble than she knows. Ingrid's dead friend keeps showing up in her dreams along with mysterious visions that feel all-too real. What's worse is now the Collective knows that Ingrid is supposed to have superpowers. They're waiting to pounce the moment Ingrid and her new superpower-wielding friends make a mistake.

When her family is threatened by Professor Jadore, Ingrid decides it's time to take matters into her own hands. A little student protest can't go wrong, she thinks. Not when her almost-boyfriend Ethan is fully supporting it. Not when her friends put an innocent student's life in danger to make it successful.

Not when a powerful alien is waiting for Ingrid to inadvertently summon him into this world.

Everything's going to be fine. Absolutely no one will get hurt this time.

...right?

Wrong, and wrong again.

THE VIOLET FOX
The Violet Fox Series #1
by Clare C. Marshall
$20.95
288 pages

YA Fantasy/Adventure
Ages 12+
ISBN: 9780987779441

Run.
That's what instinct told me.
But to save the secrets of my people
and to protect my brother
I have to become the enemy.

There are two kinds of people in the land of Marlenia. The Marlenians, who live on the surface, and the Freetors, who are forced to live underground.

The war between them ended two hundred years ago, but the Freetors still fight for the right to live under the sun. Fifteen-year-old Kiera Driscoll embodies the Freetors' hopes as the Violet Fox. In a violet cape and mask, she sneaks around Marlenia City stealing food and freeing her people from slavery.

Then the Elders task her with a secret mission: retrieve a stolen tome that contains the secrets of Freetor magic, something the Marlenians both fear and covet. Kiera must disguise herself as a noblewoman and infiltrate the Marlenian castle before the Freetor-hating Advisor finds out her real identity, before her brother is imprisoned because of the secrets he hides, and before she falls any more in love with the prince she's supposed to hate.

More is happening in the castle than she realizes, and Kiera is faced with a difficult choice. Will she be loyal to her people and their fight for freedom, or will she be loyal to her heart?

WITHIN
by Clare C. Marshall

$11.99
192 pages

YA Supernatural/Thriller
Ages 16+
ISBN: 9780987779403

Trinity Hartell's life changed after the accident. Left with irreversible brain damage, she becomes a burden to her mother, a cause for heartbreak for her boyfriend Zack, and a flattened obstacle for her jealous best friend, Ellie.

But then she starts writing. Perhaps it's a coincidence that the psychotic, murderous protagonist of her novel bears a striking similarity to the charming Wiley Dalton, a mayoral candidate in the upcoming election.

Or, perhaps not...

www.ingramcontent.com/pod-product-compliance
Lightning Source LLC
Chambersburg PA
CBHW020608300426
44113CB00007B/557